SEA CHANGE

Equipping Rural Churches
for the Tides of Cultural Upheaval

by
JONATHAN HOWARD DAVIS

Sea Change: Equipping Rural Churches For The Tides Of Cultural Upheaval
Copyright © 2021 by Jonathan Howard Davis. All right reserved.

No part of this book may be used or reproduced in any manner whatsoever without written permission, except in the case of brief quotations embodied in critical articles and reviews. For more information, e-mail all inquiries to info@freilingpublishing.com.

Freiling Publishing
P.O. Box 1264, Warrenton, VA 20188

ISBN: 978-1-956267-04-4 (Print)

Printed in the United States of America

ACKNOWLEDGEMENTS

This book began with a lifelong dream of obtaining my doctoral education, and I am especially beholden to each of my professors, especially Dr. Larry Baker for recruiting me to the program at Logsdon Seminary and Dr. Wally Goodman for serving as my faculty supervisor throughout the seminar portion of the program. I am also grateful to my committee members, Dr. Bob Dale, Dr. James Heflin, and Dr. Goodman, who have taken time to meet with me by phone and in person and added a great deal to the final form and structure of the project that eventually became this book. I am a better pastor, a sharper thinker, a more fluid writer, and even a better father and spouse because of each of these men.

Additionally, I would like to thank my family. My wonderful wife Audrey has been a constant by my side and has lent her support in countless ways over these past few years. I am also grateful to my sons, who each inspire me daily to continue in my research and writing. In terms of family, I also thank my parents, who instilled in me from an early age that the pursuit of knowledge and learning was vital to a godly and productive life and who supported me in each step of my faith and education pilgrimage. I also thank Carol Davis and Tara Smith for the use of their beautiful home for a personal writing retreat. Carol and Tara's generosity, love, and joy are a true beacon of light in my life. Also, this book would not have been possible without the kind and loving church family of Beale Memorial Baptist

Church. Their willingness to participate in the ministry research project remains an incredible gift.

Finally, when some scholars and authors had their eyes glaze over when I began excitedly describing my doctoral project and research, others took remarkably kind interest and even showed support in various forms. I'm thankful to J. R. Woodward of the V3 Church Planting Movement, Leadership Coach Eddie Hammett, Don Fawcett of the Heart of Texas Baptist Area (ret.), Brian Williams of the Baptist General Association of Virginia, Marv Knox of Fellowship Southwest, Brad Thie of Duke's Thriving Rural Communities Initiative, Tony Jones of Fuller and United Theological Seminaries (respectively), Brian McLaren, and the late Phyllis Tickle. Each of these individuals gave of their time personally in emails or transformative conversations that benefited this project. Others even extended opportunities to share my ideas and work with a wider network, for which I am incredibly grateful.

This book is the result not only of my own labor and time but also of the kindness and generosity of numerous people, who have encouraged, prodded, corrected, championed, dreamed, labored, and even opened doors along the way. Along this writing journey, it seems (sometimes hourly) that heavenly blessings abound. I am thankful for the support and encouragement of professors and mentors, family, friends, my former congregation, and colleagues. My life and this book are enriched immeasurably by each of them.

—Jonathan Davis
Spring 2021, Georgetown, Texas

LIST OF ABBREVIATIONS

BMBC   Beale Memorial Baptist Church

EMC   Emerging Church Movement

ESV   English Standard Version

KJV   King James Version

MSG   The Message Bible

NIV   New International Version

NKJV   New King James Version

NRSV   New Revised Standard Version

SBLGNT   Society of Biblical Literature Greek New Testament

CONTENTS

Acknowledgements iii

List of Abbreviations v

Introduction: Stirring Waters In Rural America 1

CHAPTER 1: STEPPING INTO RURAL CURRENTS . . . 9
   Thinking Theologically About Rural Places in Metropolitan Society . . 10
   Rural Communities, Institutions, and Environments 16
   Rural Populations and Peoples 19
   Rural Economy and Socioeconomic Well-Being 22

CHAPTER 2: THE POSTMODERN TIDE IN RURAL CHURCHES 27
   Pragmatism over Idealism 34
   Possible Critiques of a Postmodern Rural Project 36
   The Rural "Other" 38

CHAPTER 3: WHEN CURRENTS COLLIDE: INTERSECTIONALITY IN RURAL MINISTRY 43
   Localized Examples from Rural Sociology 45
   A Case Study in Spatial Relations 47
   Multigenerational Dynamics in Rural Communities 51
   Implications for Rural Churches 54

CHAPTER 4: EQUIPPING RURAL CHURCHES TO SET SAIL 57
   Helping Train and Equip Leaders 61

    Blurring the Lines and Changing the Scripts. 66
    Preparedness to Minister in Postmodern Culture 74
    Story as the Key to Confident Vision. 80

CHAPTER 5: THE BIBLE: OUR NAVIGATIONAL CHART FOR THE POSTMODERN TIDE. . 83
    A Pastoral Theology for Postmodern Rural Ministry 87
    The Smallness of the Kingdom 95
    Theology of the Periphery 103

CHAPTER 6: CHECKING THE FORECAST: EMERGING RURAL CULTURE 109
    The Emergent Church in Rural Communities? 111
    Possible Dangers of Postmodernity for Rural Churches 119
    A Robust View of the gospel 122
    What's Emerging in Your Context? 124

CHAPTER 7: HARNESSING THE TIDE: EMPOWERING THE RURAL CHURCH . 127
    Empowered for Faithfulness 129
    Empowered to Weather Change. 133

CHAPTER 8: TACKING AND GYBING: SAILING INTO THE WINDS OF CONGREGATIONAL CHANGE 139
    Deep Change as Adaptation 142
    Church-Size Dynamics and Change 144
    Clergy Burnout and Change 146
    Strategies for Leading Change in Rural Churches. 147
    Resistance to Change 155

CHAPTER 9: PASSAGE PLANNING: METHODS OF DATA COLLECTION. 159
    The Quantitative Questionnaire 163
    The Qualitative Questionnaire 165
    Provocative Proposals for BMBC 166
    Celebrating and Sharing the Stories 167

    Utilizing Survey Monkey 168

CHAPTER 10: SAILING TO CORINTH: NAVIGATING THE "TIDES OF FAITH" 171

CHAPTER 11: THE TIDE OF TOLERANCE – BRIDGING VAST DIFFERENCES . . . 173

CHAPTER 12: THE TIDE OF AUTHENTICITY: BRIDGING OUR BELIEFS AND OUR ACTIONS . . 183
    An Authenticity Deficit?. 186

CHAPTER 13: THE TIDE OF INDIVIDUALISM: BRIDGING SPIRITUAL GIFTS WITH MINISTRY . . 195
    Individuality in Western Culture 197
    Individuality Versus Divine Uniqueness. 198
    Rural Diversity and Individualism 201

CHAPTER 14: THE TIDE OF SKEPTICISM: BRIDGING FAITH AND DOUBT 205
    Atheism in Rural Communities 207
    Skepticism and Christlike Love? 211

CHAPTER 15: THE TIDE OF GREEN: BRIDGING CREATION CARE WITH PRACTICAL MINISTRY 215

CHAPTER 16: THE TIDE OF SOLIDARITY: BRIDGING THE HEART OF GOD WITH CULTURE 227

CHAPTER 17: REPORT FROM THE VOYAGE: ANALYSIS AND DISCUSSION OF FINDINGS . . . 239
    Quantitative Questionnaire 240
    Tides of Faith Message Series 246
    Church Vision Day and Qualitative Questionnaire 247
    Vision Day 248

CHAPTER 18: CHARTING A NEW COURSE THROUGH THE TIDES: SUMMARY AND CONCLUSIONS **251**
    Harnessing the Tide Instead of Fighting It 251
    Since the Project .255
    Essex County Homeless Organization 255
    National Baptist – Muslim Dialogue 256
    A Rural Church Going Green 257
    Teacher Appreciation Banquet 258

EPILOGUE **259**
    Appendix 1. Quantitative Questionnaire 260
    Appendix 2. Qualitative Questionnaire 264
    Appendix 3. Vision Workshop 267
    Appendix 4. Vision Day Feedback Form 270

FOOTNOTES **271**
    Works Consulted .271

Endnotes .281

Introduction

STIRRING WATERS IN RURAL AMERICA

"Tides do what tides do – they turn."

– Derek Landy

The idea that "in a small-town, things never change" is a myth. The tides of change are always upon us, even when we fail to realize it. Many local people can recount changes in rural communities over many decades, but the overall feeling of the town (and those from beyond town) is often that their own community is relatively immutable. For decades now, a great current has been flowing through culture. Even if the waters look glassy on the surface as they often do in the morning on a rural pond, the moving current is deep, and many may not readily see it. Many locals across rural America feel the economy has stagnated, nothing ever changes, and there are few places for young professionals to find work. Even in the past year with the stock market going strong throughout a worldwide health pandemic, major gains and record highs for indexed companies and their shareholders did not often translate into impacts in rural communities. There is a disconnect between Wall Street and Main Street. Moreover, there is often a disconnect between denominational offices and publishing houses (almost always located in metropolitan centers) and the vast majority of the churches they serve. There is movement underneath the water's surface, but many wrongly assume the water is stagnant.

Many older adults grieve the fact that their children and grandchildren no longer live locally due to the fact that there are no jobs for them. Many times in rural communities, the best and brightest are encouraged to go to college and even graduate school, only to find that there are no jobs in their chosen field back in their rural communities. Many of these young people never move home, and rural sociologists have long termed this phenomenon as "brain drain."[1] While many business owners in rural towns have passed on their companies to second, third, and even fourth generations of family, other business owners, however, have struggled since a few big box stores and fast food chains came to town. For many, it seems that their rural community has never changed, yet for others, it seems things are ever-changing.

Certainly, people migrate less to and from rural areas. Small-town residents may enjoy quaint shopping districts or relatively decent schools systems, and church may still prove important for many. The popular idea that small towns never change exists because of what sociologists label as "rural mystique." In a way, "the mystique is composed of treasured or almost sacred elements. It is an idealized form of community that stands in contrast to urban life. It is the antithesis of the modern urban world, somehow more moral, virtuous and simple."[2] Small-town culture is often, however, more than an idealized projection of some rural mythology. In an increasingly globalized world, small towns like the one your church may exist in change at a more rapid pace than perhaps ever before.

On a visit to the local family-owned lumber mill (which is now run by a fourth generation), the owners told of how their son, after obtaining a business degree at a university, devised a way to sell Virginia hardwood in emerging markets like China and India. What amounted to a mostly local company only a few years ago is now a global enterprise with clients in multiple countries in far parts of the world. Many lifelong residents may not realize that the lumber mill has changed so rapidly in only a few years because it has always been there, and many assume things never change in a small town. When people coalesce around rural mystique, they may assume their community will always remain untouched by the outside world. Not so – the tide always presses inland.

One rather humorous example of rural mystique comes from a document titled *Manifesto on Rural Life* from the National Catholic Rural Life Conference in 1939. In discussing rural people, the authors write, "Some object to the association of modern conveniences and labor saving devices with culture, perhaps because certain groups identify culture with the bathtub, electric lighting, electric power, and other mechanical devices."[3] Many felt that urban progress was not needed in the simple rural way of life; urban culture was vain, and rural culture was pure. Rural areas, however, are not so insulated from urban centers. Technology, entertainment, theology, and values all transfer from urban environments to rural ones and likewise from rural to urban as populations shift. Rural towns and rural churches do not exist on an island or in a silo, untouched by the rest of the world. As change occurs in society, small towns and their populations are all affected. There is no stopping the tide.

Why Write This Book?

I was not always interested in rural ministry. The fact is, I wasn't always interested in ministry, but that is a story for another book. As a first-time author, many readers may wonder about my interest in writing this book. It is quite likely you have never heard my name before, and I want to take a minute before we go any further to share my background with you as the reader.

After seminary, Audrey and I moved from Virginia back to Texas where we grew up. Over the course of several years, we both served at churches in the Houston area in youth and children's ministry. As one who was a youth minister for over a decade, I became fascinated with all of the ways that students in my youth ministry viewed the world. I especially found their questions interesting – questions that were very much frowned upon by their own elders and the church. As a youth minister, I sensed almost 20 years ago that there was a great undercurrent of cultural change sweeping through our society.

When I began my doctoral studies at Logsdon Seminary in San Antonio, Texas, I was serving as a youth pastor and worship leader at a small church on the north side of Houston. As I began thinking about what my focus would be for my doctoral project and research, I was drawn to the subject of postmodernity (more on that term later) and also to studying cultural change and its impact on my students. Many of the most meaningful conversations I had with students were when they were wrestling with their own inherited faith and beliefs. In other words, they were trying to discern what they believed was true, and like most healthy adolescents, they questioned the authority and teaching of their church and the authority of their parents.

Perhaps more than anything, I perceived that my students struggled to embrace truth with a capital "T." They were comfortable living with ambiguity and difference and strongly resisted believing propositional truth claims just because the preacher (or youth minister) told them it was so. To be clear, I found this to be incredibly healthy on the part of the students. I have known a large number of adults in churches through the years who have never really deliberated their own faith. These adults – and there are many of them – live with a borrowed and often shallow faith because they have never done the difficult work of truly considering and weighing why they believe what they believe.

As I progressed in my doctoral studies, I began to feel God's call away from youth ministry and worship leading and toward serving as a pastor. This is deeply ironic because early on in my ministry, I used to declare, "God will never call me to be a pastor!" Yeah … I ate those words. (Maybe next time I'll declare, "God would never call me to be independently wealthy and live on my own Caribbean island!") In any case, God called me to become a pastor, and that call was clear in my heart.

The church that called me to serve as their pastor was Urbanna Baptist Church in Urbanna, Virginia (I'm rooted in the Baptist tradition). Urbanna was a town with more sailboats than people. We moved from the Houston metropolitan area with over six million residents to Urbanna with just over 600 residents. This was a huge sea change for me and my family. As you might imagine, my ministry context was suddenly quite different. I was set to continue in my doctoral studies even after we moved to Virginia, but I needed (in my mind) to hit a reset button. It didn't seem like postmodernity and cultural change had much to do with my new place of service. Urbanna is a quaint little fishing and crabbing village on a river near the Chesapeake Bay, and at first glance, not much has changed there in nearly 400 years.

As I got to know the congregants, especially the younger families and youth, I realized quickly that the same shifting values I saw in the urban/suburban context existed in the rural context. The proliferation of technology has a lot to do with this.

A few hundred years ago, it might have taken days or weeks for news to travel from the eastern seaboard to the Midwest. There are numerous accounts, post American Civil War, for instance, of battles and skirmishes, well after the surrender at Appomattox. Today, news and values travel over the airwaves into rural communities via satellite television and cell phone towers. A Tweet, Facebook update, or Instagram post can travel the world instantaneously, and 24-hour cable news blares non-stop in the homes of many rural congregants.

As we got settled into our new church in a serene and idyllic community, we witnessed firsthand the sea changes of culture and globalization sweeping through our community. The students in my small-town church, it turns out, held many of the same values and asked many of the same tough questions as students in my large suburban youth group. I began to realize that postmodernity and cultural change are impacting rural communities just as much as urban and suburban ones. What I realized when examining the literature was that while many people were writing and thinking about postmodernity's impact on the Church, and many were writing about rural ministry, nobody I stumbled across at the time was writing and researching the impact of postmodernity on rural churches. In that realization, I had finally stumbled upon a project that has fascinated me for nearly a decade, and the book you now hold in your hands is the result.

Before the pandemic struck, I was on target to release this book at a much earlier date. After finishing my doctoral writing in the fall of 2019, I was invited to present at the National Outreach Summit in Colorado Springz, Colorado, as a small church specialist. After that event, I was in communication with several potential publishing houses, and then in January of 2020, COVID-19 reared its head. Literally, all of my focus and attention shifted at that time to the church and caring for my parishioners. Since the pandemic began, my own family has been uprooted and moved across the country to help care for sick relatives. Family members have contracted (and thankfully recovered from) COVID-19, and my wife Audrey lost her grandmother – who is now rejoicing with the angels in heaven. While the book was timely and I greatly desired to get this research out, life circumstances prevented me from doing so. This book is the culmination of a near decade-long journey of research and learning, trial and error, and ministry or reflection on ministry.

Coming out of the pandemic, I think the book is just as relevant as before 2020, and perhaps more so. The pace of cultural change has arguably accelerated as a result of the pandemic, and rural communities feel the deep impacts of these shifting currents.[4] In some cases, the impact felt may be that they are getting left behind, especially as rapid change relates to technology. In our rural community, as the pandemic emerged and schools shut down, one major challenge that emerged was the lack of internet access for many in the community. Having no broadband internet made virtual classes and streaming video nearly impossible for large swaths of the community. The school system came up with a work around though and quickly made mobile hotspots out of misspelled that would have otherwise sat in storage for the year. Populations in metropolitan areas are now used to using services like Door Dash and Shipt for food and grocery delivery, while many in rural communities still drive 30 minutes to an hour to reach a grocery store and live with cell phone coverage that can barely handle smartphones. If anything, the pace of change in our society has revealed disparities between urban and rural communities when it comes to healthcare, access to technology (which means access to education), and jobs creation. No wonder rural pastor and author Glenn Daman titled his 2018 rural ministry book *The Forgotten Church*. There is, however, much to celebrate about rural communities and churches. This book will lay out the case that rural communities and congregations are better equipped to navigate the postmodern tide than many people may realize.

Chapter One
STEPPING INTO RURAL CURRENTS

"The sea, once it casts its spell, holds one in its net of wonder forever."

– Jacques Cousteau

When I was a young teen, my family moved from the Houston area to a tiny town called North Zulch, Texas. It was actually the first time I moved from the Houston area to a small rural community. We lived on a red-clay washboard road called Emu Lane because at the end of the road was an emu farm. In the late 90s, the emu industry was burgeoning in Texas, and some thought the emu with its lean red meat would one day replace beef. Even as a 13-year-old, I knew that was a tough sell in a historic cattle state like Texas. On Emu Lane, we lived in a singlewide trailer, and I don't remember knowing a single neighbor.

Growing up in north Houston suburbs, we had relatively small yards. On Emu Lane, however, I remember we had nearly 10 acres of land. My little brother and I loved it! We could make trails in the woods behind our home, leading down to a creek. We could ride our bikes as far as we desired. I especially remember enjoying setting up coke cans (soda and pop for all you non-Texans) on a sawhorse and using them for target practice with a pellet gun and a .22 bolt-action long rifle my PawPaw gave us. We weren't rich, but I remember feeling a sense of freedom on that 10 acres that I never enjoyed living in Houston suburbs. As we move forward in this chapter, I invite you to explore with me the possible breadth of what it means to be rural and what it means to be the rural church. We will begin to explore a few theological themes which we will continue unpacking along our journey in this book. As we step into rural currents, I invite you to think and dream creatively about how God may be calling your church to live in an exciting and important ministry context.

Thinking Theologically About Rural Places in Metropolitan Society

To many, rural is an idea, and one that is difficult to articulate. Sociologists often use the term "rurality" to discuss rural matters. Most ministers in rural churches have likely never thought deeply about what rurality entails for them and their ministries. World-renown rural-studies expert Paul Cloke (University of Bristol, UK) explains well how rural is just as much of an idea as it is a hard set of demographic numbers. In exploring the idea and concept of rurality, he writes:

> The idea of rurality seems to be firmly entrenched in popular discourses about space, place, and society in the Western world. Although the precise nomenclature devoted to the idea is often context-specific – witness the sometimes subtle but always important differences in terms such as rural, countryside, country, wilderness, outback, agriculture and so on – the

concept of rurality lives on in the popular imagination and everyday practices of the contemporary world. The rural stands as both a significant imaginative space, connected with all kinds of cultural meanings ranging from the idyllic to the oppressive, and as a material object of lifestyle desire for some people – a place to move to, farm in, visit for a vacation, encounter different forms of nature, and generally practise alternatives to the city.[5]

Many ministers and congregants in rural congregations may be drawn to their own ideas of what it means to be a rural church and to live as rural people. According to the World Economic Forum, since the beginning of the COVID-19 pandemic, many in urban centers have moved to more rural locations in an effort to embrace social distancing as a lifestyle change.[6] In fact, the same report indicates that as of 2020, "nearly half of all U.S. adults said they'd prefer to live in a small town or rural area." Many, it seems, buy into the idea of the rurality that Cloke describes, imagining rural life to be simpler, safer, and cleaner.

Rural people and places, however, are more than an idea or an ideal. Defining the term "rural" is critical before proceeding. The working definition many sociologists use comes from the U.S. Census Bureau. A "Nonmetro Non-core" county is a nonmetropolitan county without a single core area containing at least 10,000 people. A "Nonmetro Micropolitan" county is a county with at least one core city of 10,000 to 49,999 persons.[7] These core population centers act as social hubs for the surrounding small towns and villages. Non-core counties are the most rural of all counties, many having less than 10,000 residents in the entire county.[8] Out of 3,142 counties in the United States, well over half (1,378) are Nonmetro Non-Core. Over 20 percent of the counties in the nation classify as Nonmetro Micropolitan which means that over 65 percent of counties in the U.S. are nonmetropolitan in population size. Most people in society live in urban settings, and "even though rural areas may only contain 15-30 percent of a nation's population, they typically contain most of its land, water, and mineral resources." Have you ever considered that your church represents an undersized population while also representing the vast majority of natural resources God provided? What an awesome responsibility and privilege!

For a few moments, I invite you to the task of theological reflection and imagination. It is one thing to read these statistics and keep moving with some knowledge of how demographers define rural places. It is another task altogether to ask, "What does this mean theologically?" Given these statistics, one possible area for theological reflection concerning rural ministry is creation care. This can be a tricky subject for a rural minister because environmental concern is often perceived as a politically divisive topic. The fact is though, in an increasingly urbanized society, rural communities represent a large portion of our natural resources. Arguably, to many in metropolitan communities, rural localities are only valued for the resources that can be extracted or produced or as a place to visit on weekend getaways. Does representing such a large portion of the world's natural resources give rural churches and people a theological or moral imperative to care deeply about creation stewardship?

We are called to steward God's creation, not to live as cogs in the wheel of extraction and production. Many might turn to the creation narratives of Scripture to seek insight into God's design for humanity's interaction with creation. We read, "Then God said, 'Let us make humankind in our image, according to our likeness; and let them have dominion over the fish of the sea, and over the birds of the air, and over the cattle, and over all the wild animals of the earth, and over every creeping thing that creeps upon the earth'."[9] The key word for creation theology seems to be the Hebrew word *hd'r'* (*radah*) which is most often translated "dominion" or "rule." Many have traditionally assumed that the word gives humanity license to dominate nature in ways that are exploitative and even thoughtless. This may be the most common use for the word as it appears in other instances in Scripture – when Joseph's brothers were angry that his dream showed Joseph ruling over them (Genesis 37:8) or when the Philistines are said to have dominion over Israel (Judges 14:4). The idea of being ruled over or dominated by someone or something is rarely a positive thought.

To only understand *hd'r'* negatively may be to miss an important part of the verse at hand. Humanity is the only part of the created order made in God's image and likeness. The Divine One, Creator of heaven and earth, has already shown dominion over every part of the natural world by virtue of speaking creation into existence. The true ruler of all creation in the passage is clearly God, so humanity's open invitation to rule the rest of creation assumes humanity itself is under the rule and dominion of God. If we are called to rule the earth and all that is in it, we would be wise to remember, "A ruler who lacks understanding is a cruel oppressor; but one who hates unjust gain will enjoy a long life."[10] Another translation states, "A tyrannical ruler lacks judgment, but he who hates ill-gotten gain will enjoy a long life."[11] Humanity may certainly rule creation, but we often lack understanding, oppressing the planet instead of stewarding it. We may indeed enjoy dominion over the earth, but we terrorize her with bad judgment and shortsighted policies, resulting in ill-gotten financial and political gain.

Theologically, rural areas and churches are at the forefront of the conversation around what it means *to redeem the dominion of humanity over the earth*. The parable of the unjust ruler in Luke 16 ends with the warning, "Whoever is faithful in a very little is faithful also in much; and whoever is dishonest in a very little is dishonest also in much."[12] Our faithfulness in caring for creation, however small the impact, is a way to be faithful in the little things. Rural churches and Christians need not change the world concerning environmental politics and policy. Rather, we must be faithful to care for what God has entrusted to us.

Another consideration demographically is that rural churches exist largely at the periphery of American Christianity. The urbanization of society and the globalization of economies push rural people to the edges of the global consciousness. One may understand that "Rural, in almost all statistical systems, is treated as residual, what is left over after urban areas have been defined." Theologically, denominationally, and vocationally, rural churches and locales exist as leftovers and afterthoughts. Theologically, this is so because cultural attention tends to reside with theologies that attract large numbers of people. Many mega churches, some that preach the prosperity gospel, are in urban areas. Rural pastors are highly unlikely to have vast media empires, TV and radio airtime, and publishing deals. That kind of attention goes to urban pastors. Denominationally, rural churches become afterthoughts because new ministry initiatives, training seminars, and resource programs mostly focus on churches in urban centers. Denominational offices are almost all in urban centers, and few denominationally held entities exist outside of cities, except Christian camps and retreat centers. Even then, the rural church is only good for what the city Christians can consume through spiritual tourism in an isolated region during a weekend retreat or summer camp. Vocationally, rural churches are often undesirable for many ministers because of smaller resources for ministry (including the pastor's salary package), the smaller acclaim that comes with pastoring a small church, and the isolation that exists for the pastor and his family in the rural environment.

Theologically, this becomes a significant issue when small town churches are viewed ecclesiologically as the leftovers, an afterthought, or un-revivable. They take on the role of the Samaritans (seen as a lesser group of people), the lepers (seen as an outcast tribe banished from mainstream theological conversation), and a remnant (a group merely serving as a reminder of times gone by that were purer and simpler). Church and denominational leaders should note that:

> In the United States [...], the rural population share, about 17 percent in 2006, accounts for almost sixty million persons, which is a large population in its own right. Moreover, the U.S. rural population exceeds the size of other important subgroups such as Hispanics (43.2 million, 14.7 percent), African Americans (40.2 million, 13.7 percent), or persons age 65 and older (37 million, 12 percent).[13]

Small town Christians and their congregations represent a significant portion of the population, and rural America presents a huge mission field! Rural churches should not be seen as insignificant, as less than urban mega churches, or even serve as reminder of our county's rural mystique, for in many ways, "what we value is the mythology and symbolism of rural places rather than their reality."[14] Small-town churches are real. They are vital. They center in communities that need the hope of the gospel and have the ability to reach one of the largest subsections of America's general population. Rural people deserve visibility for the real people they are and not simply defined as anti-urban. Viewing people for who they truly are is one way the theology of *imago Dei* may exist more fully within the Church.

Rural Communities, Institutions, and Environments

Understanding the culture of any group entails grasping the unique qualities of the communities, institutions, and environments of the culture. Rural culture is no different. One theologically rich theme in rural culture is community. Many theologians and seminaries have discussed the importance of church as *community*. Bonhoeffer's *Life Together* comes to mind. In rural culture, community is vital. In fact, "Being a part of a community implies a long-term, continuous social interaction that contributes to the formation of personal identity [...]."[15] Many rural families have occupied their homes and communities for generations. A deeply embedded sense of community exists in many small towns, especially among those who were born and raised in the area. Churches can capitalize on this as centers for community building. Indeed, "Community also involves commitment to a shared culture, including shared values, norms and meanings. As a result, community has moral authority."[16] Only when the Church functions *as* community, and participates *in* the community does the Church hold moral authority of any kind in the lives of people. Exploration of what it means to be the people of God may prove fruitful for small-town pastors.

One possible theological exercise may be to explore the Early Church and ways the believers functioned as ecclesial community. Acts 4:32-5:11 is a great example of what community meant for early Christ followers. The believers held all things in common and met each other's needs. Luke held up this ideal Christian community as an example for all communities that followed. Barnabas encouraged the community by his generosity, selling a field and bringing the proceeds for ministry. Ananias and Sapphira were less generous and tried to

Chapter One: STEPPING INTO RURAL CURRENTS

lie before the church and before God about their commitment to the community, for which severe judgment ensued. By living in radical community, the Church gained moral authority in the lives of Christians and increased in influence daily. Rural churches should seek to live in community and be active in the community surrounding the church, looking to the Early Church as the prototype for Christian community.

Another theological theme closely tied to environmental concerns is *justice and fairness*. Many rural communities survive through resource extraction. Extraction of fossil fuels like coal and oil, lumber for construction and paper, wildlife by way of fishing or crabbing, water from aquifers and dams, and even renewable resources like solar and wind are all ways that rural areas support urban areas. Rural ministers should be mindful that, "The development and extraction of natural resources in nearly every instance involves some degree of conflict over the control of resources, the rights of local communities and residents, and private interests "versus" the public good."[17] Sometimes, very little of the fortunes made from resource extraction actually benefit small-town people. In a rural town close to water, a developer may come in and want to build a large resort, but lifetime residents may oppose it for fear of the culture dramatically changing. Oftentimes, tax breaks for large corporations and private investors have more say over the future of a town than the long-term residents. In this instance, remembering the prophets in Scripture might prove valuable. They cried for justice for the poor and oppressed, and challenged economic and spiritual systems that perpetuated injustice.

Amos 5 comes to mind. Martin Luther King, Jr., quoted this passage in his *I Have a Dream* speech. The prophet rebukes those who would extract natural and agricultural resources on the backs of poor rural people:

> Therefore because you trample on the poor
>   and take from them levies of grain,
> you have built houses of hewn stone,
>   but you shall not live in them;
> you have planted pleasant vineyards,
>   but you shall not drink their wine.
> For I know how many are your transgressions,
>   and how great are your sins—
> you who afflict the righteous, who take a bribe,
>   and push aside the needy in the gate.[18]

The extracted resources in Amos 5 are a tax to nobility and not the result of a free market economy, but in many ways, major corporations in rural communities perpetuate the ancient cycle of patronage. Many people in rural areas live in abject poverty. This is often because the wages at the factories, farms, and mines are too low to support a family. Companies that make billions in yearly profits do so because of worker neglect or because the companies neglect to sow back into the communities from which their profits are reaped. Many rural communities cry out, "Let justice roll down like waters and righteousness like an ever-flowing stream."[19] Theologians and pastors should carefully explore themes of justice and fairness when considering rural ecclesiology.

Issues of justice, as we have been reminded of so many times in recent years, often touch on how minority groups are treated. It seems reasonable that one cannot speak of justice without naming oppression. Some rural churches, particularly those primarily made up of racial minorities, may view issues of justice as critical to their mission as a church. Rev. Dr. Leonard Edloe pastors a primarily black church in rural Virginia and also teaches ethics to graduate students at an area seminary. Edloe is a personal friend who I deeply admire and respect, and one of his passions is the rural black church which was a major focus of his own studies and research. He writes of justice issues facing the black community in rural America:

> There are a lot of Theo-Ethical issues that we face in our community, however, from my viewpoint, the Rural Black Church remains silent. We lack in many instances both the facilities and the finances to bring about change in our communities because of structural racism that is embedded in our communities. Our farmers can't get loans. The same holds true for those who wish to start businesses. The Rural Black Church must embrace advocacy and tear down the theologies, some that are in our Churches, to bring a little bit of heaven right here on earth. The silence is deafening. Many avoid the Church because of that silence. We must open our eyes and realize the one that we say that we follow was a radical. That is why Jesus was a victim of capital punishment. It is past time to give up slave holder theology whose sole purpose was to make us good slaves. We must move to the abundant life that Jesus wants us to have.[20]

As you provide leadership in your own rural community, what would it look like for you to explore conversation with local voices like Dr. Edloe? As Martin Luther King, Jr. stated in a 1963 interview, the most segregated hour of the week is still the 11:00 hour on Sunday morning in many of our communities. How is God calling us to listen to one another and learn what brothers and sisters in Christ experience in their own lives? Perhaps our own idea of what it means to be rural people of God needs challenging and questioning.

Rural Populations and Peoples

Many assumptions exist concerning rural culture, and there seems to be two polarities of thought concerning rural towns. Some people hold up rural life as idyllic, buying into stereotypes of open spaces, rugged individualism, and peaceful landscapes. Others seem to distain the thought of rural living, judging small towns as disconnected from the larger world, scared of change, and lagging behind in technology and other comforts readily available in urban environments. Two theological themes emerging here are prudence and discernment. Too often, assumptions about rural culture exist due to inaccurate information, ignorance, or lazy thinking. For example, "Popular associations with rural community life include strong images of public safety, informal social control, and low risk of crime, but the truth does not conform to the *rural mystique*. In fact, rural youth are almost as likely as urban youth to participate in criminal behavior."[21] When considering rural ministry, we must see things for what they are, not what we wish they were. Rural sociologist Ruth Panelli (University of Otago, New Zealand) writes that moving past rural mystique and idealism means a "commitment to deconstruct dominant narratives of rural life (e.g. as productive or idyllic or harmonious/safe)."[22] Rural communities are not bastions of productivity for those who cannot find work or for the black farmer who cannot get a loan. They are not idyllic for those experiencing rural poverty or domestic abuse at the hands of their spouse. They are not harmonious and safe for the rural homeless, who are often ignored or even driven into metropolitan areas under the auspices of "taking them somewhere where they can get the help they need." Tired stereotypes and tropes are not helpful to ministers who serve in rural contexts. The last two years have brought a sea change in cultural conversations regarding sexual assault, racial equality and justice, economic disparity, the nature of truth, and even what it means to be the Church in light of a pandemic. None of these issues is only a metropolitan or suburban issue, and they also impact rural people and places. Small towns are mission fields where God's work may be fruitful if ministry strategies and theologies address the true needs of local people.

Theologically, another theme for small-town churches to consider is *diaspora and change*. In Scripture, one of the key problems the people of God faced was dispersement and separation, often against their will. Jewish people ended up living in non-Jewish states and struggled to maintain religious and cultural identity while integrating into their new places of residence. Three community-level challenges that affect everyone in a small town are: 1) Youth Out-Migration and Brain Drain, 2) Retirement In-Migration, and 3) Natural Decrease.[23] Youth who make good grades in high school are likely to move away from their small town to attend college. After college, most of these youth are unlikely to move back home because the degrees they have earned tend to not match the agricultural and service-based job opportunities that exist in small towns. In many small towns, the best and brightest leave for college and never return. Small towns that are amenity rich (close to water, near a metropolitan area, in a scenic mountain range, possessing an artistic community, etc.) are likely to attract retirees. Often, these retirees move from metropolitan areas where values may be contrary to values imbedded in the small town. Retiree in-migrants may view certain kinds of economic development as beneficial and natural since they have been accustomed to urban sprawl, while the long-time residents of the town might strongly resist big box retailers and new road projects for fear that local families will suffer economically. Finally, as small towns tend to attract aging populations and deal with youth out-migration, they may suffer a slow death, literally. Natural decrease can leave shops on Main Street empty and farmhouses rotting in fields. The threat of diaspora and change is palpable in many small towns as young residents move away and adopt metropolitan values and lifestyles, retirees in-migrate and challenge community norms, and long-time residents pass away, resulting in cultural loss. An exploration of biblical diaspora may prove useful for rural congregations, providing an opportunity for congregants to identify with similar struggles that appear in the canon.

Rural Economy and Socioeconomic Well-Being

In considering the economies of rural localities, one should also consider how those economies contribute to or detract from the well-being of rural people. Theologically, the theme of *shalom* may become powerful, reminding us that God desires wholeness and peace for our communities. As people who serve the Prince of Peace, we should consider ways to bring God's wholeness and healing to our towns and parishes. In the Scripture, the word שָׁלוֹם (*shalom*) emerges as an important concept. The word is most often translated "peace" but may also translate as "completeness," "prosperity," "welfare," "well-being," or "wholeness." What might it look like for rural churches to seek God's shalom in their spheres of influence? The words "globalization" and "rural" may seem an unlikely pair, but the trend toward a globalized economy has major implications for small towns. Pastors and theologians should consider that "Globalization entails a fundamental transformation of the world's economy from an international federation of independent nation states to an emerging vision of the world as a globally organized and managed free trade, free enterprise economy pursued by largely unaccountable political and economic elites."[24] Churches that usher in or participate in shalom are churches that must be comfortable with ministering to people forgotten by the leaders of the world economy. International corporations not only come to rural communities without the consent of residents, they often abruptly pull out in order to move jobs into cheaper labor markets, leaving behind a small town with a completely altered economy.

Churches might consider ways to support an alternate economy not dependent on the whims of profit-minded corporate offices in cities far away. One example of creating an alternate economy might be to move back to a trade-and-barter system for certain goods and services. Brown and Schafft cite a 2007 "study of informal work in rural Pennsylvania [which] found that about 46 percent of surveyed households engaged in informal work, including activities such as household repair, personal services, landscaping, car repair, and selling items at flea markets and yard sales."[25] Rural churches could keep a list of people with specific skills who were willing to share or trade for other skills. This would not be a way for churches to encourage people not to pay taxes, but rather a way for churches to encourage members to bless each other by mutually serving one another out of Christian love. Another example of creating an alternate economy might be planting a community garden where people could freely benefit from the healing work of gardening and the healthy produce of the plants.

This kind of informal economy may also deeply appeal to a rural community's sense of morality. The moral culture of many rural communities is "built around the value of hard labor for its own sake, with survival and masculine pride often being its only rewards. Poverty per se [is] not looked down upon, but rather poverty in the absence of work."[26] When these goals are not met, many males may fall into depression and even abuse alcohol and drugs, making it more difficult to find employment. The way many families cope with the lack of work is through informal work like childcare and auto repair, and self-provision like gardening, fishing, woodcutting, and hunting.[27] In one rural logging community in California:

> [...] moral worth has evolved into a form of symbolic capital. This "moral capital" allows the poor to create distinctions among themselves in the absence of significant economic capital. Perceptions of individuals' moral worth are often based on their coping behaviors,

including how much they do or do not work and their involvement in illegal activities. A person's moral status contributes to more than just his or her reputation, however. Those who are perceived as having lower moral worth are often denied access to the community's increasingly rare jobs, as well as to many forms of community-level charity. Thus, moral capital can be traded for economic capital in the form of job opportunities and charity or social capital in the form of community ties and social support.[28]

The ease with which families are able to cope with rural poverty in an impoverished community has little to do with government or church programs or even job training, but with the moral capital people are able to trade with for goods, service, and even job opportunities.

Religion seemingly plays little impact on the morality of most people in some rural communities. This may come as a surprise to the reader because of the stereotype that the church still holds dramatic influence in small-town America. However, rural sociologist Jennifer Sherman (Washington State University) says that according to her research, religious sources and ideas of morality are "less significant in [rural communities] than are many of the more secular and culturally based ideas."[29] These secular and culturally based ideas especially include a strong work ethic and rugged individualism. For many in rural America, "the moral values on which they daily judge themselves and others tend to be based more in notions of self-discipline and masculine work ethics than in church doctrines such as loving one's neighbor."[30] Sherman is not arguing that ideas like hard work and individualism cannot be found in religion but observing that her research respondents "do not attribute [these ideas] to religious teachings or church sources."[31] Moreover, people in Sherman's research project considered their morals to be traditional values, which calls into question whether or not the church has *ever* enjoyed an often assumed influence in rural America. When we talk about a post-Christian world, we can perhaps now include many rural communities. As Christian pastors and church leaders, we can no longer afford to make assumptions of our privilege and influence in our rural communities.

As ecclesiastical entities, rural and small-town churches have social capital at their disposal. Social capital is the influence an organization can bring to bear because of the good will or trust they build in the community. One of the challenges to bringing shalom to rural communities is simply getting the larger culture to recognize the needs of rural communities and their citizens. In rural locales, "poverty as a social issue is frequently under-recognized. It is therefore worthy of paying close attention to how particular characteristics of different places — spatial, social, political, and economic — may in turn differently shape the causes and consequences of poverty."[32] By speaking out on behalf of rural people and the challenges they face, churches may play a unique role in denominational and political life within local municipalities and even nations. Rural churches may be small compared to their urban counterparts, but the overwhelming fact remains that as many as 200,000 churches exist in the nonmetropolitan counties in the United States.[33] Think of the influence those churches would have if they unified in some way to rally for the purpose of bringing shalom to rural families and communities!

It is imperative that theological themes relevant to rural culture spring forth in the life of rural congregations. Themes like *imago Dei* and *missio Dei*, creation care, community, justice and fairness, diaspora and change, and shalom may provide a lifetime of ministry initiatives, conversations, and sermon series for any minister or church. Rural congregations might immensely benefit from further exploring these theological themes. The twenty-first century brings unique challenges for small towns, and churches determined to maintain resilience while exploring avenues of positive transformation are likely to survive the transition into the decades ahead. Rural churches could be some of the best laboratories for incarnational experimentation, resulting in thoughtful ecclesiology, and astute ministers will take note of the unique opportunities and challenges facing their congregations. The tides are shifting in rural communities, and we might do well to consider exactly what forces are at play. It seems as if rural communities are shifting along with the rest of culture and society. To navigate the changing sea, we must understand the deep impulses with which we are dealing. It is time to explore the postmodern tide.

Chapter Two
THE POSTMODERN TIDE IN RURAL CHURCHES

> *"We must free ourselves of the hope that the sea will ever rest. We must learn to sail in high winds."*
>
> – Aristotle Onassis, Shipping Magnate

In some ways, tides are visible, and in other ways, they are great movements below the surface, below what is viewable to the naked eye. A new tidal movement is presently upon rural churches, even if people do not yet see it. One significant shift in emerging culture has nothing to do with technology like high-speed internet, green-energy solar panels, or even a more globalized economy. The shift is more philosophical (under the surface, playing on the tidal metaphor) and moving *away* from what Nancy Murphy and others have termed *foundationalism* as a way of thinking. According to Murphy, foundationalism is "first, the assumption that knowledge systems must include a class of beliefs that are somehow immune from challenge; and, second, the assumption that all reasoning within the system proceeds in one direction only—from that set of special, indubitable beliefs to others, but not the reverse."[34] Scholars and journalists have labeled this shift *postmodernity*, which has been widely written about and analyzed in various fields of study, beginning with Lyotard in 1979.[35] Küng critiques postmodernism as an answer to modernity believing it "is no way out of the crisis. For while postmodernism proclaims an end to modernity, it only has 'radical pluralism' or relativism to offer as an alternative […]."[36] The tide no doubt holds the power to erode. Suffice it to say, some views on postmodernism seem optimistic and others more fatalistic. Some embrace the tide, and some fear it. The same is true in your church.

The last church I pastored was in a rural Virginia community called Tappahannock, an old Rappahannock tribal name meaning "the tide rises and falls." Because of the church's location (across from a tidal riverfront), the imagery of water and tides runs deep in the area's cultural memory. In many ways, the number of residents in the community rises and recedes, like the tide, based on the seasons. In the warm months, seasonal residents come to live on the water and recreate in the area. Tidal movements are constant, and residents get so used to living near a tidal waterway, the tides often go unnoticed (like cultural movements). When the tide recedes, things appear on the shoreline that you might not see otherwise (like oyster shells, crab shells, coins, and beautiful sand beaches); likewise, when culture shifts away from allegiance to God's kingdom and cultural Christianity loses hegemony, the church may discover unknown gifts within her midst.

When the tides come in, all ships rise with the water level; in the same way, cultural change shifts our church – whether we like it or not. Boat owners should tie off their vessels to docks with enough slack in the line for the vessel to adjust as the water level rises and falls, and churches with built-in flexibility can move slightly when cultural change comes without becoming unanchored from biblical and spiritual moorings. The tide exists beyond our control, and forces that we often do not see or have any leverage over (the moon, the sun, gravity) move vast amounts of water daily. In the same way, cultural tides are beyond the control of any one person or church, and there are forces far beyond us that lead to great movements in humanity – like postmodernity.

While argument exists over the very term *postmodern*, the consensus of Christian scholarship seems to be that postmodernity creeps upon us, if it is not already here. Drew Dyck, editorial manager of Christianity Today International, included postmodern as a category of church "leavers" in his book, *Generation Ex-Christian: Why Young Adults Are Leaving the Faith...And How to Bring Them Back*.[37] If Christianity Today (as arguably a sample of the pulse of American evangelicalism) is comfortable with the term *postmodern*, then it seems the term and all of its implications are now widespread topics for dialogue and debate within American Christianity. Indeed, writings proliferate concerning postmodernity in the church, including theological works from the postmodern perspective, practical works with ideas for how churches can minister in a postmodern world, and books warning people about even the dangers of postmodernity for Christendom. A simple Google search with the term "postmodern church" yields over 800,000 results![38]

As postmodernity permeates urban environments, and suburban and rural churches begin to deal with postmodernity and its implications for theology and ministry, rural churches will inevitably face postmodernity and all of its implications for life and faith. Rural families in the 1930s could not foresee a time when rural homesteads might have a bathtub, a sink with running water, electricity, light bulbs, and modern kitchen appliances, not to mention things that had not been invented yet like computers, internet, and video-streaming services like Netflix for home entertainment. Twenty years ago, the owners of Tappahannock Lumber Company could not have foreseen a son coming home from college and leading the company into developing markets around the world. In the same way, many people in your rural church today might find it unlikely that they (or their children and neighbors) may soon move away from viewing faith as a bounded set of propositional truth claims to a more holistic view, taking on "a degree of circularity—of nonlinear reasoning—in the internal justification of the tradition, as theologians, biblical scholars, and others seek coherence among doctrinal claims, textual interpretations, and interpretations of history of that very tradition."[39] Rural faith, in the future, may increasingly be seen as a rich tapestry of interwoven philosophies, histories, and theological streams, and the fundamentalism that grips many rural churches might give way to more postmodern outlooks as those values continue to transfer into rural communities from urban ones. The tide has the ability to pound away and even shape hardened rocks, given enough time.

A century ago, rural life as we know it was unimaginable, yet change moves forward. Currently, there is a national initiative to provide broadband internet to every community and county in the United States, which means that within a decade, every household in America might have access to high-speed internet.[40] This will cause a dramatic shift for small towns and small-town churches as new avenues open economically and educationally to rural populations and new values proliferate into rural areas over the internet. Technology and the rapid dissemination of knowledge go hand in hand with the spread of postmodernity, and many rural churches may soon feel the effects of entering (or being forced into) what Küng calls "another entire constellation."[41] You can safely conclude that your church will

Chapter Two: THE POSTMODERN TIDE IN RURAL CHURCHES

not remain untouched by such an overarching social movement, and the sooner your congregation considers this movement and possible responses (both individually and culturally) the better.

A great example of competing values in a rural context is the imaginary Pottersville from the classic movie, *It's a Wonderful Life*. Mr. Potter is a man with modern values, whose dreams of profit and growth clash with the idealized and traditional values of rural Bedford Falls. Near the end of the film, protagonist George Bailey considers suicide, and a guardian angel named Clarence shows him what the town might look like without George's presence. Bailey is shown a vision of Bedford Falls being renamed Pottersville and containing every vanity conceivable, including casinos and brothels. In the film, modernity is shown to lead to moral and social ruin, and traditional values are celebrated as pure and ideal.[42]

This struggle still exists in small towns, especially in locales where modernity *has* brought ruin, like towns where resource extraction runs dry which leads to mine and mill closures. Another preliminary conclusion and a challenge adding to the complexity is that these small towns like Tappahannock now exist amid an increasingly postmodern world. The town was historically a port village for the English crown 400 years ago and then transitioned to a waterman's town for fishing and oyster harvesting 100 years ago. As overfishing and overharvesting occurred, the state has regulated industries to the point that it is no longer economical for sole proprietors to make a living as watermen. Tappahannock does attract industries of various sorts and boasts a regional airport. Most of the economy currently is retail and service related as Tappahannock has become a regional hub for commerce, surrounded by even more rural communities whose residents drive to Tappahannock for goods and services. Your rural community may be situated in a different location, but it no doubt shares similarities with this tidal waterway community in Virginia.

Many rural communities have seen rapid and unsettling changes in the last 20 years. Boarded up storefronts and dilapidated buildings dot the landscape of many small towns, perhaps where an oil field dried up or where industrial agriculture has replaced family-owned farms. It seems other rural communities have been luckier and have become regional hubs for commerce and shopping. But even in these communities, the arrival of big box stores and suburban chain restaurants often signals the demise of locally owned businesses. In these cases, it may seem like things are fine because the veneer of economic development masks the fact that many small business owners may be facing bankruptcy. In fact, many rural towns have a vision to become "a regional commercial, industrial, and employment center while keeping a small town feeling."[43] It seems many rural leaders are seeking continued and measured economic development without ruining the rural character of the locality.

As rural churches desire to give voice to the love of Jesus, they should consider what it may mean to have a vision for God's kingdom in their local context. This vision may include doing ministry beyond the four walls, reaching new people groups with the love and news of Jesus, and serving the community in varied ways. Some churches may catch a vision that includes leading in certain ethical conversations that arise as the local community continues to develop, such as fair and affordable housing, the need to maintain a high level of creation stewardship within the community, prison and sentence reform, and a Christ-like concern for the poor in the region who are not lifted by rising economic tides. What, if anything, will emerge in your congregation's life and faith as the surrounding community grapples with ever increasing change?

Chapter Two: THE POSTMODERN TIDE IN RURAL CHURCHES

In many ways, twenty-first century Christianity centers in reimagining *faith* in the postmodern context. This is not to say that the substance of our faith, Jesus, should ever change, only that people increasingly approach faith in different ways that may fundamentally impact your own congregation's approach to ministry. About a year ago, my wife's grandmother moved in with my in-laws and needed to downsize her possessions so she could comfortably live in the room they had prepared for her. She knows how much I love to cook and graciously offered to let me have all of her recipes. In case you were wondering, when a 90-year-old grandma offers to give you her entire box of recipes, the proper response is, "Thanks, Grandma!" As I dug through the box, my wife and I began to chuckle at the names of many desserts. One handwritten card had the words "Sinful Pumpkin Pie" written at the top. Another had the popular "Devil's Food Cake" recipe. Never mind questions about why angel food cake is white and devil's food cake is black (perhaps that's another book altogether). What made me grin and even shake my head a little is thinking about how the conservative and Puritanical influences of my childhood led upstanding Christian women to create desserts with such names and how scandalous they must have felt when they went to a dinner party or church potluck with their sinful devil food. I have yet to see someone bring a "Better Than Sex Cake" to a church potluck. Here you may rightfully ask, "Why does Jonathan feel compelled to share this anecdotal information?" A fair question indeed.

The point is this – Christianity has lost enough privilege in our culture and there is so much injustice in the world, it seems hard to imagine younger Christians sitting around and sheepishly blushing at the names of desserts. They may be more inclined to deconstruct the name of the cake itself. Does your faith make you blush about words like sin, devil, or sex? Because those words certainly don't make anyone in our culture blush. Society is now so different from society of 50, 30, or even 10 years ago that churches who take the same approach to ministry as they took in the past are doomed to struggle in unhelpful ways.

The complexity of contemporary society could be good news for emerging theology in your rural community. Increasingly, many Christians (and not only the post progressive) care deeply about economic justice, racial justice, sexual justice, environmental justice, and women's justice.[44] Not only is society at large more socially complex than just a few decades ago, but because of globalization and the rapid transfer of values from urban to rural locales, increasingly "rural change is becoming more complex in nature," including changes affecting your own church and the surrounding region.[45] Instead of only increasing the kingdom of God through focusing on the eternal, rural churches should also seek to increase God's reign in tangible ways on earth. This, of course, requires relationships and community because "the justice that people need is a moving target."[46] Through living in community and building intentional relationships, rural churches can seek justice in multiple ways.

Pragmatism over Idealism

Rural communities of faith will increasingly need to decide how to approach the gospel in the twenty-first century. A challenge for rural churches and people is to view the culture in small towns the way it actually exists, not through the lens of an idealized past. One author acknowledges, "We've got to realize that in our emerging culture, we are now in a different culture and we need to view it and the people in it as a missionary would. Christians are now foreigners in a post-Christian culture, and we have got to wake up to this reality."[47] Viewing our culture as a *mission*

Chapter Two: THE POSTMODERN TIDE IN RURAL CHURCHES

field rather than *Christian* may prove challenging for some church members because such an outlook acknowledges that change has already occurred. At this juncture in time, it is normal to hear people talk of a "post-Christian Europe," but one could arguably use the same descriptor of North America.

This inherently cuts against the notion that nothing ever changes in small towns or that rural communities are somehow culturally pure compared to more urban locales. I once pastored in a rural Virginia community called Urbanna, which had more sailboats and crab pots than people. A local historian observes of this colonial village that "today, the 600 or so people who live in the incorporated limits of Urbanna are on sacred ground where Native Americans, British Tories, American Patriots, slaves and masters, and Union and Confederate troops once trod."[48] A cursory glance of your own community's history may reveal that change has always been afoot, whether acknowledged or not.

Not only does postmodernity impact small-town churches through value exchanges due to spatial relation[49] to urban environments, Christianity does not enjoy the same influence it once did in rural America. For a small-town church, this reality may prove a difficult reality to embrace. Despite rural stereotypes, it seems that in rural areas, "the most dominant forms of morality [...] are drawn mostly from cultural rather than religious sources and images. While religious doctrines are important as well, they inform only a small portion of the moral pronouncements, judgments, and decisions that make up much of the day-to-day fabric of social life" in small-town America.[50] Wherever you live in North America, religion is not as important or privileged as it was in the past.

For the people who attend your church on a regular basis, Christianity has an impact on their lives, but as in the city, empirical research confirms most people in your small community likely do not attend church regularly or attribute Christianity to the moral choices they make each day. Rural churches and congregants should face the reality of their eroding influence in the community because organized religion's influence wanes in the larger culture. In fact, the church itself is arguably a microcosm of the larger culture. One underlying assumption then is that this reality may possibly reverse through creative ministry focused on bridging the gap between 1) traditional, modern, and postmodern values and the gap between 2) an idealized approach focused on a mythic past and a pragmatic approach focused on present realities and future possibilities.

Possible Critiques of a Postmodern Rural Project

Any attempt to address emerging culture in rural churches is itself open to criticism from rural studies leaders and those who identify as postmodern. In the first case, rural studies leaders around the country have not often thought of the field in terms of postmodernity.[51] As previously stated, scholarly articles examining postmodernity in the rural context prove scarce.

Secondly, emerging church leaders may not appreciate such a treatment because they generally dislike it when people are placed in categories like rural and urban. One example comes from an online conversation in the Emerging Village Community where one respondent asked, "What would be postmodern would be to rethink whether the categories 'urban' and 'rural' really mean anything, and insofar as they have meaning, who do those meanings serve? How do those categories obscure the universal human condition that exists in all of us?"[52] To be sure, these are excellent questions. He was making the argument that the project was faulty from the start, beginning with modern categories of thinking about social groups. He further states:

> Postmodern thinking is an attempt to start at this kind of conceptual level. Christianity and postmodernity don't mix well, even among Christian pomo [postmodern] sympathizers because evangelical Protestantism begins with the self at the center of its theology, not with the church or the communion of saints. But even here, a categorical flip is not sufficient — the latter way of thinking has its own traps. These are some of the problems I see with thinkers that want to be emergent; they're mapping on top of a philosophy that starts from a different center.[53]

The process of developing a ministry plan to equip rural congregations for ministry in the emerging culture will persistently present challenges and even invite critique from multiple angles.

Despite potential concerns among some about using the term "rural," countless believers surely experience life and church in ways that differ significantly from their metropolitan counterparts. The evidence is the body of writing in both rural sociology and rural ministry. To pretend these differences do not exist would not serve the purpose of a ministry project centered on cultural adaption for rural churches.

A postmodern move, it seems, might consist of a more holistic approach, viewing the experiences of rural congregations in a larger web of social fabric. This moves away from the foundationalism Murphy discusses but stops short of the relativism displayed by Peterson and others. It seems that "for holists, in contrast, there is no preferred direction of reasoning, and the kinds of connections among beliefs in the web are many – strict logical implication, weaker probabilistic arguments, arguments 'forward' to further conclusions, arguments 'backward' to presuppositions."[54]

To view rural churches as a part of a larger social fabric, one might consider how rural and urban studies scholars make distinctions between rural and urban and consider the ways rural and urban locales overlap. In an increasingly postmodern rural context like Tappahannock with population flow between the rural Essex County and surrounding communities, values now transfer from urban to suburban environments more rapidly.

The Rural "Other"

Rural sociologists and theologians often argue that metropolitan and urban people frequently view rural people and towns as "others," those who are foreign and backwards, as those who are less than and second tier.[55] Rural ministry author and theologian Glenn Daman argues that rural Americans have largely been forgotten in our rapidly urbanizing context. It seems "many people tend to view the resistance of rural people to progressivism as being backwards and naïve, stuck in a mentality that existed thirty years ago."[56] As urban and rural populations move further from each other and seem more distant, not only geographically but politically, isolation sets in for both, often leading people in rural and urban contexts to form stereotypes of what "rural" and "urban" people do, say, and think.

Chapter Two: THE POSTMODERN TIDE IN RURAL CHURCHES

This means "when we fail to understand and value a culture and people, we will eventually devalue and probably ridicule them."[57] The people in your church may experience status as the rural "other" in their places of work or when they visit a doctor in the city. Many church members who commute to metropolitan areas for work may receive questions from co-workers as to why they choose to live in a small, seemingly backwards town like (insert your community's name here). A parishioner I knew at a former church loved living in our rural community and dutifully commuted daily to her job at the state supreme court. Her co-workers often teased her about being from a small town and derided rural living. In doing so, they made the mistake of basing their views of rural communities on mythical assumptions and personal biases concerning rural places and people. A close view of your rural community, however, may indeed show that the region does not meet many popular assumptions about rural spaces.

While your rural location may be idyllic in some ways, for the poor, it may seem less optimal. The community may present as a caring small town where everybody knows their neighbor, but the rural homeless may see a different town as they themselves bear the status of "other" in a community that has itself been effectively "othered" by society at large. A postmodern view of a rural community realizes "rurality can no longer be regarded as a single space, but a multiplicity of social spaces that overlap the same geographic area."[58] The people of your church and your ministry context do not fit neatly into stereotypical or idyllic molds of "rural" that often pervade urban culture.

One missional challenge in the increasingly postmodern rural context is to consider how God calls us to minister to rural "others" while being seen *as* the rural "other." Populations that may have the status of "other" in our context include those with mental health issues, the homeless, asylum seekers, religious minorities, children, and even animals like crabs and fish which may face negative impacts from eco-tourism.[59] How is God calling you to minister to the rural "others" in your midst? Jesus often exhibited radical hospitality to those "othered" individuals in his own culture, and all of our churches will do well to follow Christ's example.

One impact of postmodernity is referred to by Fritz Kling as "a global Monoculture [...], emerging as multinational-corporations create common world tastes around logos, products, advertising slogans, stars, songs, brand names, jingles, and trademarks."[60] Many rural communities have several empty buildings and store fronts that once housed locally owned hardware and grocery stores. According to longtime Tappahannock residents, since around the time Walmart and Lowe's came to town, many stores sit vacant, and many longtime local shop owners closed their family-owned businesses. In many ways, Applebee's and other national foodservice chains have replaced locally owned eateries and locally sourced menus.

It seems that in succumbing to the monoculture of globalization, rural Christians have something of an identity crisis, particularly those longtime community members who have seen radical shifts in the community during their lifetime. It is telling and informative that Kling names monoculture as a global current which is shaping the world (per his monograph's title). Perhaps the exploration of postmodernity as a tidal shift is not far off.

Monoculture even impacts churches in terms of curriculum offerings from major publishers like Group!, Smyth and Helwys, Abingdon, or Lifeway with nearly every church between New York City and Miami doing one of the same four or five

Chapter Two: THE POSTMODERN TIDE IN RURAL CHURCHES

Vacation Bible School curriculums each year. How can a unique rural church maintain a unique call and outlook when even denominational publishing houses enable and perpetuate the trend of monoculture in church life?

One final observation concerning the postmodern wave in rural churches and rural "othering" is that urban areas often view rural places as areas for future colonization and resource extraction or destinations for recreational getaways. A postmodern approach to ministry might require small-town churches to find their own identity apart from denominationalism or apart from urban church programs and strategies. If we could "decenter the city as the unit of analysis,"[61] then we might stop comparing ourselves to urban and suburban churches, stop succumbing to Christian monoculture, and develop a more uniquely incarnational approach to ministry in the community where God has planted us.

The postmodern wave is creeping into your own rural congregation. Congregations can, however, respond nimbly and thoughtfully, finding ways to use the tide to our advantage for the sake of the kingdom. We can also respond with fear, deciding to respond in reactionary ways to the changes around us, perhaps with the feeling of constantly bailing water from the boat or sailing against prevailing winds. The third possible response to postmodernity is to do nothing which may certainly bring death from drowning in a wake of cultural change. As I see it, rural churches in post-Christian North America can set sail in faith, bail water in panic, or drown a slow death.

Chapter Three
WHEN CURRENTS COLLIDE: INTERSECTIONALITY IN RURAL MINISTRY

> *"Life is like the sea. Its tides and currents sometimes take a man to distant shores that he never dreamed existed."*
>
> – Jocelyn Murray, *The English Pirate*

Numerous differences exist between ministry in urban and rural environments. Part of the challenge in these differences comes not only from different cultures in urban and rural places but also the spatial relationship of rural and urban to one another. Many contemporary philosophers and theologians claim that we live in an emerging era that is moving beyond modernity. Some call this postmodernity, while others call the new era hypermodernity. Generally speaking, modernity often entails efficiency, reason, and the compartmentalization of life, while postmodernity focuses on natural processes, experience, and holism. The philosophical trend of postmodernity is beginning to impact people everywhere, including rural populations.

Inmigration is a term that means the transfer of populations within a country or border. When people move from urban locales to rural communities or when white flight leads people to move from an inner city to a suburb, social scientists refer to these movements of people within national borders as inmigration. As rural areas experience inmigration from college graduates returning home, retirees moving from urban places (more likely), and from families moving out of the city to escape unaffordable housing, values between urban and rural locations are transferring at a rate unseen by previous generations. This is also true as rural communities now have media delivered from around the world (like cable television and internet-based news services) straight into their living rooms. Another reason for the transfer of typically urban values into rural locales is the rise of commuting and telecommuting. Many urban workers are now able to live in rural locations, enjoying the benefits of the urban economy while also taking advantage of all rural living has to offer.

In order to form a model for rural and small town ministry in the twenty-first century, one should grapple with these trends, attempting to understand technological, philosophical, economic, and sociological impacts of the spatial relation between urban and rural cities, towns, and villages. In this chapter, using the article "Postmodern Values in Rural Peripheries" by Éva G. Fekete and Katalin Liptak and the book *Critical Rural Theory: Structure, Space, Culture* by Thomas, Lowe, Fulkerson, and Smith as guides, we will: 1) identify localized examples of the broad rural cultural norms, 2) explore the relationship rural communities have to surrounding urban centers, 3) unpack rural cultural dynamics which are multi-generational, and 4) identify how these cultural realities relate to our ministry settings.

Through examining your local context and the spatial relation of your community to surrounding urban centers, you will gain a clearer sense for how postmodernity may be affecting the parishioners of the church as well as the community.

There are certainly urban places where postmodernity seems evident. Churches fully embracing postmodernism seem to concentrate in highly urban, extremely diverse, and demographically young environments. I do not claim that small town and rural places are already postmodern in their outlook and mentality, but there is a seemingly strong correlation between trends in contemporary society and younger parishioners at many rural congregations. The question is not, "Is my rural church postmodern?" or "Can postmodern worship and ministry exist in our small town?" but rather, "To what extent does postmodernity affect my context, and how should our ministry adjust accordingly to stay vibrant in the rapidly evolving culture of our time?" This is a question every church should ask, no matter their denominational and theological tradition and no matter their local context.

Localized Examples from Rural Sociology

Rural and urban communities both occupy unique spaces in culture and society. In many ways, the two have been identified and defined by their differences. It is not enough, however, to simply define rural by all that urban is not. In our current culture, there is an increasing overlap of these spaces and how they occupy our lives. The study of how spaces like urban and rural intersect is called "spatial relations." To truly understand the twenty-first century rural context, it can prove incredibly helpful to identify ways our churches and the people in them relate to those in different contexts.

A postmodern approach to understanding the spatial relation of rural and urban locales might observe, "The city does not end at the city line or at the last exurb, but rather is part of a continuous web of social relations that as a whole represent the urban system." Rural towns connect to cities through a giant web of interaction—economically, politically, and spatially. This idea of an interconnected web is extremely similar to Nancy Murphy's conversation about all knowledge and experience as a web.[62] Instead of compartmentalizing knowledge, philosophy, theology, economics, politics, or spatial experience into urban *or* rural, a postmodern approach to rural and urban relations realizes that rural and urban do not exist in separate compartments but are part of an interconnected whole.

Additionally, a postmodern approach to rural/urban relations realizes that while rural places may not all identify with postmodern values, they are still affected deeply by these values because of the web of connection existing between the city and the countryside. A postmodernist approach to rural ministry will "not look to sciences but to the humanities. In essence, postmodernist approaches seem different from earlier sociological approaches to [spatiality] because the aim is different; whereas a social science approach attempts to explain the phenomenon, the humanities approach is to critique the phenomenon."[63] In this sense, one way many small towns and rural locales feel impacted by postmodernism in urban life is that in some ways, their very existence stands a critique of postmodern philosophy and values. This assumption, which is made by many, is only true if rural values and postmodern values differ.

People's values should be considered when discussing postmodernism's impact on rural culture. Curiously, when sampled, people in rural areas are attracted to traditional and postmodern values more than modern values.[64] Traditional values identified by Fekete and Liptak include self-sufficiency, love of nature, the importance of family, respect for the elderly, friendliness to strangers, respect for tradition itself, and love for the community. Note that traditional values do not inherently lean toward one political side or another as many espouse. Modern values identify as reason over emotion, order, feats of engineering, efficiency, growth, and innovation. Finally, postmodern values are described as emotion and aesthetics over reason, environmental concern, strong preference for diversity, building individual identities, preserving and promoting cultural heritage, social/communal participation, solidarity, and tolerance.[65] While not identical, traditional and postmodern values may prove complimentary in numerous ways. Postmodernism often gets oversimplified into moral relativism, hipster clothing trends, and decadent city life. This reductionist approach to describing postmodern values and people risks missing the similarities those with postmodern values may have with those maintaining traditional values. Perhaps surprisingly, postmodernism may already have more of an affect on the rural young than many realize. Our models for rural ministry should take into account the spatial relation between rural and urban, including the ever-increasing transfer of values.

A Case Study in Spatial Relations

As mentioned in the introduction to this book, I became engrossed in studying rural ministry after moving from the

Houston metropolitan area (>6 million population) to Urbanna, Virginia (<700 population). I felt that in order to understand my ministry context, I needed to study more about rural culture in general and learn specific local history that made my context beautiful and unique. Urbanna serves as a great case study for understanding how spatial relations works and can be of value to those leading rural churches.

Urbanna, Virginia, is a small town of about 600 permanent residents with a rich heritage. The distinction of permanent residents is important because Urbanna is a tourist destination. There is an RV and motorhome campground on the outskirts of town that has 5,000 residents during warmer seasons. Some small towns base their economies on manufacturing, resource extraction, or agriculture, but others like Urbanna increasingly rely on rural tourism. Urbanna means "Town of Anne" in old English, as in Queen Anne. Urbanna has been in existence since the 1600s when settlers at Jamestown commissioned the settlement as a tobacco port and warehousing station. The original tobacco warehouse still stands and serves as the town's welcome center and museum. As the town grew and tobacco became a smaller part of the Virginian economy, resource extraction from the Chesapeake Bay became the mainstay of the local economy. Watermen fished and harvested oysters for generations until overfishing and competing economies of scale due to globalization caused a drastic reduction in the industry a few decades ago. One matriarch church member (now deceased) fondly recalled that her husband paid for their home with the cash from a single day's catch in the mid-1950s! Not so these days. The famous Virginian Arthur Lee is a native son of Urbanna, and his Lansdowne estate still stands in the middle of town. Lee was perhaps the first American spy, a diplomat to Spain and France during the Revolutionary War, and a Virginian

Chapter Three: WHEN CURRENTS COLLIDE: INTERSECTIONALITY IN RURAL MINISTRY

Delegate to the First Continental Congress. Lee's home and grave, along with numerous other landmarks in town, is on the National Register of Historic Places. Baptist preacher John Waller was once imprisoned in Urbanna for preaching without a license from the Commonwealth which in part led Thomas Jefferson and James Madison to craft freedom of speech and religion into the Virginia and United States Constitutions, respectively.

This incredibly rich heritage makes Urbanna a delightful place to live, but it also means that many here buy into the "myth of a happier past."[66] People in Urbanna celebrate the past, as they should, but this celebratory posture often leads to idealism that prevents people from seeing things as they really exist today. Significantly, "changes in the countryside are not a new phenomenon, and neither is the nostalgic yearning for the idyllic pastoral past."[67] In other words, people in small towns have always longed for the "good ol' days." When considering the history of Urbanna, the town has been constantly changing for nearly 400 years! Industries have come and gone. A town that was once an outpost of English colonialism is now certifiable Americana. Civil War troops set up camp on the edge of town. Slavery was abolished. The town once had a school of its own, but now children go to the county school. The list could continue. Any notion that Urbanna is a small town where things never change is nothing more than a mythological narrative. Things have been constantly changing and evolving here for nearly four centuries!

Spatially, this change can be understood by Urbanna's relation to surrounding urban centers. Urbanna is about one hour east of Richmond (Virginia's capital), an hour northwest of Yorktown and Norfolk (the center of Virginia's military industrial economic sector), and 45 minutes from Williamsburg (a major education, shopping, and tourism hub). With each of these major metropolitan areas a short distance from Urbanna, their impact on the town shows in multiple ways. Through observation one realizes:

> [...] the countryside is undergoing dramatic changes such as the decline of agriculture and the rise of new communication and transportation technologies that link rural areas to the rest of the world in new ways, while at the same time many urban areas are expanding their boundaries to incorporate the hinterlands and many rural residents are migrating to the city in search of employment.[68]

The changes in our culture, including evolving technology, new types of commerce, and new health care models, all directly influence Urbanna. Each of the surrounding metropolitan areas holds immense influence over towns like Urbanna. Rural towns tend to have little say over statewide economic and political policies.

One might assume that cultural influence only travels one way, from urban to rural, but "when rural areas are able to avoid political-economic co-optation, they are better able to engage in cultural innovation. Thus, in contrast to the stereotypical view of the rural as a passive recipient of cultural change, we see rural areas as potentially active agents of cultural innovation that can in turn influence urban areas."[69] As a small-town congregation, your church has the ability to innovate in ways that may provide examples for city and suburban churches. This may especially prove true in the case of ministering to people of both traditional and postmodern mentalities, as both exist in your small town.

Chapter Three: WHEN CURRENTS COLLIDE: INTERSECTIONALITY IN RURAL MINISTRY

Multigenerational Dynamics in Rural Communities

Naming ways that traditional and postmodern values complement each other is critical to understanding how rural churches may reach multiple generations simultaneously. In some ways, the values are ones aligning with age ranges, but this does not always hold true. Let us return momentarily to Fekete and Liptak. It is worth mentioning that their article was a result of a study performed in rural communities in Hungary and Transylvania. Postmodernism is currently more influential in Europe than in the United States, so the article is perhaps a forecast of things to come here. A study from Hungary and Transylvania may seem obscure, and perhaps it is, but it is the only study of its kind I have discovered that analyzes the possibility (and reality) of postmodernity in rural locales.

At this point, many academics specializing in rural studies have begun to observe and explore the impact of postmodernity on rural communities, but Fekete and Liptak's study still stands alone as some of the most groundbreaking research in this area. They state as a result of their empirical analysis, "[...] we can conclude that besides the presence of traditional values, postmodern values are also spreading in the examined rural areas. The latter came partly from urban scale of values, but traditional values probably could directly turn over to them, too."[70] This once again highlights the transfer of values between urban and rural places. Their claim is that traditional and postmodern values may actually be *interchangeable*, which flies in the face of many underlying assumptions people have about traditional and postmodern culture. How are these values so complementary, and what does it mean for churches in small towns?

First, self-sufficiency, a traditional value (TV), and building individual identities, a postmodern value (PV), complement each other nicely. Together, these values focus on the individual and on attaining moral and social capital through building up oneself. Perhaps a combined ethos here can be named as *Individual Capital*. For traditionalists, Individual Capital (and sometimes morality itself) comes through self-sufficiency. Postmoderns build Individual Capital by celebrating individuality and expression of self. Both traditionalists and postmodernists desire Individual Capital and create such capital through focusing on self. Additional shared values include love of nature (TV) and environmental concern (PV). These shared values combine as *Creation Stewardship*. Traditionalists may love and appreciate nature and show passion for conservationism, while postmodernists likely buy into global-warming/climate-change politics and desire sweeping social change through green energy. Churches that can find ways to appeal to the traditionalist's desire for conservation and the postmodernist's desire for going green (without being political) will have a winning Creation Stewardship ministry initiative.

Another set of shared values is respect for tradition (TV) and preserving and promoting cultural heritage (PV). Combined, they become *Legacy Celebration*. Traditionalists have a strong respect for legacy and a desire to leave a legacy for future generations. Postmodernists feel a sense of wonder and awe toward the distant past, especially the ancient. Legacy Celebration meets both felt needs, giving traditionalists the opportunity to pass on cherished traditions while feeding the postmodern sense of respect for heritage and culture preservation. Finally, love for the community (TV) combined with social/communal participation (PV) may be described simply as *Love of Neighbor*. This value is not only engrained in traditionalists and postmodernists, but it is a key New Testament ethic/commandment. Also, through Love of Neighbor, traditionalists and postmodernists can meet their need *for* community while meeting the needs *of* the community.

In highlighting the shared values of *Individual Capital, Creation Stewardship, Legacy Celebration, and Love of Neighbor,* churches in rural areas may reach those in the community with traditional and postmodern values. The one disadvantage here is that people with modern values still live in small towns. They just aren't the majority. Finding ways to serve the traditional population while reaching the emerging generation may lead to isolating those with modern values from our ministry. There are no easy answers here, so it is critical to strive for balance in ministry programs and initiatives.

When these values converge in local churchwork, powerful and transformative ministry can take place. At another rural church I pastored, Beale Memorial Baptist Church, after preaching a sermon on creation care as a part of a stewardship sermon series, a leader in the church came to me and stated that as a result of my sermon, he wanted to donate solar panels to the church in his deceased mother's honor. The fact that the gentleman's contribution gained the support of everyone in the church was perhaps an incredible merging of different value systems that may have seemed the same on the surface. This generous gift helped people in our own congregation with different worldviews find shared identity around *Individual Capital, Creation Stewardship, Legacy Celebration, and Love of Neighbor.* After the solar panels were installed, our church saved significantly on energy costs, and we were able to reallocate funds that once went to utilities to missional ministry.

Implications for Rural Churches

Odds are, your church has many people who classify as traditionalists as well as some with more of a postmodern mentality. These two groups represent an overwhelming number of people in many rural churches. Spatially, most small towns are situated between multiple metropolitan areas so there is considerable travel, commerce, and value exchange within those regions. The fact that some rural communities are tourist destinations (hunting, camping, fishing, skiing, oceanfront, whale watching, hiking, vineyards, pumpkin patch farms, etc.) further increases value exchange in many towns. Your church would do well to view your community as you actually exist and not according to the community's own mythology. Because of the high rate of value exchange existing in communities like Urbanna, Virginia, the values of the community are ever evolving.

Many rural churches seem to combat low institutional self-esteem. This may be because too often, rural "is conceived as a space to be moved into, not as a space already integral to the functioning of the system."[71] This leads people to say things like, "We are headed back to civilization," when leaving a small town. The idea that rural places are uncivilized may lead to churches that feel ill equipped to reach the world for Christ. After all, society constantly tells them how insignificant they are. Unfortunately, this is sometimes even true in the way resources are allocated denominationally with projects, rallies, and conferences tending to center in metropolitan areas. While this may be unavoidable in many ways (a major youth conference requires a giant block of hotel rooms reserved months in advance), the effect may be that small-town churches feel like they are constantly participating in the exciting ministries of

Chapter Three: WHEN CURRENTS COLLIDE: INTERSECTIONALITY IN RURAL MINISTRY

urban Christians while never creating and owning exciting ministries at home. There are numerous opportunities for creative ministry in rural churches, especially between those holding traditional and postmodern values. By taking advantage of these opportunities, your church can increase its influence regionally and promote a positive self-image.

Additionally, many stereotypes exist concerning small towns which can affect the way our church views itself. Rural people are not all conservative, not all rednecks, not all farmers, not all traditional, not all old, and not all poor. In fact, some aspects of rural culture may simply be a "significant resistance to urban hegemony."[72] Realizing that much of the culture in our church exists because of the way our town spatially relates to urban centers is eye opening. Since traditional values and postmodern values have much in common, opportunity exists to break free from rural stereotypes with the way we do ministry. Many assume that "all the exciting ministry" happens in the city, perhaps in a re-gentrifying neighborhood or some exotically wealthy suburb. To the contrary, small-town churches are actually positioned to become wonderful laboratories for ministerial and cultural collaboration and may lead as examples for existing urban churches. This brings an exciting invitation to consider fresh ways of ushering in the gospel to your own community and the world through the ministry of your church.

Chapter Four
EQUIPPING RURAL CHURCHES TO SET SAIL

> *"The fishermen know that the sea is dangerous and the storm terrible, but they have never found these dangers sufficient reason for remaining ashore."*
>
> – Vincent Van Gogh

There is little question that rural culture is presently experiencing rapid change. The notion that things never change in rural communities is a myth. In fact, "rural communities have never been insulated from social and economic change under way in broader society."[73] With postmodernity impacting urban and suburban communities, rural communities should also brace for impact and find ways to adapt. Throughout history, God has walked with God's people no matter the era or epoch in which they live. Your church is no different. Perhaps as a first step in equipping ourselves to ride the wave of rural postmodernity, we should realize that God has proven faithful over thousands of years through untold amounts of cultural, political, and sociological changes. Realizing God's faithfulness in past generations may place us on a more solid footing moving forward.

As in any community, your community has its own unique challenges and culture. You church will best ride the tide of postmodernity if it grapples with how postmodernity affects the immediate local context. This is not only postmodern in the sense of focusing on the unique individual nature of the community but also true to emerging sociological understandings. A rural river community may experience life and identity according to the water. Rivers have great power and can provide bounty in terms of beauty, fishing, and even tourism. In many cases, a local river has been the lifeblood of a community for hundreds or even thousands of years. Other "rural areas embrace ski slopes, mines, manufacturing, farms, retirement communities, Native American reservations, bedroom communities, and much, much more."[74] Take a minute to think about your rural community. What local features or industries are the lifeblood of your community?

By recognizing the challenges and gifts of our ministry setting, we can embrace the notion that "in the twenty-first century, rural communities differ more from each other than they do, on average, from urban areas."[75] In celebrating and naming our past, we can also dream about a future in which our congregations exist and thrive based on our unique history and context. Context weighs too important to ignore or minimize. Context then may invite us to celebrate and embrace it because "the diversity found among rural communities extends to the problems felt as each responds to the social and economic change under way."[76] By naming and celebrating our context as *sui generis*, every rural church can find freedom in pursuing her own creative responses to emerging rural culture. If spiritual leaders intend to promote a vibrant and healthy congregational future as rural cultural emergence proliferates, four key issues should be addressed.

First, a greater need exists for training and building up leaders to share in the work of ministry. Rural congregations need to foster a culture of communal participation in key ministry functions, namely in intergenerational ministry, pastoral care, and small-group Bible study leaders. From fostering more communal leadership and ministry, the church may increase the diversity of leadership which will assist in helping postmodern people build healthy individual identities as they see others like themselves in leadership, be that in gender, race, or socioeconomic standing.

Second, there exists a need to examine faith and its nature, especially in terms of the postmodern turn. One key concern among many rural congregants may be characterized as a crisis of faith. People are not worried as much about their own faith (which in many ways stems from a modern foundationalist approach); they are, however, deeply worried about the faith of their children and grandchildren and more generally the future of the Christian faith. This worry materializes in conversations about a desire for children and grandchildren to have a closer walk with God, in anxiety about attracting young families to church, and in confusion and shock at the direction of our nation. This shock and often profound disillusionment may stem from concerns regarding gay marriage, the decline of Christian influence in public life, the actual religious diversity of our populace, or even the rise of populism and white nationalism.

Third, there is a need for the congregation to examine its preparedness to minister to emerging rural culture. Many churches (both rural and urban) often perform ministry as if existing in a cultural vacuum. This often transpires through filling the calendar with programs and events without regard to cultural context, community needs, or even the congregation's stated mission and vision. In some ways, your rural church may be well equipped to minister to emerging culture, and in other ways, there are certainly growth edges, i.e., diversity, solidarity with the poor and oppressed, or increasing environmental stewardship. Examining and naming strengths and growth edges will help the church respond effectively to the challenge of rural cultural change. Additionally, in an increasingly pluralistic culture, church leadership and members should take on the posture of embedded missionaries to the town and county.

Fourth, there is a need to identify positive stories and themes in congregational life with the goal of creating communal self-awareness leading to fresh vision and mission action. By identifying spiritual and communal themes in congregational life, the postmodern values of appealing to emotion and cultural heritage can be met. Story is incredibly powerful, and through telling stories, the elders in the church with traditional values may emotionally appeal to rural postmoderns. Additionally, in identifying overarching congregational metanarratives, a fresh sense of congregational identity may emerge, making the congregation healthier and more adaptive. These stories and congregational themes are now named and celebrated as a result of analyzing people's personal recollections of congregational life and identifying overarching themes in all of the corporate and personal interviews completed as a part of my research. The remainder of the chapter shall explore each of the above issues in more depth.

Chapter Four: EQUIPPING RURAL CHURCHES TO SET SAIL

Helping Train and Equip Leaders

As a small-town church with seemingly flat-lined attendance and giving patterns, we found our church needed to *better train and build up leaders to share in the work of ministry. Coming out of a worldwide pandemic, this is even more true.* In any kind of leadership, church, or community development, training and equipping people to share in the work proves paramount. Leadership training in the emerging context may not manifest as simply as adopting a model of leadership from the mostly secular leadership studies field. Christian leadership involves cultivating a foundation of deliberative theological reflection and deep conviction.[77]

Church leadership, including pastors, might do well to realize that "without a spiritual foundation, leadership is just another job."[78] Equipping your church's leaders for emerging rural ministry may not involve a drive to get more people serving on committees as much as it may involve creating space for people to introspectively reflect on their own theology, core convictions, and even doubts. As people are freed to lead from their convictions, they will serve with an unparalleled level of authenticity, which highly appeals to the postmodern mindset.

One possibility for forming healthy leaders is inviting leaders to focus on discerning their own inherited and deliberative theology, values, and core beliefs. By calling leaders to think theologically, we can exponentially increase our ability to ride the postmodern wave in ways that simply adopting a secular leadership theory model might prove woefully inadequate. In the postmodern era, church leaders may find that "deliberative theological reflection carries us forward when our embedded theology proves inadequate."[79] After all, the church is primarily a theological entity in nature, rooting common life, worship, and "leadership in the mysteries of God's Trinitarian nature."[80] For our churches to confront the challenges of postmodernity primarily in non-theological ways would run counter to the very essence of the Church as the redeemed, baptized, called, and sent body of Christ.

When considering defining Christian leadership in the postmodern epoch, one might describe the task as Tod Bolsinger does, "Christian leadership in uncharted territory."[81] Bolsinger calls for Christian leaders to raise their awareness of emerging culture as it exists, imploring leaders not to ignore developing realities. It seems for Bolsinger, "we are in uncharted terrain trying to lead dying churches into a post-Christian culture that now considers church [an] optional, out of touch, and irrelevant relic of the past."[82] If we continue to believe that Christianity takes precedent in people's lives or that the population in our increasingly emerging culture will somehow give blind loyalty to the church, we may function as decidedly unprepared for the rising tide of postmodernity.

Bolsinger reminds his readers "in a Christendom world, vision was about seeing possibilities ahead, communicating, and excitement. In uncharted territory where no one knows what's ahead, vision is about accurately seeing ourselves and defining reality."[83] Christian leadership in emerging rural life is about helping the church find its own unique identity and inviting people to respond to the present reality of life and ministry. In the past, the vast majority of churches have structured leadership around making plans, naming goals, and executing strategy. This paradigm alone will not carry us into the future. It seems that Christian leaders, if they are leading the church well, may necessarily "make hard choices about what to preserve and to let go."[84] Such leadership may prove challenging and uncomfortable at times.

Chapter Four: EQUIPPING RURAL CHURCHES TO SET SAIL

Christian leadership in the postmodern era may prove successful if the shift from maintenance to mission is navigated successfully.[85] Indeed, "some leaders and congregations who are still concerned about leadership *in* the church may choose to deny discovered or suspected realities and do nothing at this point."[86] This may functionally play out when a deacon body or elder board recognizes slumping patterns in attendance and giving, and instead of naming reality and dreaming about missional engagement, the leaders pivot to attempting to grow existing programs, insist on another stewardship sermon series, or hire staff to "attract more young people." If your church's leadership capacity is to grow and even thrive, then the church might highly consider strategies like "asking and empowering rather than telling," "building teams and communities rather than buildings," "empowering laypersons for ministry rather than enlisting them in program maintenance," "discernment rather than declaring," "connecting the dots of life rather than connecting with church programs," and "creating non-threatening entry points that build community."[87]

If the leadership at your church was to become outwardly focused on missional living instead of inwardly focused on program maintenance, then community engagement and potential for gospel impact might exponentially increase. In rural communities that may face engrained power structures, circular reasoning, and idealized allegiance to now defunct cultural norms, rural churches like may provide strong leadership in the community, especially if they are one of the healthier institutions in the community. It seems, "the rural church needs to take the initiative sometimes; often it is the only viable institution left in a community. It needs to take the lead in economic, social, and spiritual nurturing and development in those communities."[88] Our rural church was the first to adopt solar energy in our community, and when our solar panels went live, it was the talk of the town. Not only did adopting a solar energy plan help our church divert significant amounts of money from utilities to local ministry, the community took notice, and the church served as a witness to what creation care and stewardship can look like when God's people lead.

Through providing spiritual leadership in an increasingly secularized and postmodern rural context, rural church leaders can potentially help entire communities overcome myths of powerlessness (by empowering the church and the community), myths of independence (by embracing dependence on God, neighbor, and creation), and overcome myths of maintaining a golden age (by looking for God's movement and power in the present).[89]

Leadership equipping in rural communities needs to focus on celebrating all people as leaders in a shared communal-leadership model rather than placing the mantle of leadership on a few chosen individuals or committees. Many rural churches have strong congregations with strong leadership, but that leadership often comes from a few select families and committees. This reality in a rural congregation is typical and unsurprising. However, to maximize potential leadership capital and success for the emerging culture, your church might do well to embrace each person in the church as a called and empowered leader.

When leadership is not shared in Christian life, it can present "inherent dysfunction," especially "when it is bound together with the penchant of churches to view their leaders as 'God's anointed' — holy men and women who are seen as untouchable and not to be questioned."[90] Shifting to communal leadership and inviting others into the decision-making process has potential not only to appeal to an increasingly postmodern populace but to also live out biblical leadership. Hirsch warns that "worldly notions of power will have disastrous effects on the church whose New Testament dynamic is based on the cruciform model of Jesus and is therefore meant to be radically non-hierarchical and polycentric."[91] Decentralizing leadership in the emerging postmodern culture may prove a valuable way of deconstructing the trappings of modernity, colonialism, and denominationalism, allowing churches and leaders to follow God's freeing Spirit into the future.

Leadership in rural churches might also consider adopting shared language concerning resistance and struggle to change. The changes in leadership style discussed above offer no quick plan. They require intentionality and commitment over a longer period. In the process of change, resistance is likely, which is normal and healthy in any church system. Instead of viewing those who resist change as the enemy within, a better (far more theological and healthy) view is "to identify with the resistance as *our* mutual predicament, as a part of our human condition that we struggle against and sometimes transcend (but never succeed in overcoming completely), and therefore as indicative of our continuing need for God and for the mercy of God."[92] Sometimes resistance to change may prove strongest when the change that comes does not meet expectations or promises made regarding the change.

Barna reminds, "Any time a major change is being made within a ministry, people expect certain outcomes to result. Sometimes those outcomes are reasonable, but sometimes they are not. When expectations are out of line with reality, the change is doomed from the start."[93] Maintaining a pastoral/leadership view that resistance to change is inevitable and the impacts of change should not be oversold may remind your church's leadership team to communicate expectations wisely regarding any proposed changes to the church's ministry. No change or program or strategy shift will magically produce incredible results overnight, and church leadership should temper any excitement concerning missional change with realistic expectations and grounded thinking. This approach might minimize whatever inevitable resistance unfolds within the church system.

Blurring the Lines and Changing the Scripts

All rural, suburban, and urban churches have *a need to examine faith and its nature, especially in terms of the postmodern turn.* The emerging age creates much anxiety and confusion for those who do not understand the reasons for nor the breadth of the new epoch. To ride the tide of postmodern cultural change, Christian leaders must grapple with the notion that "postmodern consciousness is disabused of the frozen meanings that suppress otherness and difference and the methods that foster this suppression."[94] Rural communities are stereotypically thought of as homogeneous places of reasonable cultural stability. These stereotypes may have some truth as rural sociology goes. However, even rural studies experts now write on the emerging diversity in rural contexts.

The increasingly blurred lines between rural and urban areas mean that traditional urban and rural social constructs no longer work in the postmodern era. In emerging rurality, one may understand that "rural areas are essentially dynamic. Far from being timeless, unchanging sites of nostalgia, they are being reconstructed economically and recomposed socially by the globalized food industry, by increasing mobility of production and people, and by niched fragmentation of consumption and the commodification of place."⁹⁵ As social structures shift and change, the way people think about faith also changes.

As postmodernity impacts rural life, increasingly "human life takes place without a script. Nothing is inscribed on the consciousness that makes sense of things. And this experience of senselessness, structured into consciousness, translates into intense anxiety."⁹⁶ Consequently, the anxiety and uncertainty people experience because of cultural tidal shifts may result in anxiety and uncertainty within the church. Many churches react out of anxiety to a disparate (or perhaps desperate) list of emerging sociological phenomena and religious realities.

The script used to say that if you open the doors on Sunday, the pews would fill. The script used to say that people ordered their midweek schedules around a Wednesday evening church meeting, complete with dinner and children's activities. The script used to say that if you raised your kids to go to church, when they became adults, they would carry on with the faith handed down to them. Perhaps your church, as is the case with countless other churches, increasingly finds itself without a livable script. This causes some to long for yesteryear or to call for the reinstatement of once successful programs. Faith and church life without a script may even cause one to move toward the foundationalist faith of fundamentalism, which bases theology around a high degree of certainty, uniformity, and "othering."

For many, faith is now a patchwork of identities and backgrounds. Indeed, "at one time, consciousness, or the self if you will, formed in a primary location like a family, a village, a single religious tradition. With this forming came a primary set of values, a certain self-understanding, a self-identity, a sense of who and what to be. In postmodern society, the person is exposed almost from the beginning to multiple social worlds, multiple symbolic universes."[97] Perhaps the key word in the above quote is "symbolic." Based on conversations with several congregants, their greatest anxiety is the sense that symbols once giving their lives meaning are changing in meaning for others, and our cultural symbols are eroding in meaning altogether.

A good example of this is the symbolic attachment of people concerning the American flag. The flag has meant national unity and pride, beckoned us to support our military, and reminded us of our best of heritage as a nation and even that we are "one nation under God." Oppositely, the flag may serve not as a symbol of unity and pride but one of racial injustice and oppression of native peoples. The flag, for some, may not call us to support our military but serve as a symbol of militarism and international meddling. The flag may represent the worst of our nation's heritage, the idolatry of civil religion, and the dangerous comingling of church and state.

In 2019 and 2020, many people in our rural community decided to no longer watch NFL games out of personal protest. Of those who do not watch games anymore, some turn the channel because of (mostly) black NFL players kneeling respectfully during the national anthem to protest what the flag now means to them. Others (perhaps the minority) no longer watch the NFL because they feel Colin Kaepernick was kept from playing due to his protest. Some people (anecdotally) cannot understand why anyone's viewpoint concerning the symbol of the flag is divergent from their own. This confusion creates anxiety on the part of both conservative and progressive individuals within the life of the community. One parallel example in church life is when people talk about religious liberty at church. Many people mean different things by the term "religious liberty," and many cannot fathom that another might view the topic differently. The symbol or idea of religious liberty may indeed prove imbued with meaning for many, but those meanings may prove divergent and diverse.

Moreover, within your own church family (and even more so across denominations!), words may hold different meanings for religiously symbolic language. Words like grace, sin, the cross, resurrection, and creation may hold different meanings for various people, even though decades ago, it seemed like everyone in the congregation was functioning with the same meanings. For some in your community, the word "marriage" may symbolize a heterosexual relationship between a man and a woman. For others in the community, the word "marriage" may symbolize something quite different, including LGBTQ equality. Words and symbols that used to have homogenous meaning in rural culture now have found themselves without a script.

The words or symbols we utilize in terms of faith give great power and great meaning, or at least they once did. Farley discusses the postmodern "need to put the expressions of the words of power in quotation marks or place the qualifier 'so-called' in front of a term. For the true postmodern, all language takes place in quotation marks."[98] People then may discuss "marriage" or the "American flag" or perhaps more vexing, "God" with the understanding that "the quotation marks show that the speaker is not naïve about the matter, has a sophisticated distance from it, exercises proper suspicion towards it."[99] A fundamental challenge to postmodern faith for all churches – particularly rural ones – is learning to operate in a culture where increasingly, terms that once held common and deep meaning across culture may now be seen by some as quaint and old fashioned. It seems:

> When the postmoderns do use some quaint term from the past like 'virtue' being 'blessed,' 'glory,' even

'chastity,' they do something to show that they are aware of its quaintness. But with the loss of words of power, quaintness applies to all such terms: thus 'tradition,' 'duty,' 'consciousness,' 'truth,' 'salvation,' 'sin,' 'God.' These too need the quotation marks that indicate we are aware that they do not quite work anymore and are not to be taken seriously.[100]

With this understanding, there is unfortunately no surprise at the rise of a term like "post-truth" in the cultural lexicon, quotes intended.

To be clear, I am *not* suggesting that the words God, salvation, sin, or marriage have no meaning for Christians. Far from it. I am simply pointing out what many others have written about concerning the postmodern turn. Some may quickly dismiss this part of the turn as moral relativism, and many have implored the church to resist postmodernity because they reduce it to nothing more. I believe such a sweeping approach is a mistake because it fails to take seriously that the postmodern turn is already here, already in our rural communities, and already in our pews.

How can Christians expect people to come to church and give allegiance to Christ when the very words that give our religious lives meaning, the words found in Scripture and the language we use to talk about the Divine, are taken as curious, fanciful, and even droll by the surrounding culture? We may need to return to an earlier time for some context on our emerging culture.

In earlier times before the Enlightenment, the modern scientific age, and the Industrial Revolution, faith of any variety was full of mystery. Part of the project of enlightenment was to demystify religion and superstition. In enlightenment thinking, it was a popular belief that everything in the universe must have a reasonable and scientific explanation. A great example of an attempt to demystify religion is the Jefferson Bible, where Thomas Jefferson removed all aspects of the gospels he deemed "contrary to reason."[101] Movements demystifying religion have had a profound impact on the power of religious word symbols. However, "separated from the word of power, the terms associated with it [a symbol] undergo disenchantment. The old contents of the symbol are displaced by new contents that have no horizon of mystery."[102] When cultural language loses power, there is disenchantment and perhaps even dissolution of symbolic language that once ordered our lives and culture, meaning once again – no script.

In helping our churches grapple with tidal shifts in human faith understandings, it may prove useful to examine a date in time preceding Jefferson and the Western enlightenment. It seems the things that give symbolic meaning to our lives derive from ritual – a father cutting the umbilical cord, a parent helping a late teen move away to college, singing the national anthem (regardless of kneeling or not), observing communion, or throwing dirt on a casket. Each of these is a ritual that gives our lives some semblance of meaning and stability.

Because of ritual, we are able to place our own stories into the context of the stories of our ancestors, the stories of our culture, and more broadly, the story of humanity itself. Arguably, the field of anthropology shows that every human culture in history has valued ritual as a form of symbolic expression imbuing deep meaning both personally and socially. The Jewish culture in history is a prime example. Our own sense of scriptural authority, in part, derives from the authority the Jewish people gave to the Torah.

Why did the Torah have such authority for ancient Jewish people? How did it become a symbol of meaning and faith that survived thousands of years and influenced three major world religions? One may understand "the Torah's authority originated in the temple ritual and was only gradually extended beyond it."[103] Watts asserts through in-depth rhetorical criticism that "it was the authority of the temple's ritual traditions that established the Pentateuch's prestige."[104] Eventually, because of Babylonian captivity, the destruction of the first temple, and *diaspora*, the text itself would take primacy as a sacred symbol of Judaism. Watts further argues:

> The origin of the religious authority of Western scriptures derived primarily from the use of old texts and books for validating rituals. The idea of scripture was grounded first and foremost in the ritual use of texts. The traditional dichotomy in Western, especially Christian, traditions between text and ritual disguises the fact that the authority of scriptures originated in ritual concerns and continues to be maintained by ritual practices.[105]

What authority or power then does Christian Scripture have in the lives of people when the frequency of participation in key rituals (corporate worship, communion, baptism, fellowship meals, child dedications or christenings, the Sabbath, or even the study of Scripture itself) is seemingly in rapid decline?

Do linguistic, philosophic, and theological symbols like "grace," "sin," "resurrection," "Scripture," and even "God" lose cultural meaning because people less frequently participate in ritual, or do people less frequently participate in ritual because past symbols lose cultural meaning and become mere relics? Perhaps for those of us in vocational ministry, this is the ultimate chicken-egg question. Perhaps the frequent decline of religious observance in the United States is directly tied to the loss of symbolic meaning concerning key Christian ideas and rituals.

Chapter Four: EQUIPPING RURAL CHURCHES TO SET SAIL

This might prove an excellent topic for further exploration in a future research project. In discussing the state of the American church, Pew observes "the growth of the 'nones' as a share of the population, coupled with their declining levels of religious observance, is tugging down the nation's overall rates of religious belief and practice."[106] "Nones" are, of course, those claiming "none" when asked about their current religious affiliation.

In Christian and Jewish history, praxis shifted and even fundamentally changed. In time, "for many communities that treasure scriptures, understanding the text and its meaning was enough, and many of the rituals mandated *in* the text fell into disuse. Instead, worship rituals *of* the text arose that reinforced its iconic place at the center of worship" (italics Watts').[107] Rituals *of* the text may certainly include reading the text in worship, and in most evangelical protestant traditions, elevating the text through proclamation and preaching is the culminating act of worship. This begs the question – what if the rituals *of* the text fall away just as rituals *in* the text? One potential answer is that the text itself would lose meaning for those no longer participating in the rituals surrounding it. Could something as simple as changing attendance patterns in a hurried consumer culture relate directly to the profound shift towards postmodernity and the symbols of faith losing cultural meaning?

Based on conversations and many years of observation, this great cultural shift leaves many rural church members and pastors reeling and anxious about the future, understandably so. Transition itself in culture may give rise to meaning because "it is possible that when societies experience transition, they interpret the loss aspect of the transition as decline."[108] Perhaps this is what leads a political candidate to declare a promise to "Make America Great Again" which taps into people's sense of profound and unexplained loss due to the postmodern transition that society presently faces. Helping people grapple with the postmodern tide in terms of faith may involve helping them deconstruct their present reality, name the symbols that give them meaning, and come to terms with their own anxiety in the contemporary course of history. Restoring the meaning of religious symbols, or even preserving the meaning, involves faithfully continuing the rituals of and within the biblical canon. Something as simple as encouraging regular worship attendance may help stem perceived negative aspects of the postmodern tide, especially the loss of religious meaning in the lives of the church family. This loss of meaning comes in myriad ways – travel ball, recreational boating culture, golf, RV-ing, and camping. In fact, a segment in American religious culture still mourns the loss of blue laws and attributes the shifting religious tide to the disappearance of such laws from culture.[109]

Preparedness to Minister in Postmodern Culture

Rural churches faces *a need for congregations to examine their preparedness to minister to emerging rural culture.* Challenges clearly abound regarding successfully ministering in an increasingly postmodern rural context. Surely "few religious communities can claim real isolation from postmodern society,"[110] and in my perspective, just as few may realize they are *presently in* postmodern society. Recall Bolsinger's definition of vison in a postmodern culture, "Vision is about accurately seeing ourselves and defining reality."[111] Unfortunately, many churches retreat from reality instead of lean into it. Instead of changing anything in the church system, naming reality might prove an initial act of disrupting homeostasis. A classic interpretation of one Hebrew proverb reads "where there is no vision, the people perish [...]."[112] If vision and prophetic leadership are rooted in a firm grasp of reality, then one can accurately claim, "Without grounding themselves in reality, the people will perish." Too many churches feel more comfortable with the traditioned past than charting a new course through unknown cultural tidal movements. In part, every church's preparedness for adapting to and thriving in postmodern culture is dependent on the church seeing itself and the surrounding community clearly.

On the pastor's part, helping the church live in reality instead of idealism or even the past may require some level of disruption that only God can orchestrate. In a way, nothing could be more Christ-like. Consider the notion that "the incarnation was a severe disruption of an existing paradigm. God chose to enter the world through the womb of a virgin Jewish peasant girl from the small village of Nazareth."[113] The story of the incarnation is the story of God's breaking into human reality. For the church to take on the incarnational nature of God in the postmodern age, the Spirit will once again call for Christ's body to break into human reality and existence in our own communities.

By using the incarnation as a model for inviting the church to ground herself in reality, pastors and lay leaders can trust God's Spirit to work, once more meeting us as we currently and presently exist. Frost and Rice continue, stating "Jesus the Messiah, God in the flesh, would disrupt the social order into which he was born. The political stasis would be rattled, power structures confronted, injustices brought to light and a strong voice given to the weak."[114] How many churches could say the same about their ministries? If this is a standard for Christ-like ministry, most congregations have great room for improvement!

Instead of bold missional incarnation grounded in human reality, churches sometimes flee or withdraw from reality. Farley identifies five ways this withdrawal transpires.[115] To paraphrase the list, reality withdrawal happens in church life when 1) a denominational network devolves to mediocrity and banality to maintain a harmonious constituency.[116] Often, issues based in reality get pushed below the surface and even allowed to fester because of denominational leaders trying to maintain harmonious balance. In my view, not only does this happen at the denominational level but also in the local church. Everything from church finance issues to human sexuality can get tamped down in favor of false unity. 2) Churches withdraw from reality when offering pseudo-programs and ministries. Farley lifts up the example of anemic religious education programs in most churches, even saying (in reference to an earlier passage) that quotations need to be placed around terms like teachers, students, and curriculum. Perhaps this is an academic's elitist view of the average Sunday school class, but in the opinion of this author, the argument holds merit. 3) Congregants may get lost in reality by becoming a face in the crowd. When sermons are reduced to generic ideas and when most members do not know each other, worship is often surface level (not focusing on any real events in the life of the church or community) and reality takes a back seat. 4) Unreality is a result of over-professionalized and indifferent clergy. This may be the opposite of the last form of reality detachment with some ministers being so focused as a learned exegete that they give no real-world application in the sermon and talk over the average congregant's reasonable level of understanding. 5) False reality and confirmation bias set in when we retreat into closed groups of thought or social status. Churches struggle periodically with drawing boundaries that are too stringent and creating isolation from different worldviews. When Christians spend so much time at church events they lose a sense of the existing reality around them, they are effectively in a self-made silo.[117] Farley states 6) the final reality withdrawal is withdrawal from the gospel itself. Each of the previous ways of isolation leads to gospel abasement.

It certainty rings true that "false professionalism, anonymity in congregational life, pseudo undertakings, conflict-avoiding institutional paralysis, and isolation from the public world will diminish the sense of the master narrative."[118] The master narrative is what Farley refers to as the gospel which is the grand story of Christianity. Gleaning knowledge and insight from Farley, one may deduce that some responsibility for a congregation's preparedness for negotiating the postmodern context falls on the minister and leadership, and some responsibility falls on the laity.

A church not grounded in reality will struggle to connect with people and struggle to help them find meaning. This impacts nothing short of a church's ability to convey cosmology, theodicy, and contextualization within the Scripture as it relates to the local community. Staying grounded in the realities of place, theological identity, heritage, and community may in fact give the gospel deeper meaning. If any church wants to excel in the emerging context, then incarnational, reality-based, gospel-centric ministry is highly desirable.

Much of what Farley described as congregational and ministerial-drift away from reality might easily be summed up in a word – authenticity. One of the best ways for rural churches to prepare for ministering in rural emerging culture is to cultivate a sense of authenticity. It seems easy to confuse a constant quest for cultural relevance as a mark of being grounded in reality and as a mark of authenticity. There is little equivalence in trying too hard to be relevant and being genuine. James Davison Hunter explains that in some Christian circles, a paradigm exists of "relevance to" the contemporary culture.[119] In striving to become relevant to culture, Christians have focused, sometimes with great success, in speaking gospel truth to cultural issues like "child labor, the labor movement, Communism, the war in Vietnam, and above all, the civil rights movement."[120] While this method of relating to culture and reality can be positive, there are also disadvantages.

Hunter discusses the advent of countless conferences and churches that strive to be relevant through slick marketing campaigns and high-dollar speakers at regularly ticketed events. In his assessment, Hunter is less than approving, saying "one cannot emphasize enough how 'celebrity' and 'spectacle' permeate these initiatives,"[121] even calling into question the motives of a few major conferences by name. For Hunter, this is not simply a question of style but of substance. Often, "these initiatives, while well rooted in a deep longing, take their cue from the culture around them and offer little clarity for the confusion of their times."[122] In attempting to attain relevance in postmodern rural culture, we need not create flashy events or programs that simply add to the cultural noise. Relevance is a matter of local incarnational presence and not of worship style, the number of programs, or the number of staff positions.

Some attempts among Christians to become relevant verge on the bizarre and seem more like publicity stunts than being grounded in incarnational reality. Frost and Rice discuss a number of stunts that churches and pastors have pulled to make a temporary impact or attract more worshippers on particular Sundays. These include a pastor that jumped his dirt bike through a ring of fire over school buses, a church that did an AR-15 raffle on Father's Day, and a Texas pastor that challenged his congregation's couples to follow him and his wife in a "Seven Days of Sex" challenge.[123]

These stunts and gimmicks may attract publicity, but they hardly fulfill or proclaim the gospel. They mistake the fleeting attention of crowds and culture for incarnational gospel reality. They miscalculate the world's tolerance for Christians and may "just as easily make followers of Jesus look foolish and arguably push nonbelievers even further from Christianity."[124] Apparently, some pastors have even been injured during such stunts. Not only may they be causing injury to the gospel through seemingly desperate attempts at outreach and proselytization, but they may also cause themselves (or worse yet, innocent bystanders) serious injury. If your church wants to do outreach locally, the church might do well to not use gimmicks that non-churched people find highly suspicious and inauthentic.

There is great irony that ministry-driven antics and gimmickry amount to little more than ecclesiological chicanery, potentially repelling the very people they purport to reach. Again, ministries should strive for relevance through authenticity. In our small town, many people have a low tolerance for showy theatrics in terms of church. They do, however, want to know if you love their grandkids, if you will show up at the hospital, or if you will provide presence during a time of grief. At a former church I pastored, there was a church just 10 miles away that performed such stunts and promoted bizarre outreach in order to attract attention. In some ways, it worked in terms of attracting interest and numbers, but I always questioned the overall depth of that ministry. We regularly had people leave our church to attend the other one, often to return within six months, hungering for more substance and deeper connection. Preparation to effectively minister to the emerging culture may include a high guardedness concerning pressure from within your church to "do things like what that other church is doing." While these requests may seem well intentioned, copying another church's questionable outreach tactics will not help increase kingdom.

Preparedness to minister to postmodernists involves obtaining authentic theology, authentic motives, and authentic relationship for the sake of an authentic gospel. Obsession with relevance and ministry gimmicks hardly leads to ministry grounded in reality. Realities of brokenness, sin, grace, love, and redemption are a significant part of the ministry of Christ Jesus. God calls the Church in the present age to enter the same realities. As the Church, we should remember that "we cannot help but alter any system we genuinely enter. Those churches that have no effect on their neighborhoods have clearly never entered them."[125] Jesus fundamentally altered humanity and its course because he fully entered the system. If we fully enter the community in Christ-like incarnational fashion instead of flitting around with self-centered programs and potentially repelling shenanigans, then the Church will position itself for long-term biblically based success in ministry within the emerging culture.

Story as the Key to Confident Vision

Riding the wave of postmodernity requires us to meet the present *need to identify positive stories and themes in congregational life with the goal of creating communal self-awareness leading to fresh vision.* Asking the right questions can bring the power of listening and the power of story into the visioning process, and more importantly, the power of God's Spirit. I truly believe that "the humble journey of listening to the religious and spiritual lives of people through pastoral ethnography can lead to a place of life-giving change within a faith community and beyond it."[126]

Chapter Four: EQUIPPING RURAL CHURCHES TO SET SAIL

The journey of learning people's stories and shared experiences is a joy that molds and forms not only the hearer but also the storyteller and the church. How can recalling your church's story and the story of people in your church lead to fresh vision?

Through story in the Old Testament, God's people maintained their identity and call from generation to generation. Through story, children learn about right and wrong. Through story, adults connect to realities outside of themselves. Through story, organizations and churches can imagine a new day and different futures. By sharing story, Christ announced and proclaimed the kingdom. The power of story to convey vision and meaning in the postmodern context is critical in congregational vision work.

In preparation for visioning in one church, I preached two sermon series that recalled the congregation's own history and our history as part of the worldwide Church. The first series, titled "Windows of Faith," was a Lenten series exploring the Bible passages depicted in the eight stained glass windows in the sanctuary. The first window depicted the birth of Christ, and each following window depicted a scene from Jesus's life and ministry, ending with a window depicting the Resurrection. Each week, beginning with the first window, the story of who purchased the window and in whose memory it was given was told. One widow gave the window depicting Christ as the Great Physician, and her husband was a well-known doctor in the area in the 1940s and '50s. The family of that widow is still in the church and had not realized the window in the sanctuary had any connection to their family. Now when they enter the sanctuary, they remember how the story of their own family intersects with the story of our church and the story of Christ.

The second sermon series was called "Past, Present, Future," where a story from our church's history was told each week.

One such story is in the year 1941 when the church had recently called a pastor who had previously served as a Baptist missionary to Japan. By the Sunday evening service on December 7, news of the attack on Pearl Harbor had reached even rural Virginia. The young pastor admitted he was devastated because he knew that people he and his wife had ministered to would likely be killed in the war that surely loomed. He reminded the church that Christian brothers and sisters lived in Japan and called the church to pray for the Japanese Church and the people of Japan in addition to the families of those who lost loved ones at Pearl Harbor. People were so upset that he called the church to pray for Japan in addition to our own country that by the summer, the pastor was at another church.

This is a powerful story that needs to be retold considering the current nativism, nationalism, and fear of "others" so rampant in our culture. By recalling our own congregational stories, the hope is to better equip the Church to explore how God calls us to respond to current cultural tides. As we recall our stories, "We hear stories and songs that move us, and move us forward toward greater justice and wholeness in the world. We discover images and words with which to co-author the future, and we develop the shared communal capacity to engage in ministries of transformation."[127] Rural churches should find ways to recall and tell their own stories as preparation for riding the tide of postmodernity, and in so doing, they may co-author a vibrant future. We are, in the task of congregational ministry, not only co-authors with fellow church members but also co-authors with God's Spirit. Navigating the tide of postmodernity requires knowing our story and locating our story in the grander story of God's movement in time and history. Your rural church has unique stories to celebrate and a unique history in your own community. How are you leaning into your story and the story of God working in your ministry?

Chapter Five

THE BIBLE: OUR NAVIGATIONAL CHART FOR THE POSTMODERN TIDE

> *"We were given the Scriptures to humble us into realizing that God is right and the rest of us are just guessing."*
>
> — Rich Mullins

To set sail in the midst of radically shifting cultural tides, one should consult navigational charts to plot a safe course of travel. The churches I have pastored have been guided primarily, as all churches, by Scripture, reason, tradition, and experience. While reason, tradition, and experience may certainly prove useful, each is minimized in some way in the postmodern era. In equipping a church to navigate the postmodern tide, one may certainly highlight theories of congregational change, rural and urban sociology, and ethnography, but an appeal to biblical theology becomes paramount. This is not an appeal to foundationalism but rather an admission that the Bible has a sacred and tethering quality in a world of uncertainty, even if the Bible itself does not provide all of the certainty we long for or claim it contains.

A large multi-campus California-based church called Eastlake appeals to postmodern people in many of their messages and praise songs. The Eastlake Band writes and records original worship music, exploring themes of unknowing and even guessing, as Rich Mullins would put it. One song titled *Keep Us All Close*, states in part,

Verse 1:
God bless our friends, God bless our enemies
All of our children, all of our families
We've got no idea what we're doing

We've tried to find You throughout the centuries
Different religions in different countries
We've got no idea what we're doing

Bridge:
We'll never make it on our own
We've got too much dark inside of us
We'll never make it on our own

Chorus:
Keep us all close, every one of us close
Don't let anyone go

Verse 2:
God bless the poor, God bless the broken-hearted
God bless the widow, God bless the long departed
We've got no idea what we're doing

Chapter Five: THE BIBLE: OUR NAVIGATIONAL CHART FOR THE POSTMODERN TIDE

God bless the Christian, God bless the atheist
God bless the Muslim, God bless the rest of us
We've got no idea what we're doing[128]

The song (sung by hundreds in worship across Eastlake's campuses) succinctly and honestly states, "We've got no idea what we're doing." Perhaps this makes you furrow your eyebrows, and you can never imagine your own church singing such a song. That's fair. This worship song, though, speaks to the way postmoderns hold all truth claims loosely. Notice how it is almost the complete opposite of *Victory in Jesus* or *Onward Christian Soldiers* – with their declarations of great certainty based in enlightenment-style foundationalism. Without relying heavily on foundationalism in an increasingly postmodern era, can our churches still find inspiration and guidance in Christian Scripture for navigating rural cultural emergence? I firmly believe the answer is a resounding yes!

One challenging task to postmodern theology is that certainty is often sought by Christians and theologians in the theological task and certainty is most *definitely avoided by the postmodern*, who grates against propositional or triumphalist truth claims. Certain theologians[129] and modern apologists can no doubt list theological rationales for avoiding postmodernity, but the task at hand is to help a congregation set sail in the postmodern context and not bail water or drown.

Certain strategies may be taken to identify theological themes that might prove meaningful in the postmodern context. Some topics of inquiry potentially bearing fruit may include theologies of justice, community, economics and poverty, creation care, empire, migration and diaspora, and mission and imago Dei. Theologically, there are several biblical passages one could highlight concerning rural ministry and emerging culture.

Historically, some have attempted to write a "rural theology,"[130] which ultimately ends up as a standpoint-style biblical criticism with many of the same strengths and weaknesses of other standpoint criticisms such as Black Theology, Womanist Theology, Queer Theology (see endnote), or Native American Theology.[131] Other examples of rural standpoint criticism and research may be found in books and collections of essays like *Rural Life and Rural Church: Theological and Empirical Perspectives* (Equinox, 2012) or *Rural Ministry: The Shape of The Renewal to Come* (Abingdon, 1998). At times, these methods prove extremely helpful to the extent they closely examine pastoral and agrarian motifs in Scripture, provide empirical research concerning the uniqueness of rural ministry, and produce valuable sociological commentary. While these approaches are *certainly* worthy of consideration and incredibly useful, the scope of this book is concerned with what is emerging in rural culture and how the 200,000 rural churches across North America might respond. This is different than exploring rural typologies. As a rule, postmodernity renders a number of typologies weak and dated. The same themes and approaches might still prove useful in particular contexts, but theologically, they may lack in shaping one's perspective on rural Christian emergence. Again, the monographs mentioned above (both old and new) do concern rural ministry, but they do not attempt to explore what postmodernity means for rural culture or how rural churches might respond to this shifting tide.

Rural people are more than a biblical typology, and contemporary rural life is more complex than simply serving as the antithesis of all that is urban. In an increasingly postmodern context, complexity and nuance prove critical. Our theological rationales for postmodern ministry can take a slightly different turn away from the typologies and stereotypes that often exist with rural theology. Arguably, a rural congregation will never

Chapter Five: THE BIBLE: OUR NAVIGATIONAL CHART FOR THE POSTMODERN TIDE

make the turn toward embracing postmodern ministry (or even finding comfort in an increasingly postmodern context) without sustained pastoral leadership. Accordingly, the rest of this chapter will explore developing a pastoral theology for a postmodern rural context.

Also, theologically speaking, not much is richer than Jesus's teaching on the kingdom of God/Heaven. One may read the parables about the kingdom and see how God's kingdom is at once small and powerful – powerful enough to subvert the ruling culture of the day. Rural churches might do well to explore the notion that the kingdom is small yet incredibly significant. In contexts where urban churches and economic hubs have great influence and cultural hegemony, where globalization and monoculture press in at every angle, and where anxiety creeps into families and lives ill equipped to handle a rapidly changing culture, the stories of the kingdom's small yet immeasurable significance may reflect the stories of a church like yours. Finally, in addition to exploring a pastoral theology for postmodern rural ministry and exploring the small-yet-significant kingdom, we will explore a theology of the periphery. God's people often do not just live but thrive on the margins of empire and culture.

A Pastoral Theology for Postmodern Rural Ministry

Perhaps a good place to start the conversation about pastoral theology is the narrative of the archetypal priest, Aaron. There is little biblical scholarship focusing solely on Aaron, who is often overshadowed by his brother Moses, not only in the text but also in the academy. Aaron exhibits (in ways) the kind of flexibility and growth desirable for any pastor in the postmodern era and also serves as an example of how not to lead. Throughout Exodus, Aaron grew and developed in his role and understanding. He functioned at different times as prophet and priest, and he showed the ability to improvise in terms of his own spiritual leadership and understanding. While not always successful, he gives us much to ponder.

Aaron, along with Moses, was called to lead the people of Israel at a turbulent time when the tides of change were potentially overwhelming. In the midst of this shifting time when God was calling the people toward freedom and a new way of life, Aaron and Moses provided co-leadership on a number of occasions. In the narrative of Exodus 7-14 which includes the plagues, the Exodus itself, and the crossing of the sea by God's people into safety, Aaron takes a central role in the story. The Bible states multiple times that "The Lord said to Moses and Aaron."[132] The word translated "said" is רָמֹאצוּ, referring to the "simple act of communicating."[133] The Lord spoke to Moses and Aaron, and they spoke to the Lord. Spiritual guides who lead God's people through uncharted territory will prove wise to communicate regularly with God and listen for the voice of YHWY.

Both leaders were willing to listen to the Lord and work together to lead the people. In a postmodern context that values true community and diversity, shared and multivocal leadership may be proven helpful. Pastoral theology in the postmodern context will consider that multiple people in the church may provide spiritual leadership and direction, and God's vision and mission for the church need not rest on the shoulders of a singular pastor/prophet. In terms of congregational change, building trust and minimizing fear related to change may indeed require shared leadership. How many congregations may be

Chapter Five: THE BIBLE: OUR NAVIGATIONAL CHART FOR THE POSTMODERN TIDE

held captive to the Pharaoh of congregational inertia or enslaved by the desire to cast anchor instead of set sail amid changing currents? Pastors will surely need at least one partner to speak that timeless Divine utterance, "Let my people go!"

Aaron's narrative is also a good model for postmodern ministry when used as a cautionary tale. Later in Exodus (chapters 32-34) when Moses is with God on the mountain, Aaron builds an altar and fashions a calf out of gold. It seems "Aaron is depicted as an important, trusted figure in the community, who fails to use his position and skills wisely at a moment of crisis." [134] Our congregations are functionally at a moment of crisis. Our people seem to desire certainty, and in the midst of their longing for certainty, pastors may be quick to acquiesce and revert to habits of comfort or even patterns of idolatry, like putting programs before people, choosing comfort and safety over walking in faith, and allowing the patterns of this world to become the patterns of the congregation.

Aaron was in a position of leadership at a moment not unlike the one churches in emerging rural culture find themselves. The voice and will of God may be difficult to discern. People have difficulty imagining a future that is not in Egypt. Given the choice between making tough decisions about the future or journeying into the unknown, they would rather die in Egypt making straw. Pastors are in an incredible position of leadership at such a time and should not fold to the pressure of those who might revert to the idols of the past. Aaron's lack of leadership and lack of nerve led to death among God's people.

Another cautionary piece to the Aaron story is that it seems after the episode in chapters 32-34, Aaron "no longer speaks, proclaims feasts to the community, or calls for action. Instead, Aaron now is someone who perceives Moses and the deity only when summoned and only in concert with others."[135] Moreover, he attempts to pass blame onto the people, neglecting his priestly role to help alleviate the people's guilt through sacrifice and mediation. When pastors neglect their role as spiritual guides and leaders in the church system, they forfeit their role as priestly figures and even as spiritual leaders in their systems. Aaron goes as far as to say, "Do not let the anger of my Lord burn hot; you know the people, that they are bent on evil."[136] As a pastoral leader, it can prove tempting to speak ill of a congregation one is unsuccessful in leading, but perhaps the problem lies with a lack of conviction in leadership. There is indeed a high cost to pay for such a failure in pastoral leadership. Aaron, in terms of the text, completely loses his voice. The glory of the Lord shone on the face of Moses, and "although the text is no longer silent about him, he remains silent within the text, offering no speech at all and engaging in no fully independent activity."[137] In a context of changing cultural tides, pastors who cannot speak with clarity and gentle leadership in the midst of great uncertainty will squander their voice and ultimately may even surrender their call. This is not to say that pastors must always act assertively or even have all the answers. Spiritual leadership is not about dictatorial control, but it does sometimes require one to act as the calm and steady presence in a system brimming with anxiety. Sometimes, such leadership not only involves navigating signs and tides but also knowing the limits of one's vessel.

Another point for pastoral theology concerning Aaron is that even when the position of high priest is created, his role is not the primary role of authority in the religious community. Pastors in a postmodern context may do well to remember that there are forces beyond their control, perhaps even God ordained, that may make them secondary in the system in terms of leadership and authority. It seems "the very fact that the instructions for the high-priesthood are communicated via a pre-existing authority figure who never loses his authority even when Aaron has been inducted as high-priest, implies already that for all its significance the high-priesthood in some areas is at least secondary to other structures."[138] For us pastors, it is helpful to consider what primary structures exist in the church that may place the pastor in a secondary role. In a congregational polity (my own tradition), this becomes apparent in that a congregation is the body that calls a pastor. As a congregation of believer-priests, the pastor is not the sole arbiter of God's Spirit for the people. Pastors may provide leadership, but there may be families or individuals in the congregation that act as primary leaders in a church. In the average small-town church, a few influential families have carried significant weight for a number of years. Pastors who do not recognize their secondary role (at times) to these pre-existing forces will frustrate and sabotage their own leadership and influence.

Aaron had an earthy one above him who called him out and ordained him.[139] Christ had a heavenly One above him who called him out and ordained him.[140] This gives a fresh perspective to the author of Hebrews writing,

> Every high priest chosen from among mortals is put in charge of things pertaining to God on their behalf, to offer gifts and sacrifices for sins. ² He is able to deal gently with the ignorant and wayward, since he himself is subject to weakness; ³ and because of this he must offer sacrifice for his own sins as well as for those of the people. ⁴ And one does not presume to take this honor, but takes it only when called by God, just as Aaron was.
>
> ⁵ So also Christ did not glorify himself in becoming a high priest, but was appointed by the one who said to him,

"You are my Son,
today I have begotten you";

⁶ as he says also in another place,

"You are a priest forever,
according to the order of Melchizedek.¹⁴¹

Even Jesus submitted to the authority of the One who called him.

Only one high priest was ever perfect, and that is Jesus Christ. This means Aaron is not only a cautionary tale but an archetype for earthly priests and pastors since none of us are perfect. In the postmodern world, there is no place for pastors being placed on moral pedestals or for pastoral virtue signaling. Such a façade is seen clearly by a postmodernist who yearns for authenticity and true community. God exhibited grace in Aaron's life by allowing him to serve in spite of his shortcomings.

Aaron exhibits spiritual co-leadership and collaboration, listening to the voice of God, periodically failing as a leader, learning to function in a secondary role in the community, and serving under the one who called him. He ultimately grows from his moment of failure and finds his proper place in the community of faith. Aaron even did all of this while wandering through the rural wilderness! In many ways, the narrative of Aaron teaches great lessons for pastoral theology in a postmodern rural context.

There is perhaps one final lesson Aaron's story may teach us concerning pastoral theology in a postmodern context. The story of Aaron's death appears in Numbers 20. After all he has been through, Aaron was denied entry into the promised land by YHWH.

Chapter Five: THE BIBLE: OUR NAVIGATIONAL CHART FOR THE POSTMODERN TIDE

> ²² They set out from Kadesh, and the Israelites, the whole congregation, came to Mount Hor. ²³ Then the Lord said to Moses and Aaron at Mount Hor, on the border of the land of Edom, ²⁴ "Let Aaron be gathered to his people. For he shall not enter the land that I have given to the Israelites, because you rebelled against my command at the waters of Meribah. ²⁵ Take Aaron and his son Eleazar, and bring them up Mount Hor; ²⁶ strip Aaron of his vestments, and put them on his son Eleazar. But Aaron shall be gathered to his people, and shall die there." ²⁷ Moses did as the Lord had commanded; they went up Mount Hor in the sight of the whole congregation. ²⁸ Moses stripped Aaron of his vestments, and put them on his son Eleazar; and Aaron died there on the top of the mountain. Moses and Eleazar came down from the mountain. ²⁹ When all the congregation saw that Aaron had died, all the house of Israel mourned for Aaron thirty days.[142]

For the original readers, perhaps it came as a shock that the first high priest did not enter into the Promised Land.

The reason given for Aaron's punishment is the lack of faith and respect shown to YHWH in the previous pericope regarding water at Meribah. Aaron fails to serve in his priestly function on behalf of his brother, allowing Moses to take matters into his own hands. This perhaps exhibited some level of doubt on Aaron's part that God would do what God promised in giving water from the rock. The Lord explicitly states "because you did not trust in me, to show my holiness before the eyes of the Israelites, therefore you shall not bring this assembly into the land that I have given them."[143] The author here may have been the Yahwist (J), but it seems more likely that authorship may have come from a post-exilic priestly source (P) – perhaps a Levite group attempting to lay claim to the high-priesthood.[144] In any case, doubt is held out as a contributing factor in Aaron not entering into the rest of the promised land.

Now, consider the above narrative in contrast with the end of Matthew's gospel, where the perfect high priest (Jesus Christ) who is ordained by the Father leaves room for doubt among the faithful, giving them the assurance of his constant presence. The Scripture reads:

> [16] Now the eleven disciples went to Galilee, to the mountain to which Jesus had directed them. [17] When they saw him, they worshiped him; but some doubted. [18] And Jesus came and said to them, "All authority in heaven and on earth has been given to me. [19] Go therefore and make disciples of all nations, baptizing them in the name of the Father and of the Son and of the Holy Spirit, [20] and teaching them to obey everything that I have commanded you. And remember, I am with you always, to the end of the age."[145]

This stands in stark relief against the passage where God is said to have kept a priest from the promised land because of a moment of doubt. In Matthew, Jesus sends out people, who have just worshipped but simultaneously exhibit doubt, to make more disciples and build the kingdom. The grace exhibited by Jesus toward those doubting the very Resurrection makes his high priesthood sharply different from the high priest who faced judgment for a single moment of doubt. If the character and nature of God are consistent and if Jesus is indeed the highest revelation of who God is, then perhaps we can safely assume that a later priestly source contributed to the story about Aaron being judged so harshly for a moment of doubt.

These passages standing in tension present two important lessons for pastoral leadership in a postmodern rural context. First, spiritual leaders with political agendas, perhaps like the late priestly source in Numbers, are often eventually found out and named. The damage these individuals cause to unity among God's people can often last for generations. Second, we need to reclaim that doubt is imbedded in the Great Commission. Jesus surely sensed the doubt of those he was sending out, and he sends them out regardless. Is there room for doubt and unknowing in our churches and ministries, or is having all of the answers and always being certain more important?

In your rural church, it may prove helpful to leave room and space for people to ask tough questions about faith, voice doubts and concerns, and openly express reservations regarding faith. Such people are the people Jesus commissions to begin his work in the world, and unfortunately, such people are the people our churches often ostracize and silence. Pastoral theology in the postmodern rural context should leave room for doubt as a complement to faith.

The Smallness of the Kingdom

One of the most frequent subjects of Jesus's teachings and ministry was the kingdom of heaven. The earliest mention of the kingdom of heaven comes early in Mark, where the reader learns "Jesus went into Galilee, proclaiming the good news of God. 'The time has come,' he said. 'The kingdom of God has come near. Repent and believe the good news!'"[146] What does this phrase "kingdom of God" mean? Whatever it means, it is central to the teaching of Christ. These are the first recorded words of Christ in the earliest of the four gospels. Christians cannot understand the teachings of Christ without considering the kingdom of God.

The phrase βασιλεία τοῦ θεοῦ or "kingdom of God" appears 53 times in the New Testament gospels, almost always on the lips of Jesus.[147] The synonymous phrase, βασιλείαν τῶν οὐρανῶν or "kingdom of heaven" appears 34 times in the gospel of Matthew.[148] The frequency of the kingdom and her mention in the Scripture calls for deep reflection on the meaning of the kingdom.

When one thinks of a kingdom, rulers and subjects, sovereignty of the state, power achieved by military might, a particular ruler like Caesar (who was a deity in Roman culture), economics and trade, or even atrocities may come to mind.

As the ancients often observed, in terms of earthly kingdoms, all roads lead to Rome. Why do all roads lead to Rome? Simply stated, Rome is an animal in need of constant feeding and a machine requiring constant maintenance. Earthly kingdoms exploit natural resources for the good of the empire. Earthly kingdoms exploit people to keep prices down and goods moving. The kingdom of Caesar keeps peace but only by power and coercion through violence. Now, consider that in the middle of the most powerful kingdom on earth, Jesus declares an alternative kingdom! That kind of thing could get you killed.

According to Jesus's words in Mark 1, realizing and understanding the kingdom of God begins with repentance. Perhaps his repentance begins with the recognition that our own earthly kingdoms are sinful. Jesus immediately calls for repentance when announcing the news of the kingdom. "Repent" here is μετανοεῖτε which means to think differently, to change one's mind or purpose, or even to abandon.[149] In saying "the kingdom of God has come near" followed by "repent and believe the good news,"[150] Jesus connects the idea of embracing God's kingdom *with* repentance. At a minimum, Jesus's invitation to the kingdom involves thinking differently. In all the many ways Christ emphasizes the kingdom in his ministry, one may safely assume that to participate in God's kingdom does not only require a shift in thinking; Jesus's call to repentance is nothing short of a radical change in purpose and an abandonment of allegiance to the kingdoms of this earth.

God presents an alternative to our broken earthy kingdoms – an alternative kingdom where the sovereignty of God trumps the sovereignty of the nation state. The kingdom of the gospel is an alternative kingdom where Jesus is Lord God and not Caesar – an alternative kingdom where the greatest among us is the servant. In this new kingdom, a symbol of violent execution and state-sponsored torture (the cross) becomes the symbol of repentance and forgiveness. Jesus calls us to abandon the kingdom of Caesar and realize a heavenly kingdom breaking into reality where people (made in God's image) and resources (God's creation) are not exploited. His kingdom is one where we love our neighbors as we love ourselves.

In contextualizing the theology of the kingdom, rural churches should consider what manifestations of earthly kingdoms look like in our context, because then we will know what Christ calls us to abandon in order to enter into his kingdom. In a former community I pastored in, racial divisions still held, dating back to English colonialism (a literal earthly kingdom) when First Nation peoples were systematically displaced and killed and slave labor fueled the economy and wealth of a new nation. In rural river communities, a sign of earthly kingdoms may come in the disparity and stratification existing between those wealthy enough to live on the river and those caught in cycles of rural poverty.

Only in the kingdoms of this world does such disparity exist with some living in excess while others suffer from lack of food, shelter, and adequate healthcare. In the kingdoms of this world, natural resources like fish, oysters, crabs, water, and lumber are plundered by corporations who only have profit in mind, and many rural communities are merely seen as an expendable cog in the wheel of urban colonization and a globalized economy. With such features of the earthly kingdom all around, one may feel overwhelmed at the scale of the earthly kingdom's influence on the local community and even the local church.

This is where the size of Christ's kingdom comes into play. Throughout the gospels, Jesus speaks of the kingdom as something that only requires a small dose to make a massive impact. The kingdom is already present in the world and may grow and flourish over time, becoming something that achieves more permanence. Matthew 13 gives the reader multiple parables to consider that all speak to the size of the kingdom. In the parable of the mustard seed, Jesus communicates the smallness of the kingdom and the potential it bears over time. Matthew records, "He put before them another parable: 'The kingdom of heaven is like a mustard seed that someone took and sowed in his field; it is the smallest of all the seeds, but when it has grown it is the greatest of shrubs and becomes a tree, so that the birds of the air come and make nests in its branches.'"[151] The word translated "smallest" is μικρότερον, whose root word is μικρός (mikros). Μικρός is often used in reference not only to size but also in regard to one's station or age.[152] In the English language, this same word is the root for words like microscopic, microwave, microbiology, and even microbrewery.

The suffix τερον is used as an addition to adjectives to make a word comparative, indicating that the subject of the adjective is more or greater than the object/s of comparison.[153] The kingdom of God then is in the smallest station compared to other kingdoms, may be in the youngest stage compared to earthly kingdoms, and may seem smaller than earthly kingdoms. Of all the kingdoms, it may seem the most meager.

This is not to say that God's kingdom is insignificant, for the parable points out that what may seem insignificant can actually prove quite significant not only in the natural order of creation but also in the economy of God. Jesus says of the mustard seed, "When it has grown it is the greatest of shrubs and becomes a tree, so that the birds of the air come and make nests in its branches."[154] In a sense, the kingdom of God grows where it is scattered (like the mustard seed), and assuming it finds fertile soil, it grows into something of useful significance. A full-grown mustard plant may reach heights of 10 feet in ideal growing conditions and can go from a seed to a full-grown plant in one growing season.[155] As a large herb taking on tree-like qualities, the mustard seed undergoes a rapid transformation and change in a short period of time. Near the Jordan River, mustard plants abound in open fields, so while in the parable a person initially sows the seed, the plant has the ability to be self-propagating and perennial after the initial seed is sown. This means if the soil is fertile, one initial planting can provide new plants and rapid growth year after year. The mustard plant in fertile soil has the ability to birth new mustard plants almost indefinitely.

In the same ways, the kingdom of God does require being sown in the hearts of people and even in society, and soil may need cultivating. After the initial seed takes root, however, it can spread on its own. The kingdom has the ability to bring rapid transformation and move from insignificance to significance. Mustard, like salt, has the ability to flavor food, and likewise, the kingdom of God brings unique flavor to our lives. Mustard plants have beautiful yellow flowers, and when in bloom, they can majestically turn a drab field into something visually beautiful. The kingdom of God has the ability to take regular soil (which is not much to look at) and produce something beautiful in a world surrounded by rocks, mountains, and thorns.

Sea Change | *Jonathan Howard Davis*

In the case of rural churches, the parable of the mustard seed bears significance for several reasons. Compared to many urban and suburban churches, most rural churches are small. The parable of the mustard seed reminds us of the kingdom principle that God can take something seemingly insignificant and make it into something beautiful. The mustard seed parable also reminds us that in the rapidly changing world, God's kingdom can also bring rapid change in fertile soil. We all might do well to consider if we prefer getting caught up in the rapid change of our world and its kingdoms or getting caught up in the rapid change that the kingdom of God may bring. Finally, in the kingdom of God, what is insignificant in the eyes of many is significant in the eyes of God. The vast majority of rural churches are not a megachurches, and they are highly unlikely to ever acquire such status, but God can take the smallness of our churches and even the smallness of our communities and use us in greatly significant ways as we allow the kingdom of God to take root in our hearts, lives, and communities. After all, the kingdom of heaven is like a mustard seed.

In addition to the mustard seed parable, there are multiple parables and sayings in the gospels where the smallness of the kingdom is brought to light by Christ Jesus. The parable of the yeast (Matthew 13:33), the parable of the lost coin (Luke 15:8-10), and the sayings about the church being salt and light (Matthew 5:13-16, Luke 8:16-18, John 8:12) all point to the idea that it only takes a small amount of the kingdom to make an impact felt throughout society and even the world. If the kingdom is small and yet significant, rural churches can find hope and even joy in the fact that God uses our churches and ministries according to the principles of the kingdom and not the principles of this world. As the postmodern tide washes upon our communities, we only have to be faithful in small ways, and that is enough. Our job is not to change the tide, resist the tide, or even ride

Chapter Five: THE BIBLE: OUR NAVIGATIONAL CHART FOR THE POSTMODERN TIDE

the tide while hanging on for dear life. Our job is to become as a mustard seed, as yeast, as salt, as a single ray of light, trusting that God's kingdom and our participation in that kingdom is far more significant that we might ever imagine.

One way the church may participate with and even help usher in God's kingdom in the postmodern era is through what Carol Howard Merrit terms "Retraditioning Spirituality." Merrit argues that for too long, churches have separated sacred and secular space, and that because of this compartmentalization, many churches are not able to be the leavening in the world God desires. She states,

> Of course, dividing the secular and the sacred can make our jobs easier as church leaders. If people believe they have to be inside a church building to encounter God, then fundraising for a new sanctuary can be much simpler. If people believe that pastors are close to God, and that God does not speak except through ordained clergy, then our jobs are much more secure. If we don't maintain that divide, then we may not know how to respond when a church member tells us he skipped Sunday services because he feels closer to God on his sail boat.[156]

In a recreational river community like where I pastored for nearly a decade, this rings incredibly true. By helping people connect with God in a variety of ways, even ways outside the church walls, we can hold the kingdom with an open hand instead of expecting that people may only experience the kingdom when they are seated in church. It is, indeed, God's kingdom and not our own. And "thus entrance into the kingdom means participation in the church; but entrance into the church is not necessarily synonymous with entrance into the kingdom."[157] If rural congregations focus on the kingdom of Heaven and helping usher in that kingdom, even in small ways, then the coming kingdom through our churches may have great impact both inside and outside the four walls.

Finally, the smallness of the kingdom serves as a wonderful critique of the spatial and economic colonialism that often exists between urban and rural areas, where urban centers primarily view rural communities as uncolonized land and places for resource extraction. In multiple ways, all roads still lead to Rome, and Houston, and Los Angeles, and Bangkok, and New Delhi, and in our case in rural Virginia — Richmond and Washington, D.C. When a rural church cultivates kingdom values and witness, we serve the least of these, we find joy in starting off small, we concentrate on local missions, providing leavening in our own back yard, and we may even find the kingdom growing and flourishing in unexpected places. Churches function in these ways, and we are able to localize our ministry in ways reflective of the kingdom Jesus preached about.

Many of the kingdom parables relate eternal truths about the kingdom in everyday occurrences in the culture of the day. While the kingdom is a great mystery, it manifests itself in ordinary ways like planting seeds or finding a lost coin. In this manner, kingdom theology is not only small in the sense of the physical size of a seed or a coin. Kingdom theology may also prove small in terms of its ability to emerge as highly localized. Jesus preached to a particular culture and contextualized the gospel of the kingdom for those he encountered. Doug Pagitt wries, "this has been one of the most compelling parts of Christianity – Jesus was not a generic messiah but was embedded in the life and dirt of culture, and was the fulfilment of particular promises. Christianity does not mandate a singular culture nor a singular worldview."[158] As we find ways to contextualize the kingdom, we are called to follow the example of Christ in announcing the Good News of the kingdom of heaven. In fact, in localizing our kingdom focus and considering our church's potential responses to the rising tide of postmodernity, taking the changes around us in small strides may not only prove the most kingdom thing we can do but also the most postmodern. For in localizing the kingdom and celebrating its smallness, we inherently begin deconstructing the sociological, political, and theological constructs of urban colonialism and the idea that bigger and faster is always better. The fact that Jesus does not mandate a singular worldview may prove shocking to some, but if the church would embrace Pagitt's argument, we may even be able to deconstruct and combat the tide of Christian mono-culture which often strips rural churches of personal autonomy and local hegemony.

Theology of the Periphery

In addition to a pastoral theology for rural emergence and a theology considering the smallness of the kingdom, a theology of the periphery is critical for emerging rural churches. Small-town congregations often find themselves at the periphery of church and denominational life, not only in terms of influence but often theologically. Rural churches and people also exist on the periphery of urban localities and centers of regional political and economic influence. In the Bible, God's people are often a people on the periphery of influence and culture. Abraham was told to inhabit a land he had never seen. The Israelites were on the periphery in Egypt. As slaves, they were always near power and centers of commerce but never had either for themselves. When Israel left Egypt, the people wandered for 40 years in the desert on the periphery of other kingdoms and even on the periphery of life itself at times. During the period of the judges, God's people were on the periphery in longing for a king like other regional nations. God's chosen people would feel on the periphery of power after they got a king, and even God was on the periphery of the king's court as exhibited by prophets like Nathan, Amos, and Elijah. Jesus was hunted as a baby, and his family became refugees on the run from a despot puppet ruler. Christ, although a Rabbi with a sizable following, remained largely on the periphery of Second Temple Judaism.

In similar ways, rural people feel on the periphery in our own culture. Like the Israelites, they may long for a king of their own, only to find a political leader does not have their best interest in mind. They may feel exiled from the halls of power and from a culture that often portrays rural people as dumb, ignorant, and even bigoted. People in our communities may feel pushed and prodded by external power forces – politically and economically. The values that pipe into rural communities on network television and over the internet often seem like threats to traditional rural values.

In an increasingly postmodern context, faith itself may become a peripheral cultural artifact. For some, "the challenge of postmodernism to the Christian faith is obvious. Postmodernists see Christian belief as working as a smokescreen for selfish motivations that Christians would be ashamed of, if they were aware of them."[159] Exactly what are these motivations? Some argue the postmodernist view (which often includes post-colonialism and deconstructionism) claims "that beneath all ultimate beliefs and ideals (including the secular ideals such as Progress, Liberalism, and Justice) is the quest to gain or retain power – especially in terms of race, class, sex, or ethnicity."[160] Christians may increasingly find themselves on the periphery in an increasingly postmodern context due to legitimate (and often confirmed in history) suspicions people have regarding the authenticity of our faith and witness.

Chapter Five: THE BIBLE: OUR NAVIGATIONAL CHART FOR THE POSTMODERN TIDE

In a sense, this objection on the part of postmodernists – of faith as a guise for power – may find similarity with the popular atheist objection to faith. Certain atheists and non-theists readily argue that according to Scripture, God is a monster, dismissing Christian and Jewish faith as wicked and violent and dismissing God as an ancient mythologic deity with some serious anger-management issues.[161] Many faithful Christians, however, will readily admit that they also do not believe in the God that atheists say they could never believe in.[162]

In the case of the postmodernist objection to faith, faithful Christians can say with *certainty* that the faith we believe in as revealed in Jesus Christ is not about earthly power of any kind, especially in terms of race, class, sex, or ethnicity. If anything, Jesus is always found in solidarity and alongside the powerless. In the postmodern age, this is perhaps the only certainty worth seeking. The people of God may confess with sincerity that "religion that is pure and undefiled before God, the Father, is this: to care for orphans and widows in their distress, and to keep oneself unstained by the world." In realizing the emerging rural culture is highly suspicious of faith, Christian individuals and churches that were once at the center of rural life may move to the periphery. However, if we authentically live out our faith, we may indeed remain in the center of community life. With the suspicion of our motives in belief on the rise, followers of Christ (and not only rural ones) must rise to the challenge of living out authentic faith in God, casting off the heavy chains of Christendom and all the baggage that comes with civil religion. Postmodernists intensely seek authenticity and can discern phony religion from afar.

In a sense, it may help the witness of our church to move from center to periphery in the community, just as the Early Church existed (and thrived) on the periphery before Constantinian rule. The church at Ephesus provides an excellent example of the Early Church on the periphery. Ephesus was an economic center and also boasted serving as the home to the temple of the goddess Diana.[163] As home for a major temple cult and as a central trading route in the Roman empire, the new church at Ephesus was certainly on the outside of typical Ephesian culture. Paul reminds the church early on in his letter that they were redeemed by God from a self-serving life and ordained by God's Spirit to serve others. He writes

> You were dead through the trespasses and sins [2] in which you once lived, following the course of this world, following the ruler of the power of the air, the spirit that is now at work among those who are disobedient. [3] All of us once lived among them in the passions of our flesh, following the desires of flesh and senses, and we were by nature children of wrath, like everyone else. [4] But God, who is rich in mercy, out of the great love with which he loved us [5] even when we were dead through our trespasses, made us alive together with Christ—by grace you have been saved— [6] and raised us up with him and seated us with him in the heavenly places in Christ Jesus, [7] so that in the ages to come he might show the immeasurable riches of his grace in kindness toward us in Christ Jesus. [8] For by grace you have been saved through faith, and this is not your own doing; it is the gift of God— [9] not the result of works, so that no one may boast. [10] For we are what he has made us, created in Christ Jesus for good works, which God prepared beforehand to be our way of life.[164]

Paul appeals to this church on the periphery to recall that they were once caught up in the center. God's call and God's grace reside on the periphery.

The center with the norms of cultural idolatry and excess is the way of darkness and disobedience in the passage. Moreover,

Paul explains that God has not given these believers the free gift of grace to allow them to boast or take up self-serving activities. The free gift of grace releases the church from activities focused on self and the desires of the flesh and instead allows the church to focus on ἔργοις ἀγαθοῖς, which translates "good works" or "good deeds." Following Christ *authentically* then requires *exactly the opposite* motives and behavior from what the postmodernist may suspect constitutes our actual motives and behavior. If we live out our calling as those who have received the free gift of grace, then even on the cultural periphery in an increasingly pluralistic context, rural churches may bear witness to the gospel of Christ and the inbreaking of the kingdom of heaven.

The Scripture is full of examples of people and cultures at positions of center or periphery.[165] As people in a rural church, we may find ourselves on the periphery of culture in some instances and at the center in other moments, not unlike the Jewish people or even Christ Jesus himself, who was at once at the center and an outsider. One powerful example of this was Jesus when he was hanging on the cross. The Roman soldiers hung a sign that read, Οὗτός ἐστιν Ἰησοῦς ὁ βασιλεὺς τῶν Ἰουδαίων,[166] or "This is Jesus, the King of the Jews."[167] At once, he is at the center and the outside. Notice the word βασιλεῦς (king), which comes from the same root as βασιλεία (kingdom). The one who proclaimed the kingdom of heaven was marked and mocked as a king in death. Jesus was at the center of God's will and salvific plan while utterly despised and rejected by humanity.

Another center/periphery moment in Matthew 27 comes with Jesus's final words, "*Eli, Eli, lema sabachthani.*"[168] In crying out in Aramaic, Jesus is placed on the periphery for the reader, who's primary language was Greek. Christ is utterly at the center of the story and utterly on the periphery, isolated by even his own language in Matthew's text. Jesus speaks as one who is at the center and as one who is completely outcast. In his saving act on the cross, he occupies both spaces equally, just as he occupied two natures in being fully God and fully human. If Jesus lived and died in the center and on the periphery, what might it look like for rural churches to be both at the center of God's will and living on the edges of culture for the sake of the gospel?

In exploring the Bible, we now have our navigational chart for the incoming postmodern tide. Through developing a pastoral theology of rural ministry using Aaron as a cautionary example, in exploring the smallness of the kingdom in the teachings of Christ, and through exploring center/periphery themes in Scripture, we can prepare to continue our journey. With the Bible as our guide for this journey called faith in Christ, it is time to check the forecast.

Chapter Six
CHECKING THE FORECAST: EMERGING RURAL CULTURE

> *"The winds, the sea, and the moving tides are what they are. If there is wonder and beauty and majesty in them, science will discover these qualities... If there is poetry in my book about the sea, it is not because I deliberately put it there, but because no one could write truthfully about the sea and leave out the poetry."*
>
> — Rachel Carson

In planning a journey over uncharted oceans, wise individuals might look up the forecast. Modern meteorological forecasting is quite accurate and can save lives both on land and at sea. In considering a model for postmodern rural ministry, an overview of previous literature will help us consider what trends and patterns have already been written about which may impact both rural and postmodern ministry.

Upon examining writings concerning postmodernity and its meaning for faith and upon also exploring writing regarding rural ministry and churches, a certain poetry emerges as intersectionality transpires between these two seemingly unrelated fields.

Many people who write about emerging culture and its impact on Christianity self-describe as emerging or emergent Christians or part of the Emerging Church Movement (ECM). In recent years, the term has largely fallen out of use. Some argue that the leaders of the Emerging Church Movement (incredibly influential in the late 90s and aughts) have simply melted into progressive mainline denominations.[169] Others on the conservative side argue the movement has fizzled out completely and declare victory over apostasy.[170] The truth, of course, is somewhere in between. Brian McLaren, one of the key leaders in the ECM, is still on Amazon's bestseller list and is still writing books.

A distinction here is necessary. *It is one thing to speak of what is emerging in culture and emerging in forms of worship and to speak of the Emerging Church Movement.* My intent is not to conflate the two because it would potentially shut down conversation for many regarding how rural churches can respond to the tidal shift of postmodernity. If you have gathered anything by reading this far, hopefully you sense that 1) the conversation I am calling for is firmly rooted in Scripture and that 2) it is an oversimplistic mistake to conflate postmodernity with pure moral relativism. Postmodernity has many gifts for the church, and while Christians may be right to wrestle with all that it means, we would be foolish to ignore the developing culture and consider what it means to be faithful in the midst of it.

The Emergent Church in Rural Communities?

Some authors exploring postmodernity and faith mention small-town churches, but only in passing. With all of this discussion regarding emerging rural culture and postmodernity, it seems critical here to discuss the ECM as it relates to rural culture. Just because postmodernity is impacting rural culture and places does not mean the ECM as a movement is on the rise in rural communities. The main argument of this book is, however, that postmodernity is on the rise in rural communities. Postmodernity is not inherently progressive or conservative. In fact, numerous scholars and theologians have written extensively around what a "post-conservative" and "post-liberal" faith might look like. One of the main impulses of postmodernity is to question the categories and labels we have been given and to even move beyond them to something more authentic and profound.

A rural young adult once came to me and Audrey for counseling. She had grown up in a church that preached the love of Jesus, but when her friend came out as a lesbian, the friend was ostracized by people in the community and even in her family. The same people in her life that had taught this young lady that the love of Christ is unconditional, now seemed to place conditions on that love. The friend that had come out was even told by her parents not to return home for Thanksgiving or Christmas, and it was clear she brought shame to her family. The young lady was mortified by watching her friend go through this and was now not only questioning every time her own family had ever said, "I love you" but also questioning everything they taught her about God. She deconstructed her own faith by beginning to ask questions about God and faith that might have been frowned upon by many in her church. This phenomenon is a process called deconstruction—an academic term for the systematic pulling apart of the belief system you were raised in. It's what happens when the questions you've pushed down your whole life finally bubble over the surface, and you're forced to stare honestly at your doubts.[171]

Many people deconstruct their faith when a crisis in life emerges. A miscarriage, a sudden death in the family, the loss of a job, or simply becoming friends with someone different from you can lead to asking deep questions about your own imbedded and inherited faith.

In one small town I pastored in, I once had a young father in my church who was disillusioned with faith. He had a number of positive experiences in the church of his childhood. Having moved from a large northern city to our small southern town, he was now struggling with the cultural expectation that he view life (and faith) through a conservative partisan lens. He was asking good questions about faith, like why some people think Christians should inherently vote a certain way, why some kinds of Christians think they alone hold claim to truth, and why so many people were "othered" by people of faith in our rural community. This faithful father, who wanted to follow Jesus authentically and raise godly children, was deconstructing his thinking and his believing – a process which led to a more mature faith. He was wisely questioning the legitimacy of categories and boxes people think and live in. If some of the people in our church had known he was asking those questions, he would have been ostracized and shunned by many.

One example of the ECM in rural communities is found in Gladys Ganiel and Gerardo Marti's interview of a lady named Savannah for their book *The Deconstructed Church: Understanding Emerging Christianity* (Oxford University Press, 2014). All they

Chapter Six: CHECKING THE FORECAST: EMERGING RURAL CULTURE

say about Savannah is that "Savannah said of her past church, a rural congregation, that 'it was definitely very into the emergent, postmodern thing,' and when her family moved, 'we were trying to find a church like that'."[172] In a book nearing 300 pages, this is the only mention of an "emerging" rural congregation. Marti and Ganiel make one more mention of rural churches in their book, and the conclusion they reach seems disheartening to the current endeavor, "Indeed, the ECM does not seem to be present in rural locations— although some isolated individuals may share some of the orientations and ideas of their emerging counterparts in cities. More importantly, the ECM is actively antisuburban, with many Emerging Christians deliberately moving out of the suburbs and exurbs and into inner cities as a lifestyle choice."[173] At first glance, it seems hard to imagine digging deeper than Marti and Ganiel did in their project, but when one talks to ECM people from around the globe, one finds that emerging churches and postmodern styles of ministry *do* exist in rural areas, although at present, they are clearly exceptions within the greater ECM.

Worth mentioning here is that the term "Emerging Church" is difficult to define for several reasons. These include the facts that emerging Christians may have institutional distrust, may dislike labels of any kind, and refer to themselves as "collectives" or "cohorts" or "gatherings" or "communities" instead of "churches." The argument for Marti and Ganiel is, "Nevertheless, [...] Emerging Christians are a discernable, transnational group who share a *religious orientation* built on a continual practice of deconstruction."[174] Emerging Christians are said to have a religious orientation rather than a religious identity. Many who may be part of an Emerging Church collective have never heard the term "Emerging Christianity." As postmodernity's impact increases in your rural community, the number of people with this particular religious orientation may indeed rise.

In many of the congregations represented in Marti and Ganiel's book, the leaders interviewed may all identify strongly with the Emerging Church movement and may even write books about Emerging Christianity or speak at conferences around the world, but they do not readily disclose this information to their congregations. One person interviewed said she went to Brian McLaren's church for a few years before she Googled his name. Of course, she was astounded at how influential and controversial her pastor was. She was also surprised to learn that he was the author of a number of bestselling books. Another observation regarding the project is that most of those thought leaders live and work in urban and affluent suburban contexts. If there were emergent rural gatherings, they would be some of the last to know.

Suffice it to say, group identity and centralization of thought or power for Emerging Christians are not as important as the sociological orientations they share. As already mentioned, the term deconstruction is often used to describe how people approach faith, meaning that people in Emerging Christianity are quite comfortable wresting with their own inherited faith. It seems that "Among Emerging Christians, the term 'deconstruction' is not consistently used and therefore not a term actively discussed except occasionally and among self-consciously philosophical members."[175] Many Emerging Christians seem unaware of the term "Emerging" or of the fact that they are practicing Christianity in deconstructionist ways. Nearly all of them are aware, however, that the churches they attend are far from typical.

Emerging Churches are often said to be pluralistic in nature. The pluralist congregations Marti and Ganiel speak of are defined as "social spaces that permit, and even foster, direct interaction between people with religiously contradictory perspectives and values systems."[176] In this way, Emerging Churches seem more open than traditional evangelical and mainline churches, as both conservative and progressive Christians do not often welcome a variety of perspectives within their midst. Emergent Churches may have liturgical elements and follow the lectionary, they may burn incense in the place of worship and place icons around the room to help people connect to the Divine, or they may have a rock band singing original songs written by community members or a jazz band that reworks familiar hymns. Emergent Churches may have ministers who robe and stole, they may meet in a pub, and they may incorporate art, dance, poetry readings, and communion into nearly every service. The point here is that Emergent Churches are incredibly diverse and may display a plurality of practices in worship and mission. To assume that all Emergent worship services are the same would be a gross mistake.

In many ways Marti and Ganiel argue that from a sociological perspective, Emergent Churches allow their participants to form authentic selves while they continue their deconversion from the faith of their youth. Marti and Ganiel state

> *Strategic religiosity conceives religious identity as dominated by assessments of appropriateness, relationality, and self-image. In the process, certain forms of religiosity and religious identity are sought out and legitimated while other forms are regulated to being less desirable, ineffectual, or merely mundane.* Overall, Emerging Christians participate (often unknowingly) in a socially enabled, collective entrepreneurial process in which a distinct, though slippery, religious orientation is being formed. In doing so, they enact a strategic religiosity in the shaping of a legitimated religious self (italics theirs).[177]

Emergent communities, therefore, provide a way for religiously disenfranchised people to find community with other people who have experienced organized religion in similar though not inherently identical ways. Who in your rural community or in your church may be going through a deconstruction of faith experience?

Emerging Churches highly value conversation and may actually use dialogical exercises as a part of the worship experience. They do not try "to settle on established positions or to reach a point where all can agree and therefore stop talking. Ongoing conversation is in itself a mechanism or a strategy to maintain a plurality of identities and positions within emerging congregations."[178] *In this regard, Emergent Christians present striking differences from the polarized Christian Left and Right, acknowledging the legitimacy of various views.* Many of the Emergent Christians interviewed by Marti and Ganiel report a heightened sense of authenticity in their current congregation compared to previous churches. People in disagreement are encouraged to respectfully dialogue and not shout each other down. In this way, Emergent Christians are seen by Marti and Ganiel as entrepreneurial because they create meaning for themselves through theologizing in a way that runs counter to the tidy systematics of modernity.

In the politicized and polarized world we live in, especially in the United States, many who study religion now write about so called "purple congregations." Purple churches are congregations with a fair mixture of republicans and democrats (or if you're in another country – conservatives and progressives). In some rural communities, purple congregations may seem on the cutting edge because they provide a space for conversation and dialogue among Christians of different theological and political bents – that is if the differences in the church are ever even named or acknowledged.

Chapter Six: CHECKING THE FORECAST: EMERGING RURAL CULTURE

While trying to deconstruct denominational practices from numerous veins of Christianity, Emerging Churches still remain loyal to a number of practices that most Christians would expect in corporate worship. One may understand "The ECM remains bound to paradigms of congregational worship that have developed over the past 2,000 years. Emerging Christians remain largely committed to prayer, singing, Scripture, and teaching in corporate settings within structured time limits."[179] Interestingly, what sets Emergent congregations apart from many others is the intentionality with which each worship element is selected each week. Thoughtfully planned worship becomes important to meaningful and authentic worship for those with an Emergent orientation.

One of the foremost leaders in the ECM was Phyllis Tickle, who passed away in 2016 after a short battle with cancer. In personal correspondence, I asked Tickle about her knowledge of emerging rural churches and groups. Her response (in part) was, "I do know that the rural groups are there. I can't, for the life of me, dredge up a single, concrete name for any of them, but I do know I have met over and over again at meetings and conferences, both the leaders and the members of such rural worshipping units."[180] Seemingly, there are conflicting reports on the possibility of emerging churches and ministries in rural settings. However, if someone as influential as Tickle indicates they are present, one can deduce that 1) postmodernity exerts impact in certain rural areas and 2) emerging ministry is possible in those areas. This is also indicative of the problem this book hopes to address – that most people writing about postmodernity as it relates to faith (whether they are conservative or progressive) tend to write from urban and suburban contexts.

In written conversation, I also reached out to Brian McLaren, mentioned earlier in this chapter. Arguably, no writer or theologian has been more influential in the conversation regarding the Emerging Church. While the term "emerging church" seems to have recently fallen out of vogue, McLaren is still writing bestselling books read by people across theological and denominational traditions. I asked McLaren two questions regarding emerging ministry and values in rural communities – 1) Have you seen any examples of emergent ministry in small towns or rural locations? 2) How can ministers serving in rural areas reach the emerging generation while also serving parishioners with highly traditional and conservative values? His response was the following:

> Yes to your first question, Jonathan. In fact, some of the most surprising experiments are taking place in these settings precisely because younger generations are being driven away in such large numbers. But your second question surfaces the problem. The people who help "emerging generations" usually can't simultaneously help the highly conservative/traditional folks.
>
> It does happen occasionally, and I could imagine it happening more. The minister would need to serve the traditional congregation well, while maintaining his/her integrity by not saying things he/she didn't believe. This is often hard, but with a lot of wisdom (wise as serpents, innocent as doves?), it can be done. Then, in his/her free time – not "on the clock," so to speak – the minister could invite some people over to his/her house or meet with them in a restaurant or coffee shop or whatever. Sometimes the people the minister would be helping in secret would be the sons and daughters of those who would fire him if they knew. That kind of ministry life isn't for everyone – but it isn't boring![181]

As one who has pastored in two rural churches, I can vouch that ministering to the traditioned church while attempting to reach out to the broader community is not for the faint of heart. The ECM may be fully present in rural communities (and you the reader may see that as good or bad), but many things are emerging in rural culture that open up countless ministry possibilities for those willing to try new things.

Possible Dangers of Postmodernity for Rural Churches

Perhaps all of this talk of helping people struggling with deep questions and wrestling with traditioned faith sounds non-threatening, but Emergence Christianity has many critiques. Tim Conder, an Emergent pastor and author, states, "Postmodernism has become the ultimate red herring in conversations between many existing churches and those doing ministry in the emerging culture. While postmodern thinking has shaped the emerging culture and many emerging churches, many in the existing church believe a postmodern understanding is antithetical to the gospel."[182] The critique most readily levelled against postmodernity and its proponents may be that the movement embraces moral relativism and individualizes faith in a way that places ultimate priority on experiential faith, thereby undermining the authority of Scripture. For many, the phrase "postmodern Christian" is an oxymoron.

Much of the writing concerning Emergence Christianity falls into one of three categories: ministering *as* postmodern Christians, ministering *to* postmodern culture, and *rejecting* postmodern culture as a threat to Christian belief. The last category is where many conservatives and evangelicals likely fall. Conder identifies three fears that many Christians have concerning the gospel and postmodernity. They are 1) Postmodernism and the loss of "truth," 2) Community and the loss of "personal faith," and 3) Cultural "accommodation" and changing the "changeless" message of the gospel."[183] To its Christian critics then, postmodernism exists in terms of what Christianity *loses*. When faith begins with belonging and conversation instead of propositions and dogma, many people feel "truth" is at stake. When people feel that "truth" is at stake, they feel ultimate "Truth" in the person of Christ is in jeopardy as well. People may also feel that the postmodern emphasis on community and belonging downplays emphasis on the personal profession of faith that has dominated evangelism in evangelical circles for decades. Mainline Christians may not struggle as much here since they generally have a more covenantal focus concerning salvation and ecclesiology.

Finally, and perhaps most important, opponents to Emergence theology believe that cultural accommodation may reach a point where the gospel itself is in danger. An example of this is the 2014 World Vision hiring controversy. The Christian relief organization announced a change in hiring policies in March 2014—they were now allowing Christian people in gay marriages to become employees.[184] The backlash from conservative Christians was furious, and within 24 hours, over 10,000 people had pulled sponsorships from children in need of clean water and food, much to the dismay of social justice-minded progressives. The same day as the World Vision decision, Al Mohler wrote on his blog:

> The worst aspect of the World Vision U.S. policy shift is the fact that it will mislead the world about the reality of sin and the urgent need of salvation. Willingly recognizing same-sex marriage and validating openly homosexual employees in their homosexuality is a grave and tragic act that confirms sinners in their sin — and that is an act that violates the gospel of Christ.[185]

Chapter Six: CHECKING THE FORECAST: EMERGING RURAL CULTURE

Influential reformed apologist John Piper wrote, "You cannot undermine biblical authority and trivialize perdition and its blood-bought remedy and expect to maintain a vibrant spiritual base."[186] To conservatives, the (arguably postmodern) stance taken by World Vision was a Cross issue, a salvation issue, an atonement issue—a gospel issue. Nearly any move made by Emergence theologians, be it a fresh atonement theory, a conversational rather than dogmatic approach on controversial social issues, or an openness to interfaith dialogue, many traditionalists unanimously cry, "The gospel is at stake!" For many rural churches, entertaining postmodern ways of approaching faith may indeed prove threatening. This doesn't change the fact, however, that the postmodern tide is coming.

Local congregations will increasingly need to decide how to approach the gospel in the twenty-first century. Emerging culture's increasing distain and distrust of institutional religion leaves the church in a seemingly precarious position. Somebody writing from the perspective of ministry *to* postmoderns writes, "We've got to realize that in our emerging culture, we are now in a different culture, and we need to view it and the people in it as a missionary would. Christians are now foreigners in a post-Christian culture, and we have got to wake up to this reality."[187] There is a strong desire by many to live as missionaries *to* emerging culture which still holds emerging culture in suspicious regard in many ways. Many churches have few postmodernists in membership or attendance, but they still feel the culture rapidly shifting around them. This even seems true in rural and small-town churches which tend to be insulated from trends in metropolitan areas. As congregations live through changing demographics, they will have to decide if simply ministering *to* postmoderns is enough. A small minority of Christians have already moved on to *fully embracing* postmodernism and all of its implications for faith.

A Robust View of the gospel

Over time, the impact of postmodernity on rural areas will increase, just as bathtubs and lightbulbs slowly made their way across the countryside. A tidal shift is on the horizon for rural churches, and none will escape the impact of emerging global culture. Such shifting tides deserves careful thought and evaluation from church leaders. In their ground-breaking research project, European sociologists Fekete and Liptak establish the core imbedded values of rural postmoderns and the strong correlation of those values to traditional values. As mentioned in an earlier chapter, the postmodern values they identified are listed as emotion and aesthetics over reason, environmental concern, strong preference for diversity, building individual identities, preserving and promoting cultural heritage, social/communal participation, solidarity, and tolerance.[188] Please take note that these values are not inherently conservative or progressive which speaks to the fact that they are deep cultural impulses that permeate all of society. If you can measure a church's affinity for these values, you may be able to gauge the church's affinity for new expressions of ministry and worship. To my knowledge, Fekete and Liptak's project remains the only scholarly attempt (or perhaps one of very few) to explore how postmodernity impacts rural localities. A survey of many of the rural ministry books in the works cited and works consulted portions of this book will also indicate a high probability that few authors or researchers focused on rural Christianity and ministry have written deeply or done a research project regarding the impacts of postmodernity on a rural congregation or network of rural congregations.

Emergence Christianity (whether you're drawn to it or not) centers in reimagining *faith* in the postmodern context. In the

Chapter Six: CHECKING THE FORECAST: EMERGING RURAL CULTURE

wake of sweeping movements for justice in regard to race and gender, every denomination and group of Christians is wrestling with what it means to respond in biblical ways, including repentance. Remember, postmodernity does not inherently mean progressive or conservative or any of the labels that have bound the church for so long.

Not only is society at large more socially complex than just a few decades ago, but because of globalization and the rapid transfer of values from urban to rural locales, increasingly, "rural change is becoming more complex in nature."[189] Instead of only increasing the kingdom of God through rescuing souls from hell, rural churches should also seek to increase God's reign in tangible ways on earth. This, of course, requires relationships and community because "the justice that people need is a moving target."[190] Through living in community and building intentional relationships, rural churches can seek godly justice in multiple ways.

One of the main reasons for tension concerning postmodernity and Christianity is arguably competing definitions of the gospel. My own rural ministry context has always been in thoroughly southern towns and in thoroughly evangelical Protestant churches – the kind of places where it might prove a true challenge to invite people to a broader understanding of the "gospel." Hill astutely observed in 1966, "All the affirmations of popular southern Protestantism grow out of one concern, the salvation of the individual."[191] One of the largest challenges to getting an evangelical small-town church to embrace a more postmodern outlook of faith is found in people's individual view of salvation itself, which is deeply embedded. Our overly individualistic and consumeristic mono-culture doesn't help. Does Jesus only save us from an eternity in hell, or could salvation have a temporal quality? What does it truly mean to participate with God's Spirit in ushering in the kingdom of heaven on earth?

The postmodern mindset challenges us to break down mental barriers in separating eschatological salvation from the church's earthly ministry. Perhaps it is true that "many of us grew up in a world where you talked about *either* salvation or social justice."[192] It seems that many, including younger ministers from across denominational and theological traditions, are shouting, "*You no longer have to choose!*"[193] What will it take for our churches to recognize the multifaceted reality of the biblical gospel?

What's Emerging in Your Context?

If we use a little imagination, any rural church may become an Emerging congregation through simply breaking modernity's trend of embracing an eschatological gospel versus an incarnational gospel, embracing both equally. Traditional, modern, and postmodern values do not exist in a cultural, social, or spatial vacuum. Understanding that *Emergence* is simply finding ways to negotiate cultural value shifts and exchanges that open up the definition of Emerging Christianity to include small-town churches that embrace forms of worship and ministry that acknowledge competing value systems in the contemporary rural context. In some churches, this might simply mean welcoming people from all political stripes as brothers in sisters in Christ – which may prove easier written than accomplished!

To equip rural churches for adapting to postmodern cultural change, issues like congregational change, values, and even the very nature of faith all emerge as appropriate areas of emphasis, teaching, and reflection. Adaption does not mean we forsake our convictions, but it may mean we evaluate them critically. Adaption does not mean we become moral relativists, but it may mean we embrace the radical grace of Jesus more fully. Adaption does not mean we are giving up on the Bible, but it may mean we listen to the Spirit more deeply when interpreting the Bible. Adaption may even look like moving from boisterous and triumphant certainty to humility and a willingness to dialogue with those we've long "othered" and ostracized in our faith communities. The fact is, the Church has adapted countless time in 2,000 years. My hope in this chapter is to invite you to consider how God may be calling you to adapt in your own rural ministry.

Rural churches will increasingly need to decide how to approach the gospel in the twenty-first century. A challenge for rural congregations and people is to view the culture in small towns the way it actually exists and not through the lens of an idealized past. One author acknowledges, "We've got to realize that in our emerging culture, we are now in a different culture, and we need to view it and the people in it as a missionary would. Christians are now foreigners in a post-Christian culture, and we have got to wake up to this reality."[194] Viewing our culture as *mission field* rather than *Christian* may prove challenging for some church members because such an outlook acknowledges that change has already occurred. This inherently cuts against the notion that nothing ever changes in our town or that our scarcely populated county is somehow culturally pure compared to more urban locales.

Not only does postmodernity impact small-town churches through value exchanges due to spatial relation to urban environments (see Chapter 2), Christianity does not enjoy the same influence it once did in rural America. For a small-town church, this may be a difficult reality to embrace. In spite of rural stereotypes, it seems that in rural areas, "The most dominant forms of morality [...] are drawn mostly from cultural rather than religious sources and images. While religious doctrines are important as well, they inform only a small portion of the moral pronouncements, judgments, and decisions that make up much of the day-to-day fabric of social life" in small-town America.[195] Read that last quote again. And then again. Let it sink in. Religion in rural America has an increasingly diminished influence on culture and even people's sense of morality. How would it change your ministry if you realized that this trend might only escalate in the years to come?

For many in rural America, Christianity has an impact on their lives, but just like in the city, most people in rural communities do not attend church regularly or attribute Christianity to the moral choices they make each day. I used to pass a local golf course on my way to church on Sunday mornings. The parking lot was more packed before 8:00 a.m. than our church would be all day between two services. Our church, like many, struggled to face the reality that our presence was perhaps not as influential in the community as it used to be because organized religion's influence wanes in the larger culture. This reality can be reversed through creative ministry focused on bridging the gap between 1) traditional, modern, and postmodern values and the gap between 2) an idealized approach focused on a mythic past and a pragmatic approach focused on present realities and future possibilities.

Chapter Seven
HARNESSING THE TIDE: EMPOWERING THE RURAL CHURCH

> *"The day will come when, after harnessing the ether, the winds, the tides, gravitation, we shall harness for God the energies of love. And, on that day, for the second time in the history of the world, man will have discovered fire."*
>
> – Pierre Teilhard de Chardin,
> Toward The Future

When my family moved to that small town of North Zulch, Texas, I was quite obviously the "new kid" on the first day of school. My status as a new resident branded me as an outsider. When I was much older and living in another rural community, many locals regularly and openly used the language of "been heres" and "come heres." People would even introduce themselves with the qualifier, "Hi, I'm _____, and I'm a come here!" This designation was clearly cast on me by my peers in the small school in North Zulch. As I recall, my freshman class had thirteen students. Of those thirteen, I was the only one who everyone hadn't known since birth.

Making designations about who is a "been here" and who is a "come here" is about one thing – power. The same is likely true for any number of designations a group casts on an outsider. With the designation as the "new kid," I was sometimes bullied and often the subject of jokes. One advantage I did enjoy from having grown up in a metropolitan suburb is that the youth basketball leagues were quite competitive. In moving to North Zulch, I found myself as one of the better players on the school team. But this also drew ire from my classmates. My family had recently made a move away from suburbia, and my parents were going through a divorce. One of the primary questions in my life was not only how to make it day to day in school (a question I suppose for any young adolescent) but also how to remain faithful as a Christian. As a young adolescent male, my temper would sometimes get the better of me when classmates pushed or taunted me. I got in more than one fight the year we lived in that town.

Some of the same temptations and challenges exist for rural churches today. When the power dynamics tilt in favor of larger churches, of "bigger" pulpits, and of big-money ministries, rural churches can feel like outsiders in their own tribes. What should power dynamics look like between rural churches and their more urban counterparts? One of the challenges I had my freshman year of high school was that I was experiencing so much change – moving from a city to a small town, parents getting divorced, leaving friends behind at my old church, puberty. It was a lot. Many rural churches might feel like all the change in our world is just too much. They may hunker down into old habits and comforts, or they may even lash out in anger if they perceive the world is taunting them. How should rural churches prepare for all the changes sweeping through our culture? The rest of this chapter will explore how rural churches can be both empowered for faithfulness and also empowered to weather change. One reality about the tide is that it is always beyond our control. Powerful forces move vast amounts of water each day, and most people hardly even notice. We can never stop the tide. The question then may be, how do we harness it?

Empowered for Faithfulness

A fruitful conversation concerning power may develop for rural churches when examining the relationship between urban and rural locations in Scripture and at present. This concept pairs nicely with Emerging theology which possesses a particular sensitivity to cultural power structures and their abuses, often promoting post-colonial and deconstructionist theological perspectives. An instance in Scripture of cultural change where urban and rural power structures are in play comes in Esther. The Persian Empire controlled much of the known world. It was an empire in which it was punishable by death to disobey the king's decrees. Several times in Esther, the "provinces" are mentioned (e.g., 1:16, 2:22, 4:3, 8:9, 8:11) as the places where God's people were scattered. Even in the midst of shifting empires and power structures, the Jewish people attempted to remain faithful to God's law.

Cultural centers of power often remain urban, and rural areas sometimes function as modern provinces of more urban populations, especially in relation to economic development, distribution of healthcare resources, and transportation. Since the advent of telecommuting, many rural communities have increasingly become bedroom communities for people who may need to be in the office only one or two days a week. Urban centers often only see rural areas in terms of the next place for a new development or a place to get away. Sociologically, this creates an imbalance of social capital. One may understand that "communities lacking social capital altogether or having a high density of only one kind are either apathetic or are at risk of being controlled by internal or external elites who may or may not have the community's best interest at heart."[196] Small towns without a strong identity may find themselves at the mercy of lobbyists, investors, developers, or legislators from urban areas with their own interests in mind for the small town and her resources (natural and human). The system of how urban and rural communities relate to each other is often one of urban colonialism with rural locations seen by their urban counterparts as only good for resource extraction (mining, farming, fishing) or recreation (the weekend home on the lake or river).

The concepts above provide both a sociological framework and a lesson in our theology of power. In Esther, God's people faced clear and present danger from a king who wanted them annihilated. Even though the provinces only served to funnel resources to the emperor and the emperor's urban centers of trade, God's people remained faithful in the hinterlands. It was said of the Jews, "There is a certain people scattered and separated among the peoples in all the provinces of your kingdom; their laws are different from those of every other people, and they do not keep the king's laws, so that it is not appropriate for the king to tolerate them."[197] The Jews were able to maintain a strong sense of identity in the face of colonialism and empire because of their willingness to remain faithful to God's law and commandments.

To have a strong sense of congregational identity, it is critical for your church to focus on its unique calling to reach area

Chapter Seven: HARNESSING THE TIDE: EMPOWERING THE RURAL CHURCH

and regional residents and remain faithful to the Lord. Remaining faithful to God's call despite the shifting power structures in culture might free your rural church to pursue bold mission, thereby leading to higher congregational self-esteem, more engagement with those who are far from God, and a greater sense of identity as God's people. This theology of power turns typical power structures upside-down; it potentially empowers rural congregations to embrace their own unique identity as God's faithful ones, not living in the narrative that they are lesser because they are smaller, too country, or not trendy enough.

Such a theology of power is postmodern in that it deconstructs historic metanarratives concerning urban and rural power relationships. Deconstructing the narrative in Esther provides a good example. On first reading, it would seem that Xerxes holds all of the power in the scenario, and he surely *was* a powerful king. From a deconstructionist perspective (and I would also argue a strong exegetical one), one might say the emperor Xerxes (the symbol of imperial and urban power) reacted to the Jews (scattered in the provinces) out of a posture of fear and indignation, meaning the problem was not the faithfulness of the Jews but the emperor's own ego. Who was more powerful — the Jews subverting imperial authority by being faithful to God or the "unenlightened despot, who possesses power but little wisdom," willing to kill thousands in order to maintain control?[198] By being faithful to God, rural churches and people may possess far more power than they realize.

This book seeks to empower the rural Church for missional engagement to more effectively minister in emerging rural culture. Critical to this endeavor is a *theology of rural empowerment*. Such a theology believes in three key ideas: *1) God* has called rural churches *"for such a time as this,"* perhaps even to rise up for their own survival. Rural congregations like yours are called and empowered to offer a prophetic corrective to the sins and excesses of many entertainment and production-driven churches in urban areas, environmentally damaging practices in global economics, manufacturing, and consumption, and the idea that only large urban congregations hold sway in conversations concerning faith and culture. Much attention, focus, and capital go into celebrating mega-churches in inner cities and suburbs, and small-town churches often feel they have little voice in Christianity. Thus, a theology of rural empowerment encourages rural congregations to embrace their unique calling, not only in their physical location but also within the context of the larger Christian church. A theology of rural empowerment also means 2) *Rural churches may control their own future, independent of urban actors.* As such, rural congregations can subvert cultural metanarratives about urban and rural power through taking pride and ownership in ministry, mission, and vision. In this way, your own rural church can live out the postmodern values of community and authenticity while capitalizing on your church's unique strengths and attributes. With great thought and care, Esther and Mordecai subverted power structures in their day, and God's people came out stronger and safer. In subverting cultural power narratives, rural churches may attract a younger demographic, sympathizing with postmodern values while strengthening their ability for missional ministry. The final stage of a theology of rural empowerment is 3) *Rural congregations are vital to the future of the Church-universal and naturally equipped to reach emerging generations.* In the scholarly treatment of rural and urban populations, "rural, in almost all statistical systems, is treated as residual, what is left over after urban areas have been defined."[199] Rural people, however, are not leftovers of urban colonies, and neither is the rural Church.

Chapter Seven: HARNESSING THE TIDE: EMPOWERING THE RURAL CHURCH

Empowered to Weather Change

If you look, you will find cultural change all over Scripture and also examples of how rural people adapted to it. Throughout the Bible, God's people change and adapt to shifting culture, changing kings and empires, and even different technologies. Prophets came declaring that God was not only the God of Israel (a particular geographic location and ethnic group) but also the God of all peoples and nations. The Bible shares accounts of people resisting cultural change, dialoging about what change means, and struggling to cope with cultural shifts. These struggles are key to the identity of God's people and shape the narratives and metanarratives of Scripture.

One example of cultural change in Jewish history comes in the Apocryphal texts of Maccabees and Sirach. As parts of the world faced cultural Hellenization, many Jews in cities had little problem adapting to cultural change, while people in rural areas struggled to adapt. Arguably, "The upper classes in Jerusalem, the Hellenizers, had long adopted Greek ways, while the poorer people of the rural areas tended to cling to the customs of their ancestors."[200] Of course, Hellenization (Greek culture overtaking the ancient world and replacing indigenous cultures) and postmodernity do not equate entirely, but both prove significant in nature, ushering in new cultural and theological paradigms. New thought patterns and cultures tend to emerge from urban environments, and many rural people often resist new ideas and philosophies or at the least become what many term "late adopters" to new technologies or ways of thought.

Additionally, it seems important to note that not every cultural change emanating from urban environments is desirable, just, theologically sound, or economically beneficial for the rural person. Rural people and communities have long critiqued urbanites in all matter of living. The critique in 1 Maccabees is that:

> ...the king sent letters by messengers to the land, to forbid burnt offerings and sacrifices and drink offerings in the sanctuary, to profane Sabbaths and festivals, to defile the sanctuary and the priests, to build altars and sacred precincts and shrines for idols, to sacrifice swine and other unclean animals, and to leave their sons uncircumcised. They were to make themselves abominable by everything unclean and profane, so that they would forget the law and change the ordinances.[201]

While many of the Greek customs and laws were acceptable, many were directly against deeply embedded Jewish traditions and beliefs, including the Covenant and the Law. Other laws were (as the passage above suggests) written expressly against the Jewish people. Interestingly, many of the Greek customs the Maccabean revolts fought against were later embraced by the Early Church, including acceptance of uncircumcised Gentiles into the faith, God's blessing on all foods that were previously deemed unclean (Acts 10-11), and even the end of ritual animal sacrifice. It might have behooved the Hasmoneans to examine how much of their resistance to change stemmed from nativism and tradition and how much from true religion – struggles that grip the world today. No doubt the Hasmonean population was persecuted, but lives were lost and blood was spilt fighting for things Christ, Peter, and Paul counted as unnecessary to the gospel. Seemingly, God's people should strike a balance between cultural accommodation and remaining true to the essence of the faith.

One way to view change theologically is through the lens of necessity. Another driving force in change often becomes creativity. When necessity and creativity meet, change becomes possible as churches, cultures, and entire religions morph and mutate. In thinking about change theologically, one should not overlook the changes that existed in Christ's day and in the time of the Early Church. We understand, for instance, "A series of major political and cultural and social changes affected all aspects of life in the Near East as well as around the Mediterranean under the Roman Empire. Religious beliefs and attitudes, in particular, underwent some dramatic transformations."[202] Change came to religion because of change in the culture, including (as the article just cited indicates) the end of ritual sacrifice. Many Christians never imagined that animal and temple sacrifice would have ended, with *or without* Christ and the cross.

In many cases, the cultural movement away from animal sacrifice came because of necessity, requiring a creative response among people of all faiths. Stroumsa goes on to say:

> In order to do justice to the dramatic nature of transformations in our period, from say, Jesus to Muhammad, one can also speak of "religious mutations." By borrowing this metaphor from the field of biology, I intend to highlight the fact that we do not only witness the passage from paganism to Christianity (to follow traditional perception), or from polytheism to monotheism. I wish to claim rather, that we can observe nothing less than a transformation of the very concept of religion.[203]

Many theologians and leaders today suggest that society is again undergoing a great mutation from modernity to so-called postmodernity. Could transformation of the very concept of religion once again materialize within human consciousness? Christians everywhere, especially those in small towns, should begin to grapple with the nature of the Bible and traditional orthodoxy as well as the nature of religious experience and

Divine revelation. If religion at its very nature is something that mutates, we must ask ourselves, "How much of what we call church are we willing to give up in order to *be* church?"[204]

In the ancient world and even fifty years ago, people more often than not fit neatly into categories of urban and rural, but postmodernity and globalization ushered in the blurring of such lines. Postmodernity and cultural change affects people in Tappahannock, not because such values are trickling down from cities (like the kingly decree in 1 Maccabees) but because lines of cultural distinction are rapidly eroding in our media-driven and technically connected world. Such rapid cultural change has ostensibly never occurred in human history, but that does not mean we are without biblical examples for consideration.

Several theological themes emerge which prove useful to the task at hand. In terms of change, biblical themes abound. Examples include wandering, journeys, the constant presence of God, diaspora, pilgrimage, and even the most significant changes of all — incarnation and resurrection. Change appears conceptually in Scripture in a number of ways, sometimes positively and sometimes negatively. In the same way, change may be viewed positively or negatively in terms of religion today. Equipping churches to *adapt to change* rather than equipping churches *for particular changes* may sound more palatable to many, and in numerous ways, this may be what is needed. However, a strong case can be made that human understanding of religion may once again undergo radical changes. In the latter case, churches should not only consider adapting to changing culture but also how they may be called to change both theologically and structurally within the new paradigm. In an idyllic rural setting, this may prove challenging. Oppositely, as culture shifts dramatically, people may rightfully cling to the certainty and assurance that "We have this hope, a sure and steadfast anchor of the soul" in Jesus Christ.[205] One necessary consideration for emerging rural ministry will be not getting so far out ahead of the congregation that nobody is willing to follow. As Southern Baptist ethicist Russell Moore once quipped, "One thing you have to remember about Southern Baptists – If you're 9 percent out in front of them, you're a trailblazer. If you're 10 percent out in front of them, you're dead."[206] Moore's idea is likely not far off. One of my hopes in writing this book is to help rural churches and pastors get a glimpse of what the future may hold for rural churches and people of faith. My hope is not to be so far out in front that people cannot hear any of what I am expressing.

My ultimate hope for you and your church is to equip your congregation to talk and think about change in healthy ways, to remind the rural Church (in a pastoral way) that things have always been changing and that God is present in the midst of change, to help leaders in the Church learn more about the dynamics of congregational change, to help the church consider what is *worth not* changing in order to give people a sense of the church as an anchor in the community, and to encourage the Church concerning change by identifying changes both culturally and congregationally that have been faced or overcome in the past. Through educating, nurturing, and encouraging, you may not change your church directly, but rather prepare your church to deal with rapid cultural change in healthy ways, both congregationally and personally.

A pastoral approach to change does not require pushing change or manufacturing change. It does, however, require a great deal of care and respect for the individual and corporate experiences of your congregants. Achieving a church-wide realization that God's people have always faced cultural change and that God does not abandon God's people would be an incredible step toward equipping the congregation for ministry in the current century. In many ways, the rural Church does not inherently need to change; they need to be empowered and encouraged. They need shepherding and patient love. They need someone to ask tough but thoughtful questions and help coach them through a discernment and visioning process.

There comes a time in every congregation though, where the need to change is evident. If we never change anything, then we never respond to the needs of the community around us. I once heard the Dean of Fuller Seminary, Tod Bolsinger, say in a presentation, that in his estimation, over 90% of churches would rather die than change. The statistic is shocking on its face, but it may not be far off. We get comfortable in our habits and ways of being. We grow fond of our theology and worldview and don't appreciate when it is challenged. We buy into the myth that things never change in a small town, and so we believe another myth – that our church should never change. The postmodern wave is already unleashed, and not responding to it in any way means the world will be passing our churches by – quite literally driving past the parking lot. Congregational change should not be forced or contrived, but one of my hopes in this book is to invite you to prayerfully consider how the Spirit might be leading your church to respond to the challenges and opportunities that exist in the emerging rural culture. If you are willing to commit to that, then read on.

Chapter Eight

TACKING AND GYBING: SAILING INTO THE WINDS OF CONGREGATIONAL CHANGE

> *"I am not afraid of storms for
> I am learning how to sail my ship."*
>
> – Louisa May Alcott

In negotiating global tides and currents on the high sea of cultural change, it is sometimes necessary to sail into or even through the wind. In sailing, the terms tacking and gybing refer to nautical maneuvers that do just that. If a vessel is tacking, it is sailing upwind, and it can look like it is zig-zagging across the water to its destination. Gybing (sometimes spelled jibbing) is a maneuver that turns a boat through the wind and can be more dangerous than tacking as it is more complicated. Just as sailors have maneuvered vessels successfully into the wind and through the wind for thousands of years, pastors and church leaders may feel powerful headwinds when leading a church to change course. One wrong move, and your main sail or even your mast can rip or break.

A possible synonym for emergence is the word change. The shift from modernity to postmodernity is a seismic shift, and any church grappling with emerging ministry in an emerging culture must inherently grapple with congregational change dynamics. Like tides bring regular change to bodies of water and shorelines, so does change as it constantly ebbs and flows in congregational life. There has been much discussion to this point of changes in culture, changes in history, and changes in biblical times. It is appropriate also to discuss the dynamics of change within congregational systems.

Not all change, of course, is needed or even desirable. Many of the changes some young ministers try and lead are purely cosmetic. I once knew a young pastor who removed the pulpit from a rural sanctuary within the first week of becoming the pastor. He also wore ragged jeans to preach in and told people he was bringing a number of changes to his rural congregation to bring in the younger families. If he had asked around a little, he would have learned that the head deacon's grandfather had made that pulpit in his own woodworking shop with reclaimed wood from a house fire that had killed several community members. The pulpit not only carried symbolic weight for the family whose relative had made it, but it also served as a reminder to the entire community that God can bring something positive from the rubble and ashes of life and that even in the midst of great tragedy and suffering, the mission and witness of the church carry on. The young pastor's reason for taking the pulpit away which he repeatedly stated to the church was, "I just don't feel comfortable preaching behind that old

Chapter Eight: TACKING AND GYBING: SAILING INTO THE WINDS OF CONGREGATIONAL CHANGE

monstrosity!" In addition to the pulpit fiasco, the new pastor's attire was offensive to many who saw jeans as work clothes for farming and wore their "Sunday best" to church as a way to honor God. Needless to say of our young pastor friend, he didn't last six months, and sadly, the church nearly split in that time.

In perhaps the original field manual for rural ministry (published after his death in 1652), George Herbert wrote in *The Country Parson* that "the Country Parson is a Lover of old Customs, if they be good, and harmless; and the rather, because Country people are much addicted to them, so that to favor them therein is to win their hearts, and to oppose them therein is to deject them."[207] Some customs give our lives and communities meaning. Pastors in rural communities will find many customs unique to the communities they serve. When I talk about leading change in rural congregations, I am not talking about doing away with these meaningful customs, as long as they do not hinder the gospel. These customs and idiosyncrasies are what give rural communities their unique charm and often bind people together. For the most part, they should be honored and celebrated by rural pastors – especially those from outside the community. Much of what many people would change in a church is customary or cosmetic. No, the change I am writing in regards to is a deeper change – the kind of change that has nothing to do with worship style or cosmetics.

The Onion is a satirical website which considers no topic off limits, and rightly so. The title of one article before the turn of this century, "I Just Don't Trust the New Pastor Yet," gives voice to Trudy, who is suspicious of the different way her new (and younger) pastor does things. At the beginning of the piece, she quips, "Pastor Logan seems like a good man. Maybe a bit too young to lead a flock, but still a good man. Nevertheless, he does a lot of things differently from Pastor Bufenkamp, and I simply cannot approve of some of them."[208] Trudy goes on to voice complaints about several things Pastor Logan does differently which are by no means greatly significant in terms of the gospel, but they are significant to Trudy. This may not read like satire at all to many in the pulpit or in the pews, but rather like real life. Change of any kind in a congregation – even good change – may cause anxiety to rise.

Numerous jokes exist about change in congregations. Don't worry. I'll spare you. Suffice it to say the anxiety congregational changes can bring often leads to people trying to deal with that anxiety, including through humor. Humor, of course, is far preferable to bullying and dysfunction. A struggle for any pastor or church leadership team desiring to lead change is how to go about it without congregational anxiety taking control of the situation and sabotaging the vision and mission of the church.

Deep Change as Adaptation

Gilbert R. Rendle discusses three types of situations calling for some level of change in congregational life. They each have their own unique qualities, and some leaders and churches may be positioned to deal with certain types of situations better than others. The first type of situation requiring a response is what Rendle terms a "Technical Situation." In technical situations, "A problem can be clearly defined and a solution can be clearly applied."[209] The maintenance committee determines the toilet needs to be replaced in the men's room because the seal is broken. The women's missionary group decides to order more promotional materials for this year's Christmas outreach because they ran out last year. A solder goes bad on a microphone cable,

Chapter Eight: TACKING AND GYBING: SAILING INTO THE WINDS OF CONGREGATIONAL CHANGE

and the worship leader needs to make a repair. These are all technical problems requiring technical solutions.

Adaptive situations are a bit different, since "the problem can be clearly defined but the solution requires learning."[210] The pastor is having problems gelling with the new youth minister, so they both agree to learn about the personality of the other through doing a Myers-Briggs assessment and share their findings. Small-group Bible studies are not as dynamic as the Sunday school director would like, so she goes to a conference to get some ideas. The church website unexpectedly crashes, and the chair of the technology team spends all day Saturday reading online help forums to work a solution. In adaptive situations, the problem at hand is clear, but learning on some level is required to address the issue.

Finally, Rendle discusses adaptive situations where both "the problem and the solution are unclear and new learning is required by all."[211] The congregation has a stellar youth program, but year after year, when students graduate high school and move to college, they seem increasingly disconnected from the faith with some even becoming agnostic. Grandparents are now wondering how to get their grandchildren interested in church again, but they have no idea why they fell away and are even less confident about how to bring them back to church. Or perhaps people at this year's state denominational gathering brought politically charged motions to the floor. It seems like everyone is anxious about something, but nobody is sure what it's about. If too many more years like this go by, people will stop coming to these meetings altogether because nobody wants to be around political infighting. Maybe a woman who has been faithful to church and God all of her life and has done everything she knows to raise her three kids to follow God experiences untold amounts of personal anguish and grief. In a six-month period, she lost her husband to a heart attack, her son to a drunk-driving accident, and her daughter to suicide. She hates coming into the sanctuary because all three of the funerals were in that space. She questions God, as any sane person would. At night when she's alone, she shouts to God, "Why me? What did I do to deserve this!?!" before crying herself to sleep. These complex situations do not have easy answers, and in each situation, people might be able to voice that something is wrong but not be able to adequately name the issue at hand.

Rendle wisely suggests that the appropriate response to adaptive situations is mutual learning by all. The wave of postmodernity coming to a rural community near you is an adaptive situation. There are no easy answers to why our culture is going in the direction it is going. People sense that something is fundamentally wrong with church being done the same way it has always been done, but nobody, including this preacher, is entirely aware of how to fix it. There are no trips to the hardware store, no weekend retreats, and no quick phone call to a denominational strategist that fully address the kind of shift that is happening in our culture, our towns, and increasingly in our churches. One of the marks of a healthy congregation in the face of an adaptive situation is "the willingness of all parties to learn to be open to changing behavior based on new learnings."[212] Hopefully, over the course of confronting difficult situations and questions, churches can become open to shifting behaviors and habits in healthy ways for the sake of the Kingdom.

Church-Size Dynamics and Change

One dynamic concerning congregational change stems from church size. The vast majority of churches in rural America

Chapter Eight: TACKING AND GYBING: SAILING INTO THE WINDS OF CONGREGATIONAL CHANGE

classify as smaller congregations. Congregations often termed as "shepherding congregations" have between 50-150 active members. They derive their name from the fact that "the primary leadership function of the pastor is akin to that of a shepherd caring for the flock. The members in such a congregation get their spiritual needs met primarily through their personal relationships with the pastor."[213] If a pastor wants to lead a small church to grow, one of the first places of resistance may be that congregants (and perhaps the pastor) don't weigh the fact that growth might lead in a shift in how the church relates to the pastor.

My last church was one of those rare small-town churches classifying as a program-sized congregation – a church "with 150-350 active members."[214] In a program-sized church, programs of spiritual feeding begin to supplement members' needs for a high-quality relationship with the pastor. There are many cells of activity in this church, and they are headed by lay leaders who take on some pastoral functions. Still, at the center of church activities, pastors now spend much of their time planning with lay leaders to ensure high-quality programs.[215]

To properly address (or lead) congregational change in a program-sized church, one might wisely work within the confines of organizational dynamics. In a program-sized church for instance, people other than the head pastor might help create and even implement ministry programs and opportunities. Also, ministering directly to key leaders and their families is not only expected in a program-sized church, it will lead toward earning the trust required to lead change of any lasting value. No matter the congregation's size, organizational dynamics and imbedded functioning weigh heavily on any effort to facilitate change.

Clergy Burnout and Change

It seems both anecdotally and through empirical research that ministry burnout is related directly to a clergyperson's ability to lead congregational vision and change. The need to work with key leaders and even delegate during leading change becomes paramount upon realization that "12% of rural clergy believe that they have accomplished very little of worth in their ministry; 17% believe that they have no positive influence over the lives of others, and 13% find that they gain no exhilaration from working with others."[216] Perhaps these bleak statistics are a clarion call for rural churches and clergy to consider the importance of change and adaption. Perhaps this percentage of clergy who feel dejected are suffering depression, or perhaps they overextend themselves in small congregations relying on a pastor for all the ministry. To make things crystal clear, a grave risk associated with leading change in a church that looks to the pastor to do everything is total burnout.

In rural communities, clergy isolation lurks as one of the top risks for burnout. In many rural churches, "some rural pastors enjoy the challenge of functioning as generalists. But the call to pastor a single pastor church can lead to burnout, brought about by a lack of privacy, deep seated feelings of isolation, and a heavy load of responsibilities."[217] Finding support through a peer group like a local ministerial alliance can help not only the pastor but also the church because with collegial support, the pastor will be more emotionally and spiritually available. Moreover, leading change in any organization might cause feelings of exhaustion in addition to isolation. Finding a supportive network of clergy and even a regional peer-learning cohort might prove wise, so that in attempting to facilitate change, the pastor maintains emotional and spiritual support from colleagues and friends.

It seems "there are a significant number of clergy working in rural ministry, who are suffering symptoms associated with emotional exhaustion and feelings of lack of personal accomplishment. In practical terms, those clergy experiencing symptoms of burnout are more likely to show a subtle disengagement" in their place of call.[218] Leading change requires discipline and drive, vision, and focus. Leading a congregation to adopt a stance of adaptiveness for ministry in the postmodern context might necessitate cultivating strong habits of personal Sabbath keeping, finding places of spiritual and emotional affirmation, and even maintaining a self-care regimen, including regular habits of exercise and attention to nutrition. The ministry plan will incorporate a self-care strategy to prevent the possible burnout that comes not only from serving as a clergyperson but potentially as a change agent in the life of the church. Engagement is the opposite of withdraw, and "those experiencing one form of burnout or another display signs of withdrawal [...]."[219] Effectively leading a congregation to *engage* more fully in the joys, challenges, and complexities of ministry in the emerging rural context makes preemption and prevention of burnout a leading concern. Wading into the tides of cultural change and leading a church to follow suit requires periods of exertion and training, but also rest.

Strategies for Leading Change in Rural Churches

In the dynamics of congregational change, also consider the role of the clergy. One excellent and generous definition of *emerging churches* defines them as "congregations that are meeting challenges of the postmodern world with creativity and vitality."[220] This definition is helpful in that it makes no theological claims about what it means to be emerging as a congregation. Surely rural churches can meet the challenge of postmodernity with creativity and vitality! One suggestion Sanguin later gives for achieving such vitality is, "The role of clergy needs to shift from personal chaplain to spiritual leader and equipper of the saints in Christ."[221] This, of course, echoes the apostle Paul in claiming the role of pastor is "to equip the saints for the work of ministry, for building up the body of Christ."[222] Unfortunately, many rural churches fall into the trap of expecting the ordained clergy to functionally *do all* of the ministry, particularly visitation ministry. The churches I have pastored were blessed with mostly functional deacon bodies (Baptist tradition), but each group had room for improvement in terms of visitation and building relationships with assigned families. Sanguin suggests that churches should make the shift to equipping laity for pastoral care for theological reasons (Ephesians 4:12) but also for a practical reason. He argues, "Cultural shifting requires immense energy and leadership," and when pastors devote almost all of their time to visitation, they simply have no time (or energy) remaining for sustained attention to visioning and change. Of course, the importance of striking a balance here seems obvious. Pastoral care remains an important aspect of one's ministry at a church of any size, and congregational size *plus* the dynamics of change remain important here. *In your church, any sustained focus on congregational emergence and change should complement a strategy for training and freeing lay people and leaders to minister.* Different denominations and traditions may embody this in different ways, but freeing the Church to actively participate in ministry is critical not only to vitality but also to leading a change process. If we want to position our congregations for vitality and creativity in the postmodern era, one of the first steps may be to equip as many lay people as possible for ministry and pastoral care.

Chapter Eight: TACKING AND GYBING: SAILING INTO THE WINDS OF CONGREGATIONAL CHANGE

Sadly, many small congregations self-sabotage when a pastor tries to lead change which always involves some level of risk. In discussing the resistance that can surface during congregational change, one author relays a personal experience that brings into relief the dynamics of resistance that often proliferate during congregational change in a rural community. Robert Stephen Reid writes,

> I was in my first pastorate in a growing congregation when a wise lay leader explained why I was experiencing such resistance even in the face of positive congregational growth. Leo Moore said to me, "You have to understand, Bob. If you try and fail, then you'll just move on, and we are left to pick up the pieces. On the other hand, if you succeed, then the denomination or some bigger church will tap you on the shoulder, and you'll be gone. Either way we're left picking up the pieces." Leo's sobering words were my first real introduction to the reason that most congregations try to keep pastors in the role of chaplain-manager rather that inviting them to become leaders. Add to this the fact that the congregation is the pastor's employer, and it becomes immediately apparent that a pastor's power, especially in a democratically religious organization, is diffuse.[223]

The above story recounts what many pastors, including this one, sometimes encounter when meeting resistance to congregational change. The dynamic described above includes congregational feelings of fear, potential abandonment, expendability, and inefficaciousness. No wonder some congregations might resist changes proposed by the pastor. *Any plan to address congregational change at your church should consider developing a pastoral perspective toward resistance arising during the change process.* Cliché ideas like "people are stuck in their ways," or "they just want to control the church," or even "there is nothing around here a few timely funerals cannot fix," seem childish when acknowledging the underlying psychological feelings and emotions of congregants at play in the church system.

Moving from a posture of chaplaincy to missional engagement is not for the impatient. True change in a church requires dedicated time, not in increments of months but of years, and "a realistic figure might be five to seven years, or sometimes longer."[224] Changing the missional posture of a congregation or the fundamental makeup of the church is a shift that alters the entire DNA of a congregation. These changes include "deep changes such as a shift to ministries that target unchurched persons, a major transition in the racial or ethnic composition of the membership, movement to a significantly different size, or the journey from a 'chaplaincy' stance to a missional posture."[225] Leading change in a rural church requires patience. It might take half a decade to usher in *one* deep change, and apart from a mighty movement of God's Spirit (which of course we always pray for), one might wonder if any wisdom comes in pursuing more than a *single* deep change in a congregation at a time. Focusing entirely on reaching even the worthiest of goals might alienate some church members, raising the level of anxiety in the church. Focusing on reaching multiple worthy goals, when those goals involve deep change, may prove catastrophic. It seems, "The most effective transformational leaders have mastered the art of leadership. They know when a congregation is ready to move forward and when it is time to slow down, regardless of any timetables that may have been previously set."[226] Pace becomes critical to successfully leading congregational change.

Part of the reason transformational leaders learn to lead at the pace a congregation is willing to move is because the *process* of change is equally (perhaps more) important than even the change itself. In a rural church, no matter the congregational size, the path toward fruitful and lasting change might involve

Chapter Eight: TACKING AND GYBING: SAILING INTO THE WINDS OF CONGREGATIONAL CHANGE

what Jung and Agria term "facilitating rather than leading. In such a model, process becomes more important than goals."[227] Allowing people to express opinions and ask questions while also giving them time to process information might all prove successful to leading congregational change. One of the biggest changes in the history of my last church was when the church moved from the colonial courthouse on the town square to her current campus nearly 11 years ago. When congregants describe changing locations, many describe the *process* of reaching the decision before talking about the new building and how it compares to the "old church," as it is called – a telling observation! Per several congregants, multiple public meetings were held over the course of several years as the church explored (and wrestled with) the idea of physically moving. People had a chance to openly voice their concerns and opinions, and everyone felt heard. If the pastor leading this change had not trusted the process and been satisfied to move at the pace people were comfortable with, then the church might still be situated in town or might even have split.

If process is so important, then identifying processes likely to bear fruit becomes paramount. In discussing change, Jung and Agria suggest that pastors and church leaders frame the conversation regarding change in one of four ways. Through 1) "Framing change as maintenance,"[228] pastors can help identify that change may actually help preserve traditional values inherent within the church/community. A pastor might make the case, for instance, that the church has always valued ministering to the less fortunate, and in order to maintain that value in the face of changing demographics, it could prove fruitful to begin an afterschool program for at-risk youth. If such a program were to begin at the church, not only would a new program bring change in terms of the weekly ministry, the families it might reach would almost certainly be more economically and ethnically diverse than the current membership, potentially bringing a much deeper change to the life of the church. Appealing to the congregation to explore deep change for the purpose of maintaining embedded values has great appeal.

Encouraging a church to alter her programs or ministry approaches may also entail 2) "Interpreting change in the context of historical patterns."[229] Your church might decide to set a goal as a church to become more engaged in local outreach and ministry which may lead to new ministry opportunities and new members. Appealing to times in the church's history when the people engaged the community in similar ways might prove a powerful motivator, capitalizing on the congregation's rich sense of history and tradition.

Another approach is 3) "Presenting change as endemic."[230] After arriving at one church, Pastor Jason and his family learned that at all three public schools (elementary, middle, and high school) lacked accreditation from the state department of education. Turns out the search committee didn't lead with that one, no doubt out of a desire to put their best foot forward. The problem of a sub-par school system was unique to that particular town and county with schools in neighboring counties receiving top marks on standardized test scores and other benchmarks. The pastor believed God was calling the church to change in some way to help address this issue by coming alongside families and school system employees to focus on a pressing need in the community. Tackling this issue would also lead the church to deal with the issues of local poverty, the church's lack of racial diversity, and the church's reputation in the community as "the snooty person's church." Perhaps Pastor Jason will be able to lead positive change through leading the congregation to focus on a missional opportunity unique to his church's community.

Chapter Eight: TACKING AND GYBING: SAILING INTO THE WINDS OF CONGREGATIONAL CHANGE

Finally, this pastor may encourage churches to embrace change by 4) "Reinforcing the change as a desire that must come from within – from the individual and the community."[231] Pastors in rural communities are often "at once insider and outsider" and might wisely choose to win over long-term members and residents (especially matriarchs and patriarchs of the church) before initiating any meaningful congregational change. In short, if the people have no desire to change, the most effective pastor in the world (potentially marked with "outsider" status) will not effect change in the least. Meaningful change in rural churches (for better or worse) will almost always be led by people who the congregation consider as "insiders," people who meet the dual criteria of long-term church member and long-term community resident. If it hasn't crossed your mind at this point, that means that if Jesus showed up at some churches on Sunday, the Lord Himself as an outsider (culturally/racially/theologically) might not be able to institute positive change in many congregations. However, when building a world changing movement, even Jesus recruited different people as His closest disciples and most trusted representatives.

One possible path toward positively leading congregational change may come in the field of appreciative inquiry (AI). Appreciative inquiry is "an organization-wide mode for initiating and discerning narratives and practices that are generative (creative and lifegiving). Then AI guides and nourishes (reconstructs) the organization along the line of its best stories."[232] The reader may recall that in the postmodern context, discerning meta-narratives that arch across history is appealing to the postmodern mindset, and postmodernists are drawn to deconstruct the varied constructs of modernity. Through AI, any church may identify her own unique and life-giving story, and after deconstructing what makes the church nourishing and life giving to her members and the community, reconstruct a positive identity that ushers in deep and lasting change. It seems many churches that experience themselves as confused, declining, or conflicted may too easily live out those constructs. Participants may attempt to change through problem-solving or blame or seek a hero pastor who is expected to provide an inspired plan. Theories about social determinism sap real choices. Endless discussions about failures focus personal and corporate energies on everything that has proven deadening, "Command and control approaches to leadership fail to engage participants fully as whole persons who can participate fully. Appreciative inquiry is built on theories that move a congregation away from deficit-based models toward the images and forces that are the most life giving."[233]

Through following principals of AI as laid out by Branson, I have attempted to help churches discuss congregational change in positive and meaningful ways that celebrate all the best stories and memories from within the life of the church. You can also focus on positive attributes of your own church in encouraging them toward an adaptive posture concerning 21st century cultural change. In doing so, we may be able to draw focus and energy away from people's fears, anxieties, and frustrations with current and past failures and construct a positive, redeeming, and joy-filled plan for where God is calling us in our next chapter as a people.

Remember the claim that an emerging church is a "congregation that [is] meeting the challenges of the postmodern world with creativity and vitality?"[234] Through framing congregational change in ways that appeal to rural people's values and using the principles of AI in developing a ministry plan, your church may indeed rise to the challenge of creatively dealing with societal change on the global and local levels.

Chapter Eight: TACKING AND GYBING: SAILING INTO THE WINDS OF CONGREGATIONAL CHANGE

Resistance to Change

Here, a final discussion of conflict and change seems in order. When change of any sort comes, conflict has potential to surface. There is wisdom in realizing biblical precedent here. *Resistance to change is, in fact, biblical.* Upon reviewing biblical patterns, it seems "every time—without exception—the people of God began to make adjustments to join God in his activity, conflict emerged."[235] Conflict, at some level then, is inherent for any congregation seeking and following the will of God because following God's will often involves "making adjustments." It is not biblical in the sense that God commands conflict. It is biblical in the sense that the witness of Scripture reminds us that people often resist change, even when God institutes the change. If people resist changes instituted by the Almighty, then what sane pastor wouldn't expect some level of resistance when leading change?

Resistance to change is also personal. Conflict, while expected whenever change creeps into society or congregational life, can sometimes leave lasting wounds. Pastors might be wise to consider, "In small, rural congregations where long-standing, intimate relationships are so very important, unresolved conflicts can be especially painful and destructive."[236] Before leading your rural church toward any deep changes, it might prove wise to discern if there is any unresolved conflict in the church and how best to resolve it. If change (however small) has potential for conflict, then encouraging a church to embrace change or even a posture of adaption toward culture might potentially open old wounds where former strife remains unresolved.

Consequently, *resistance to change is often emotional.* In discussing resistance to change, Ried cautions, "Leaders provide followers with good reasons to go on the journey, but they need to appeal to the heart as well as the head. Resistance will gain a strong foothold if leaders fall into the trap of assuming that facts speak for themselves."[237] In a world that increasingly uses terms like "post-truth" and "alternative facts" to describe how people perceive reality, one thing pastors and church leaders can learn from our emerging culture is that appealing to facts to the detriment of appealing to people's deep internal emotions might lead to various levels of resistance among a constituency – whether political or congregational. Whenever conflict is at hand concerning change, congregational leaders should pay careful attention to the emotions people exhibit and appeal to their emotions in stating the case for change. Also worth noting is that emotions may be positive or negative. Perhaps through lovingly addressing people's negative emotions while casting vision based on their positive emotions, a pastor, deacon body, elder board, session, or church council may effect change despite some resistance on the part of certain parishioners.

Finally, it pays to realize that *resistance to change is inevitable*. Anecdotally, it seems some people have a natural inclination against change. Churches are made of people. Therefore, it stands to reason that some people in every church might resist change of one variety or another. If anything, we know:

> Leading change is hard, and it is hard on pastors. What is apparent is that pastors become leaders rather than congregational managers when they take up the responsibility to become the vision bearer for "making something happen" in the life of the congregation, and then take responsibility for preparing for resistance that will inevitably occur along the journey.[238]

In encouraging a congregation to embrace an adaptive posture to the emerging rural culture, it helps to know that resistance to change is biblical (in the sense that if we follow God's will

Chapter Eight: TACKING AND GYBING: SAILING INTO THE WINDS OF CONGREGATIONAL CHANGE

as a church, some may resist), to know that that some people take change personally (particularly if already wounded in some way), that resistance is often deeply emotional because change is often deeply emotional, and that resistance to change is inevitable in many ways.

Even though resistance to change is a given, the resistance might come from non-stereotypical quarters. Buttrick presents the notion that "elderly persons are often open to a changing world in ways that their children may not be."[239] Pastor Susan's church began a contemporary worship service (with a full band) only a few weeks before her arrival as the new minister of First United Methodist Church. Much to the surprise of many, a number of elderly people happily attended because they enjoyed the music and the casual atmosphere. One ninety-year-old man commented (on the way out the door one Sunday) that he loved the praise choruses and their uplifting nature and appreciated that he could come in casual attire because dress shoes now hurt his feet. Many younger pastors may incorrectly assume that older members automatically position themselves as resistant to change, when in fact, the elderly may emerge as early adopters. Buttrick observes that many "elderly looking back know they have been foolish and have been forgiven over and over again, as have their grandparents and their parents; as a result, they have found a kind of tender tolerance towards themselves and others."[240] In a rural congregation, elderly people open to change are also, in some cases, the patriarchs and matriarchs in the church, giving them a certain social and leadership capital that a young pastor may never acquire. In terms of dealing with resistance to change, it becomes paramount not to make assumptions about who might resist or embrace change, and it's also paramount to rely on elderly members open to change to help ease the anxiety of some of their younger biological and church family members, respectively.

Chapter Nine
PASSAGE PLANNING: METHODS OF DATA COLLECTION

> *The universe lies before you on the floor, in the air, in the mysterious bodies of your dancers, in your mind. From this voyage no one returns poor or weary.*
>
> – Agnes de Mille

Before navigating the tides, it pays to study our navigational chart and view the forecast. The world of sailing uses the term "passage planning" which simply means developing a more comprehensive plan for the journey. This will bring together a navigable plan, also taking into consideration other elements like time, the actual route, possible alternative routes, navigation dangers, and more. In developing methods for data collection, several pitfalls and alternatives were indeed considered when developing the project's implementation.

What if you could measure the extent to which your own rural church or community had affinity for postmodern values? As stated at the outset of this book, the research and writing contained in this text largely originated with my own Doctor of Ministry project at Logsdon Seminary. In the project, there were several goals and objectives as part of the ministry project implemented at my church. In consultation with my project committee, I developed two assessment tools to help measure my congregation's value systems. I measured traditional, modern, and postmodern values within the church by administering a church-wide questionnaire.

It hopefully seems obvious at this point that people's values enter into consideration when discussing postmodernism's impact on rural culture. It seems many people in rural areas are attracted to traditional and postmodern values more than modern values.[241] As identified by Fekete and Liptak, traditional values include self-sufficiency, love of nature, the importance of family, respect for the elderly, friendliness to strangers, a respect for tradition itself, and love for the community. As mentioned in previous chapters, traditional values do not inherently lean toward one political side or another, as many may espouse. Modern values identify as reason over emotion, order, feats of engineering, efficiency, growth, and innovation. Finally, postmodern values are described as emotion and aesthetics over reason, environmental concern, strong preference for diversity, building individual identities, preserving and promoting cultural heritage, social/communal participation, solidarity, and tolerance.[242] In their original study, Fekete and Liptak measured how people perceive these values by using visual representations of each value and asking people which picture or image they feel most drawn toward.

One early attempt to measure the difference between rural and urban values and culture came from Lee Taylor of Cornell University in 1968. His book, *Urban-Rural Problems*, Taylor states that urban life and modem science provide many of the answers –

Chapter Nine: PASSAGE PLANNING: METHODS OF DATA COLLECTION

not to the problems of rural people, but rather to the *problem of* rural people. Parts of the book may read rather shockingly to the contemporary reader. One early passage describing the problem of "low-income people" tellingly describes poor people and people of color as their own worst enemy and describes poverty in ways that are now widely seen as racist and demonstrably false. In describing the urban poor, Taylor states, "Slum people are characteristically economically poor, dark-skinned or otherwise minority types, inadequately educated, and occupationally depressed. They are often emotionally disturbed, have little motivation, and have low aspirations."[243] Six pages into the monograph, Taylor categorically stereotypes poor people of color as poor, lazy, dumb, and mentally ill and categorically labels them as "slum people." Many may not realize the current narratives appearing in white nationalist and far-right conservative media were being written about by an Ivy League professor in the sixties. Nowhere in the chapter on poverty does he mention the systemic abuse and dehumanization of black people in our culture. Nowhere in the chapter on education does he mention integration in his multi-page explanation of school consolidation. He goes so far as to describe those rural people in-migrating to urban locales as "the residue of the rural population."[244] All 110 pages of the book use quantitative data, and not a single page has a personal story or account from a rural or urban person sharing their unique perspective on the matter.

My own project also utilized quantitative data, but it also attempted to recognize that a purely quantitative approach may make for dry and even jaded analysis that misses large themes potentially emerging from human story and recollection. A helpful passage plan in the postmodern era ideally includes personal story as a means of data collection. Taylor's monograph serves as a prime example of how *not* to approach rural-urban studies in the 21st century (or the 20th century, for that matter) and also serves as an admonition to listen to the experiences of people before passing judgment based purely on quantitative research or analysis.

Any assessment of our church's capability to adapt to postmodern emergence needed to define what "postmodern emergence" actually meant. As explored in Chapter Six, naming emerging postmodern values is notoriously difficult since emerging Christians tend to shy away from propositional truth claims, categorical thinking, and nicely packaged labels. In fact, "The lack of coherence among emerging Christians contributes to the frustration of their more conservative counterparts who work within theological structures furnished with tidy, holistic frames of critique that finely distinguish between 'correct' and 'incorrect' varieties of modern Christianity."[245] How does one measure a church's feelings about values and movements that seem incoherent, much less their readiness to adapt to such values? One approach is to find a large sample of emerging Christians and determine their commonalities. More on that shortly.

In desiring to name postmodern values (or for that matter, rural values) one should remember, "The city does not end at the city line or at the last exurb, but rather is part of a continuous web of social relations that as a whole represent the urban system."[246] Rural towns connect to cities through a giant web of interaction—economically, politically, relationally, and spatially. This idea of an interconnected web is extremely similar to Nancy Murphy's conversation about all knowledge and experience as a web.[247] Instead of compartmentalizing knowledge, philosophy, theology, economics, politics, or spatial experience into urban *or* rural, a postmodern approach to rural and urban relations realizes that rural and urban do not exist in separate compartments but are part of an interconnected whole.

Additionally, a postmodern approach to rural/urban relations realizes that while rural places do not all identify with postmodern values, they are still deeply affected by these values because of the web of connection existing between the city and countryside. A postmodern approach to rural ministry might "[...] not look to sciences but to the humanities. In essence, postmodernist approaches seem different from earlier sociological approaches to [spatiality] because the aim is different. Whereas a social science approach attempts to explain the phenomenon, the humanities approach is to critique the phenomenon."[248] In this sense, small towns and rural locales often feel impacted by postmodernism in urban life because their very existence stands in some ways as a critique of more urban postmodern philosophy and values. This assumption (made by many) is only true if rural values and postmodern values prove antithetical to each other.

The Quantitative Questionnaire

The ministry project included one congregational assessment questionnaire designed to gather quantitative data about congregational comfort with traditional, modern, and postmodern values, as defined by Fekete and Liptak. The questionnaire served as a pre-test and a post-test for the ministry project *between two different focus groups* to measure the impact of the preaching, training, and Bible-study materials. The language for these questions kept the layperson in mind and attempted to measure certain embedded values and theological positions. One focus group was made up of deacons and church council members, and the other focus group was made up of congregants willing to participate in the project.

One may understand "the term survey refers to a method of data collection, whether it takes place in the field, in a lab, among the participants of a case study"[249] or in a ministry project. The field base for the research was, of course, my congregation – Beale Memorial Baptist Church (BMBC).
I cannot thank them enough for serving as willing participants in this process of discovery! The questions on the quantitative questionnaire measured data, including the respondent's age, how long the respondent had lived in the town or county, their feelings about cultural and ecclesial change, their values (traditional, modern, or postmodern) as mentioned previously, and their perception about the values of other generations. The questions were structured in various ways, such as ranking, multiple choice, simple "yes" or "no" questions, and Likert scales.[250] In section 2.a of the quantitative questionnaire, questions measured people's comfort with congregational change and their leanings toward postmodern, traditional, and modern values. Multiple choice answers were weighed based on people's feelings about congregational change with answers most strongly reflecting resistance to change weighing one point and answers showing total embrace of change weighing three points. Section 2.b allowed respondents to rank modern, traditional, and postmodern values according to their affinity to those values. Section 3 of the questionnaire measured agreement or disagreement with statements regarding generational values and leadership on a 10-point Likert scale. Finally, each focus group was given an assessment of their readiness for ministry in emerging culture based on their overall responses. Based on weighted scores and averages, each focus group had areas for growth and improvement in navigating postmodern tidal forces. Analysis between pre-test and post-test questionnaires showed how each focus group evolved in their own understanding over the duration of the project. Based on the overall assessment,

Chapter Nine: PASSAGE PLANNING: METHODS OF DATA COLLECTION

the church council and deacon focus group was tasked with devising a plan for implementation to address potential growth areas for ministry in a postmodern context.

The Qualitative Questionnaire

After administration of the initial quantitative questionnaire, participants in each focus group were invited to participate in an ethnographic qualitative survey instrument.[251] Working with willing participants, a qualitative exercise using ethnographic techniques assisted the church in identifying individual narratives and micronarratives within BMBC. At a Saturday church-wide workshop, trained facilitators served as interviewers. Through appreciative inquiry, the questions in this questionnaire focused on how a sample of congregants might view congregational change positively and explore potential positive feelings they may have had about rapidly changing culture, if any. Emerging people highly value relationships and story, and by incorporating story-telling and relationship-building into the ministry project, a foundation was laid for further progress in ministering effectively in an emerging rural culture. Leading thinkers in postmodern thought emphasize "the deconstruction of overarching metanarratives and the influence of context on the written texts."[252] In a modern paradigm, churches and denominations focus on reinforcing agreed upon theological boundaries, often valuing uniformity within the group. The metanarratives of Scripture and church life (beliefs) often preexist as litmus tests and boundaries. In these churches, being welcomed may require buying into exact beliefs and propositions. However, in the postmodern context, "belonging before believing" is paramount for seekers and skeptics.[253] Through a series of in-person interviews in small groups,

BMBC began to unpack the *micronarratives* of the congregation, learning each interviewee's individual truth, thereby opening the congregation's ability to view individual "microstories and truth as story."[254] This allowed for identifying broader themes that the congregation may synergize around, helping us to develop what Branson terms as "provocative proposals concerning possible futures."[255]

Provocative Proposals for BMBC

What some churches need to imagine and dream is what appreciative inquiry proponents term as "provocative proposals." One may understand provocative proposals as "an imaginative statement about the future, crafted as if it were already experiential and generative."[256] In order to lead the church to craft provocative proposals about our future, a series of meetings and brainstorming sessions provided opportunities for congregants to help identify themes emerging from the stories people told during the research process, inviting the church to dream about a positive future in which we handle changing cultural tides with grace and excitement. As an example of one potential provocative proposal, the need for more racial diversity may emerge as fresh vision for our church. A provocative proposal concerning this might read, "Beal Memorial Baptist Church is the most racially diverse congregation within a 45-minute drive from town. Their commitment to welcoming people of all backgrounds became apparent several years ago when they leaned into their call to become a church of regional influence and embrace the shifting demographics of their community. When Beale hired a young African-American as a minister to seniors, people really began to notice a change in the passion the church had for reflecting the true diversity of the body of Christ." By listening to people's stories and memories of ministry at Beale and identifying emerging themes, the church had opportunity to shape provocative proposals that would enliven the people's "sanctified imaginations, stretching the status quo by pushing boundaries."[257] In this sense, BMBC may *become* an emerging rural congregation as they imagine and eventually step into a new future. After the Saturday workshop, members of the deacon body read BMBC's provocative proposals aloud during worship over several weeks. When the provocative proposal was read aloud in worship, a lay leader also led a prayer time concerning the proposal, helping the church seek discernment for our emerging future.

Celebrating and Sharing the Stories

One may understand, "Allowing people to tell their stories of life in [the] community, including the good, the bad, and the ugly, is a critical pastoral task that can help people heal and free them to move on with strength and vigor."[258] In desiring to equip BMBC for adapting to cultural change in the 21st century (postmodernity), it seemed prudent on many levels to invite people to share their stories. Not only can sharing story help open new ways of viewing truth for people in a congregation, but it can assist pastors in facilitating conversations that will lead churches into a healthy future. Additionally, pastoral theology for rural emergence, a theology of the smallness of the Kingdom and a theology of the periphery, took seriously the individual narratives of rural people and BMBC as a congregation.

The qualitative survey primarily sought to record a congregant's positively stated memories of church in the past and encouraged them to voice positive dreams concerning the future of Beale. By examining someone's feelings about church as it used to be and their feelings about church as it exists (or might exist in the future), individual micronarratives emerged, helping create conversation and dialogue about what change, adaptation, and empowerment means for BMBC. *Upon collection of the qualitative surveys, the church's history committee shared people's memories of BMBC and devised a creative way to display the memories in a "living history exhibit."*

Utilizing Survey Monkey

One method of data collection utilized for the quantitative survey was the web-based service Survey Monkey. This developed in consultation with the leaders of the church who suggested that an electronic delivery method for the qualitative questionnaire would garner a much higher participation rate among respondents. Survey Monkey is one of the largest, free, online-survey platforms. According to the company webpage, "Every day, 3 million people around the world use our platform, whether it's to ask 10 employees about a company barbecue or 10,000 consumers about the next big product. That's because we've built a platform that's simple for a survey novice to use, but powerful enough for a pro."[259] In designing a Survey Monkey questionnaire, I was able to craft and design the questionnaire in a digital format, making the survey deliverable by email, text message, or Facebook messenger and embedding the survey on our church website. Paper copies of the questionnaire were made available for those not comfortable enough with digital delivery systems. Through utilizing Survey Monkey, the ease of collecting and interpreting data was greatly heightened. It remains true that, "As leaders, we grow in faith

Chapter Nine: PASSAGE PLANNING: METHODS OF DATA COLLECTION

and maturity when we weave our life stories into a larger faith story."[260] Using Survey Monkey somewhat changed how the questionnaire answers were scored and weighted. However, because of Survey Monkey, I believe that survey participation and completion rates were heightened for both the pre-test and post-test questionnaires, thereby allowing more people to tell their own stories and weave those stories into a larger whole. Because of the ease in navigating the data, outputting questions, and collecting responses, I was also better able to focus on retelling the stories the congregation told of themselves. The final chapter of this book summarizes the findings of the ministry project, which are fascinating and inspiring.

Chapter Ten
SAILING TO CORINTH: NAVIGATING THE "TIDES OF FAITH"

> *There is a tide in the affairs of men, which taken at the flood, leads on to fortune. Omitted, all the voyage of their life is bound in shallows and in miseries. On such a full sea are we now afloat. And we must take the current when it serves, or lose our ventures.*
>
> – William Shakespeare

Hopefully by this point, the reader gets a sense that exploring postmodernity in rural culture is not incongruent with sound exegetical work. I am making the argument that we should not avoid postmodernity like the plague because of our reading of Scripture. In fact, quite the opposite! We may be able to lean into postmodernity with gratitude to God for the gifts it brings in ministry – precisely because of our reading of Scripture. The tides of cultural change are nothing new for God's people, and considering how early Christ followers dealt with similar issues has the power to become inspiring and instructive for today's emerging rural churches.

The next part of this book lays out a biblical case for how to approach key postmodern impulses and includes an exegetical exploration of passages in First and Second Corinthians, unpacking six unique cultural tides that every rural congregation must navigate. These sweeping tides include tolerance, authenticity, individualism, skepticism, going green, and solidarity. The Church at Corinth navigated the same tides in their own time, though under different circumstances. The following six chapters explore these cultural movements in depth. At the beginning of each chapter is a selected text from Paul's letter to the Church at Corinth. I highly encourage you to read the passage in full before engaging with the chapter that follows.

Chapter Eleven
THE TIDE OF TOLERANCE – BRIDGING VAST DIFFERENCES

"Tolerance is another word for indifference."

– W. Somerset Maugham

Key Text: 1 Corinthians 10:14-33

The town I was living in when implementing my doctoral project was called Tappahannock, which means the tide rises and falls, and because of the church's location across from a tidal riverfront, the imagery of water and tides runs deep in the area's cultural memory. In many ways, the number of the residents in the community rises and recedes, like the tide, based on the seasons. In the warm months, many people come to live on the water and recreate in the area. Tidal movements are constant, and many people get so used to living near a tidal waterway, the tides often go unnoticed (like cultural movements). When the tide recedes, things appear on the shoreline that you might not see otherwise, such as oyster shells, crab shells, coins, and beautiful sand beaches; likewise, when culture shifts away from allegiance to Christendom, the church may discover unknown gifts within her midst.

When the tides come in, all ships rise with the water level; in the same way, cultural change shifts our church – whether we like it or not. Boats must be tied to docks with enough slack in the line for the vessel to adjust as the water level rises and falls, and churches with built-in flexibility can move slightly when cultural change comes without becoming unanchored from biblical and spiritual moorings. The tide exists beyond our control, and forces that we often do not see or have any leverage over (the moon, the sun, gravity) move vast amounts of water daily. In the same way, cultural tides are beyond the control of any one person or church, and there are forces far beyond us that lead to great movements in humanity.

One of the great tidal shifts presently in our culture is the trend of tolerance. We live in a culture and a society that has always valued tolerance to an extent, but as a cultural value, tolerance is influencing everything from fashion and pop music to politics and law. Many people, and perhaps many readers, celebrate the rise of tolerance in our culture. What would it mean to think about tolerance from a theological vantage point? The Oxford Dictionary defines tolerance as "the ability or willingness to tolerate the existence of opinions or behavior that one dislikes or disagrees with."[261] Is tolerance not desirable, at least on some level?

In 1 Corinthians 10, Paul writes to the Corinthians, "[14] Therefore, my dear friends, flee from the worship of idols. [15] I speak as to sensible people; judge for yourselves what I say. [16] The cup of blessing that we bless, is it not a sharing in the blood of Christ? The bread that we break, is it not a sharing in the body of Christ? ¹⁷ Because there is one bread, we who are many are one body, for we all partake of the one bread."²⁶²

Paul teaches that food sacrificed to idols has been shared in worship just like communion bread and wine. First-century Corinth was a cosmopolitan city with a variety of thriving pagan religions and cults. Now, we do not have a lot of food sacrificed to idols in our grocery stores, but we have goods in all of our stores that wouldn't exist without idolatry. The idolatry of greed and profit means that clothes sold in many American stores are made in what amounts to sweat shops, often using child labor. The idolatry of work sells us on bigger homes, nicer cars, and more money in the bank, while we simultaneously sacrifice our relationships, our joy, and even our sanity. The idolatry of power leads us to sacrifice our dignity, our decency, and our democracy, all in the name of influence. The idolatry of information and control leads us to worship at the feet of talking heads on 24-hour news channels where we sacrifice being able to see the humanity in another; we sacrifice time better spent with family; we sacrifice the arts of understanding and listening all on the altar of identity politics and anger.

When we look at our culture, there are plenty of idols to go around. How can we share in the act of communion (reenacting the sacrifice of Christ) and yet sacrifice so much to the idols of culture? Paul writes in verses 21-22, "You cannot drink the cup of the Lord and the cup of demons. You cannot partake of the table of the Lord and the table of demons. Or are we provoking the Lord to jealousy? Are we stronger than he?" While calling believers to abstain from food sacrificed to idols and encouraging Christians to be careful of the foods they eat, Paul also seems to write to the Corinthians that a certain level of tolerance is desirable for Christians living in a largely pagan world. Perhaps there is a lesson for us in this passage as we increasingly live in a pagan world. Many scholars of religion readily argue (and have for decades) that in America, Christendom is dead.

On March 21, 1969, an English preacher and scholar name Rev. G.R. Beaseley-Murray delivered the Diamond Jubilee Lecture to the London Baptist Preachers' Association. His lecture was titled, "Evangelising the Post-Christian Man." In arguing that Europe was in an emerging post-Christian context, he raised the example of plummeting church attendance among Swedish Christians (3% of the population at the time) and also the increasingly scarce numbers in London and the surrounding areas. He reported that according to census and polling data in 1886, the percentage of Londoners attending weekly worship was roughly 30%, but only 2% of present day Londoners (in 1969) frequented a church on Sundays.[263] Before the COVID19 pandemic hit, Pew Research announced that the "decline of Christianity continues at a rapid pace,"[264] and a study publicized by Outreach Magazine claimed that attendance of weekly worship in the United States was down to 17.7% (a much lower number than those usually reported by Pew and Gallup).[265] Fifty-two years after Beaseley-Murray's lecture, the United States seems on track to meet the same statistics that have long existed in post-Christian Europe. It remains to be seen to what extent a global pandemic may hasten the process.

Christendom was that period of history when the church enjoyed reign and influence in society. In Christendom, pews filled because the church's power, reputation, and control of society was all-encompassing. Increasingly, however, we live in a culture where the church enjoys fewer privileges and far less influence than 50 years ago. In a culture increasingly more disconnected

Chapter Eleven: THE TIDE OF TOLERANCE – BRIDGING VAST DIFFERENCES

from traditional religious moors, we might ask on first reading of 1 Corinthians 10, is the Apostle Paul calling for tolerance?

For many Christians, tolerance may be a dirty word. Several disadvantages to the tide of tolerance in culture exist. First, the Bible warns in numerous places that God's people should not tolerate ungodliness in the temple or in the nation. Biblically speaking, there is a time to not show tolerance. The church should wisely use discernment concerning when to speak out and when to remain silent for the sake of the gospel. Consequently, certain kinds of tolerance in the church may lead to moral relativism, causing our rural churches to lose our moorings to Scripture and God. Second, tolerance has been politicized to the point that the very word may prove off-putting. For some, the word tolerance is now a dog whistle that calls people to defend their own power and interest, on both the left and the right. Third, tolerance may be undesirable if coming from a posture of entitlement and arrogance. If tolerance is merely the powerful granting favor to the week or the few, then tolerance is no true freedom.

Early Virginia Baptist John Leland made just such an argument in contending for religious freedom. He argued that tolerance was not freedom at all, and true liberty called for an even more robust social contract. In 1790, he wrote:

> The notion of a Christian commonwealth should be exploded forever. Government should protect every man in thinking and speaking freely, and see that one does not abuse another. The liberty I contend for is more than toleration. The very idea of toleration is despicable; it supposes that some have a pre-eminence above the rest to grant indulgence, whereas all should be equally free, Jews, Turks [Muslims], Pagans and Christians.[266]

In arguing for religious liberty and what would ultimately become the First Amendment in the U.S. Bill of Rights, Pastor Leland realized that if Christianity had been recognized as the state religion (as in England), all Christians would not be free from the tyranny of the majority, much less those of other faiths. As much as some in our present age might lift up tolerance, Leland knew that it had its downsides as a form of public policy. Tolerance often leads to one group seeking advantage over the other.

Paul reminds Christians not to become polluted by the pagan world surrounding them, but then he says, "All things are lawful, but not all things are beneficial. All things are lawful, but not all things build up. Do not seek your own advantage, but that of the other ." What if our response to living in an increasingly pagan culture was to "not seek our own advantage, but that of the other?" Talk about counter-cultural! This posture toward the world, instead of a defensive one, might provide a way for churches to increase Christ's reputation in our communities.

One of the great problems with American Christianity is when many people look at the church or look at evangelicals (or Baptists, my own tradition), they see little more than a group of people trying to seek advantage for themselves. In being sensitive to the beliefs of others, Paul encourages spiritual maturity and some measure of tolerance for the sake of the gospel. This means, biblically speaking, the conscience of a Christian remains clean when *certain* choices are made for the benefit of another. This is part of what it means to die to self, which Paul discusses elsewhere. Paul continues, "'For the earth and its fullness are the Lord's.' If an unbeliever invites you to a meal and you are disposed to go, eat whatever is set before you without raising any question on the ground of conscience."

Chapter Eleven: THE TIDE OF TOLERANCE – BRIDGING VAST DIFFERENCES

In verse 26, Paul references Psalm 24. Often, when citing a Bible verse, the author intends to draw our attention not only to the verse quoted but also to an entire chapter or narrative. In Psalm 24, the entire first verse reads, "The earth is the Lord's and all that is in it, the world, and those who live in it." Contextually, the phrase "the earth is the Lord's" can be taken to mean all the *people* of the earth and not only the food mentioned in the passage. The understanding that all the people of the earth are the Lord's (even if they are not *in* the Lord's saving grace) may be a foundation for Christian tolerance. The foreigner is the Lord's. The Republican is the Lord's. The Democrat is the Lord's. Your gay nephew is the Lord's. The Muslim is the Lord's. The Buddhist is the Lord's. The felon or the prisoner is the Lord's.

To say everyone is "the Lord's" does not mean everyone is saved; it means we acknowledge that God is sovereign – that God created all of us. When the "other" is understood as "the Lord's," then Christians may exhibit openness toward others as an expression of trusting God's sovereignty, and showing love to neighbor and stranger alike is fulfilling the second great commandment. Paul concludes the passage in saying, "So, whether you eat or drink, or whatever you do, do everything for the glory of God. Give no offense to Jews or to Greeks or to the church of God, just as I try to please everyone in everything I do, not seeking my own advantage, but that of many, so that they may be saved." It cannot be overstated that for Paul, the purpose of showing love and hospitality toward all people is *"so that they may be saved."* How do you see God's saving grace at work in a culture that is increasingly embracing tolerance? Where is your rural church's place in all this, and where is our place as individuals?

Perhaps tolerance is the wrong word. Maybe humility, sensitivity, or even empathy would be better. No, none of these words will do. God's church is not the church of tolerance. God's church is established wholly and fully by God's redeeming grace! Perhaps somebody reading here is thinking, "I can't believe this guy is endorsing tolerance!" If that is you, allow me to explain further and just keep reading. What I am trying to encourage is for us to live faithfully according to Scripture. I believe that while our culture may be leaning into the value of tolerance, Paul is encouraging us to *embrace a value far more radical* — the value of God's redeeming grace. Think about it. To tolerate people means little more than to endure the pain they cause you. To tolerate people also means little more than to begrudge their existence because their very existence gets to you. Tolerance means little more than that we reluctantly and resentfully allow people to deviate from whatever it is *we* believe. The more I think about it, tolerance does not seem to be what Paul is calling the Corinthian church to embrace. God's grace is *far* more profound.

We live in a world that embraces a gospel of tolerance. But the gospel of Christ is the news of grace! To show grace to people means you consider them before yourself. To show grace to people means we see them as "the Lord's," fully made in God's image. Grace means we are willing to bridge whatever gap exists between the church and the world with self-giving love, even to the point of death (Philippians 2:8). In many ways, our culture is selling us a lie – the lie that tolerance bridges vast cultural differences. *Only grace can truly bridge these differences. Only grace can bridge the chasm between God and humanity.* How is God calling you and your rural church to bridge vast cultural differences for the sake of the gospel?

Jesus taught that Christians are not responsible for the beliefs of others (Luke 9:1-6). When the disciples were told to shake the dust from their feet upon encountering an unfriendly town, perhaps it was not because of spite, but rather a form of relinquishing responsibility for the future of those who rejected the message of the Kingdom of God. Anecdotally, many rural church-goers worry a great deal about their kids and grandkids' salvation, especially if those kids and grandkids are not the church-going type. What would it look like for you to release any responsibility you might feel for their eternal destiny into the hands of God? Jesus taught that even when rejected, Christians should love everybody and curse nobody (Luke 9:49-56). What would it look like for your rural church to love everybody and curse nobody, compassionately acknowledging diversity in the world and showing kindness to those different from you? A church that embraces Christ's radical grace instead of mere cultural tolerance has the potential to change the world!

Chapter Twelve

THE TIDE OF AUTHENTICITY: BRIDGING OUR BELIEFS AND OUR ACTIONS

> *"Authenticity is a collection of choices that we have to make every day. It's about the choice to show up and be real. The choice to be honest. The choice to let our true selves be seen."*
>
> – Brene Brown,
> *The Gifts of Imperfection*

Key Text: 1 Corinthians 11:17-34

Kevin was new to youth ministry and had been volunteering with the students at his rural church for several months. Getting to minister to the students was such a blessing. He felt like he was making great relationships that would lead to discipleship opportunities. The church's motto was, "The Most Loving Place in Town," and Kevin felt drawn to that vision because he felt it was a great representation of what a biblical church should be. In fact, he had developed an entire Wednesday teaching series around what it would mean for the youth ministry to be the most loving place in town for area teens. So far, it was well received, and the students really seemed to be engaged.

One day, two older high school students who were dating came to Kevin and said they needed to speak with him. In the conversation that ensued, Kevin was told that the young lady was pregnant. Both teens were visibly worried about what would happen if their parents discovered their news. Pregnant teen girls did not have a good reputation at the local high school, and the couple had a mutual friend a few years ago who went through the same thing. According to this friend who had since dropped out of school to raise her little one, being a young teenage mom in this small town was hell. Kevin offered to meet with the teens' parents when they broke the news and to also meet again soon to continue the conversation. He also promised to find out if there were any resources in the local community for the young couple.

Later that week, the church had a Sunday evening business meeting, and the church was set to pass a budget for the new year. Kevin was surprised to know that a contentious subject that evening was if the congregation should continue to financially support the Christian crisis pregnancy center in town. The church had given the center money for several years under the former pastor's leadership, much to the chagrin of many church members. In the business meeting, a few people spoke in favor of continuing the funding, but for the most part, person after person stood up and argued against funding the

Chapter Twelve: THE TIDE OF AUTHENTICITY: BRIDGING OUR BELIEFS AND OUR ACTIONS

center for nearly 30 minutes. Some of the arguments made included that the church "didn't need to support young people who were sleeping around," that the church "should be funding abstinence-only programs and ensuring kids don't have sex before marriage," and that "partnering with the crisis pregnancy center amounted to partnering with apostate denominational groups because there was no telling what church a volunteer might invite somebody to join."

Nobody knew what Kevin knew – that he was counseling the teenage daughter and son of two of the families in the business meeting through an unexpected pregnancy. Two of the strongest opponents in opposition to funding the crisis pregnancy center were the parents of each of the respective teens. One of the fathers, a deacon in the church, was one of the ones most strongly opposed. Kevin had a sinking feeling in his stomach as an overwhelming majority of people in the business meeting that night voted to defund the crisis pregnancy center. Kevin also wondered deeply if his church was really "The Most Loving Place in Town" and how the parents of these teens might react when finding out their children's news. It was the first time it occurred to Kevin that 1) his church was, perhaps, not as pro-life as they claimed, and 2) that purity culture could actually lead to judgement toward those the church was called to love. Kevin was now beginning to question the authenticity of the church he loved and wondering if what the church said out loud really aligned with the church's practice of faith. The pastor had talked about forgiveness and hope just before communion that same morning, but Kevin didn't get the sense that anyone approached the crisis pregnancy center with forgiveness and hope in mind. It seemed clear that the conversation these students needed to have with their parents might be fraught with pain and punitive reactivity on the part of the parents.

An Authenticity Deficit?

One could fairly say that in the emerging postmodern era, the world is not in search of religion. The world is not in search of a belief system. The world is in search of authenticity. Another word for authentic is genuine. People want a faith that's real, a faith that's thoughtful in its approach, and a faith that doesn't gloss over difficult questions or social circumstances. In 1 Corinthians 11, Paul needs to address a church that has an authenticity deficit. The lack of genuine faith and practice largely stemmed from how the Church at Corinth practiced communion. He writes in verses 17 and 18, "In the following directives I have no praise for you, for your meetings do more harm than good. In the first place, I hear that when you come together as a church, there are divisions among you, and to some extent I believe it." When our faith is not genuine, it shows. When our faith is not genuine, it does great harm.

Paul further tells the Church at Corinth, "No doubt there have to be differences among you to show which of you have God's approval." In small towns and rural communities, which often lack as much diversity as big cities, our differences can sometimes become even more pronounced because we find the need to compare ourselves to others. Somebody else's sin, family dysfunction, job, education, neighborhood, race, spouse, wardrobe, or car has nothing to do with how much God loves anyone. Sherman indicates that in many poor rural communities, people's sense of morality may serve as "one of the few remaining axes" upon which to base social hierarchy.[267] It seems, "When jobs, incomes, and other sources of identity are stripped away, it is still possible to find ways [for rural people] to define themselves and their entire community as morally upstanding. Thus morality often becomes a dominant

Chapter Twelve: THE TIDE OF AUTHENTICITY: BRIDGING OUR BELIEFS AND OUR ACTIONS

social force and social boundary marker" in many rural communities.[268] Sherman goes onto argue that people's sense of morality (which is not inherently based on any religious principles or beliefs) may serve as one of the only markers of individuality in communities "which are relatively homogenous and lacking in sufficient other sources upon which to base social distinctions." The kind of judgmental moralism that played out in Kevin's rural church may not have as much to do with biblical principles or the love and grace of Jesus as it does with members of the church and community needing to distinguish themselves from others as "moral," precisely because of the fact that in their rural community, not much distinguishes anybody.

Many rural churches may struggle with a false sense of moralism because it is a way for members to feel distinct in their own communities. This posture, though, may prove unhelpful in living out God's forgiveness and grace. Whenever there are divisions in the church, we may say we are "The Most Loving Place in Town," while in reality, we are anything but. Communion became a farce within the Corinthian congregation. The church was going through outward acts of worship, but divisions in the church, particularly between the rich and the poor, rendered the act of communion meaningless, making a mockery of a holy and worshipful act. In verses 21-22, Paul continues:

> For when you are eating, some of you go ahead with your own private suppers. As a result, one person remains hungry and another gets drunk. [22] Don't you have homes to eat and drink in? Or do you despise the church of God by humiliating those who have nothing? What shall I say to you? Shall I praise you? Certainly not in this matter!

Authenticity is not just about being true to oneself; it is fundamentally about character. Here is a place for a critical distinction – piety steeped in moralism (as exhibited by many in Kevin's church) may be fundamentally different from character, particularly the character of Christ.

Stephen Joseph (Professor of Psychology, Health, and Social care at the University of Nottingham, UK) writes about seven traits of an authentic person. According to Dr. Joseph, authentic people 1) have realistic perceptions of reality, 2) are accepting of themselves and of other people, 3) are thoughtful, 4) have a non-hostile sense of humor, 5) are able to express their emotions freely and clearly, 6) are open to learning from their mistakes, and 7) understand their motivations. This is what is means to be true to oneself. The same might be said of authentic people and authentic churches. Conversely, inauthentic people 1) are self-deceptive and unrealistic in their perceptions of reality, 2) look to others for approval and to feel valued, 3) are highly judgmental of other people, 4) do not think things through clearly, 5) have a hostile sense of humor, 6) are not open to learning from their mistakes, and 7) do not understand their motivations.[269] The world could certainly use more authentic people and churches.

The Oxford dictionary defines authentic as "made or done in a way that faithfully resembles an original."[270] Did the faith of the Corinthian church or their practice of communion seem authentic? Paul writes:

> [23] For I received from the Lord what I also passed on to you: The Lord Jesus, on the night he was betrayed, took bread, [24] and when he had given thanks, he broke it and said, "This is my body, which is for you; do this in remembrance of me."

Chapter Twelve: THE TIDE OF AUTHENTICITY: BRIDGING OUR BELIEFS AND OUR ACTIONS

> [25] In the same way, after supper he took the cup, saying, "This cup is the new covenant in my blood; do this, whenever you drink it, in remembrance of me."
>
> [26] For whenever you eat this bread and drink this cup, you proclaim the Lord's death until he comes.

Being an authentic church isn't just about standing up loudly for our beliefs and assaulting the world with theological or moralistic hand grenades. Authenticity is not just "telling it like it is." Authentic church happens when our beliefs are also informed by the character of Christ, who was willing to sacrifice His very life so that we might abundantly live.

> [27] So then, whoever eats the bread or drinks the cup of the Lord in an unworthy manner will be guilty of sinning against the body and blood of the Lord.
>
> [28] Everyone ought to examine themselves before they eat of the bread and drink from the cup. [29] For those who eat and drink without discerning the body of Christ eat and drink judgment on themselves.

The act of worship was inauthentic because they were lacking the character of Christ.

"Discerning the body" in verse 29 is possibly a play on words. We should discern the true meaning of communion, but we should also discern the needs of others in the body of Christ. Discernment is about truly hearing and truly seeing whatever or whoever lies before us. How might Kevin's church have discerned differently? Remember the first mark of authenticity? Have realistic perceptions of reality. The Corinthians failed to maintain a reverent attitude toward communion, reveling instead in food and drink. They failed to show love to one another and failed to extend grace to everyone in their midst. Observing communion in such a phony manner impacted their ministry deeply, including their ability to engage others with the gospel.

One study by Barna Research indicates of those outside the church, 91% view Christians as anti-homosexual, 87% view Christians as judgmental, and 85% view Christians as hypocritical. The same study also found that those outside the faith view Christians as too old fashioned, too involved in politics, out of touch with reality, insensitive to others, boring, and confusing.[271] Notice that one of the critiques of American Christians is that they are out of touch with reality. One of the problems in attracting younger people to our church or to any church is that many young people increasingly find the church inauthentic in witness and practice. I wonder how many were turned off to the Church at Corinth because of their practices of exclusion around the Lord's Table?

In the case of the teens in Kevin's church, the students sat down with their parents to tell them the news of the pregnancy, and Kevin was present with them. He went to – you guessed it – the crisis pregnancy center for information on how to guide parents through a conversation. Both sets of parents were shocked and responded in unhelpful ways. The girl's parents shamed her and made sure that all of her prenatal visits were in the next town over. The young lady ended up dropping out of school and church in her third trimester – the looks from other kids at school were too much to bear, as too were the snide comments from some older people in her church. She had the baby and now struggles as a single mom, working part-time jobs to pay for formula and diapers. The young man faced pressure from his parents to marry the girl. The boy was not ready to enter into marriage or become a father and never sees his son because his parents insisted he cut off all communication with the young mother.

Chapter Twelve: THE TIDE OF AUTHENTICITY: BRIDGING OUR BELIEFS AND OUR ACTIONS

Both the young parents feel a heightened sense of isolation because there has been pressure on their peers to distance themselves from any further relationship, due to the fact that all of the adults in their lives and their church judge them as moral and social deviants.

Was Kevin's church "The Most Loving Place in Town?" Perhaps the story rings true for you, as the rate of teen pregnancy in rural communities is well above that of teens in metropolitan areas.[272] Pregnant teens and young expectant couples in rural communities often experience "social isolation, lack of educational and economic opportunities, and limited access to health services," not to mention the pressure they may experience in their religious settings or at home.[273] Perhaps like the teenagers in Kevin's story, you have witnessed young people in your own context experience the pain and stigma of "othering" that often comes with teen pregnancy.

Whatever our beliefs, people are looking for us to live them in an authentic way without any hint of hypocrisy. Rural churches should strive to be a place where all people, no matter their station in life, will be treated fairly and with Christ's love. Communion is a reminder that God's grace applies equally to all of us. Authenticity is ultimately not only about character but also about seeing others. Paul writes, "29 For those who eat and drink without discerning the body of Christ eat and drink judgment on themselves." Authentic faith not only requires seeing God clearly in Christ Jesus but also seeing the image of God in others. When our faith and actions lack the character of Christ, we pass judgment on ourselves.

A former student of mine who was in sixth grade when I was the youth minister posted a remarkable story on Facebook recently. Levi was always a bright young man and is now in the graduate program for mechanical and nuclear engineering at Virginia Commonwealth University. Hear his account (which I share with permission):

> Earlier today I was walking back from the Richmond Folk Festival with friends. As we are making our way back to the car we cross a bridge. I see ahead of me a man that was looking over the bridge, and I had a funny feeling. I pass him, and think maybe it's nothing. But I knew something was wrong, I turned back, approached him, and asked if he was okay. "I'm thinking about jumping". There was so much sadness and defeat behind his eyes and words. I had the feeling, but to hear the words caught me off guard. I talked to him, listened to his story. I eventually got him to get off the bridge, and contacted authorities. All he wanted was to be heard. This PSA is to let everyone know: you are loved. Life is hard. Sometimes things get rough and you internalize all the wrong, but wear a face that says it's okay. Talk to somebody. Tell your story. If you don't know who to talk to, there are resources out there. If you want, you can talk to me. If everything is going okay in your life, be ready to listen. Not only for family and friends, but also the man with watery eyes on the bridge. So many people walk by and convince themselves it's probably nothing. That could be true, but that doesn't matter. People need people.[274]

How does your rural church let people who are hurting and scared know, "You are loved by God, and you are loved by us?" With the opioid epidemic, rising cases of rural depression and suicide, and rural poverty and homelessness, there are millions of hurting people in our rural communities who desperately need God's mercy, grace, and love.

Are we so busy playing church that we don't take the time to see others or even see those in our midst? What are some

Chapter Twelve: THE TIDE OF AUTHENTICITY: BRIDGING OUR BELIEFS AND OUR ACTIONS

ways we can demonstrate the authenticity of our faith to our local community outside of worship? Who do we exclude from the table of the Lord? Do we despise the Church of God by humiliating those who have nothing? How do we make sure our worship isn't simply going through the motions of Christian faith? How can we thoughtfully incorporate the fundamental character of Christ into our ministries and also into our personal lives? Rural churches that embrace authenticity as a moral value rooted in the way of Jesus will have a much greater probability for vibrant ministry in the emerging rural culture.

Chapter Thirteen
THE TIDE OF INDIVIDUALISM: BRIDGING SPIRITUAL GIFTS WITH MINISTRY

> *"Snowflakes fascinate me... Millions of them falling gently to the ground... And they say that no two of them are alike! Each one completely different from all the others... The last of the rugged individualists!"*
>
> – Charles M. Schulz

Key Text: 1 Corinthians 12:4-27

If your church is like the rural churches I've pastored, you may have a person in your church that stands out from the congregation in terms of their personality. They may be a character of sorts, but they are loved by the church, and the congregation considers them as one of their own – no matter the level of difference. Such was the case with Alvin. In the town of Urbanna, Virginia, Alvin was a fixture. He had suffered oxygen damage during childbirth because his umbilical cord was wrapped around his neck. Due to this circumstance, Alvin lived with health issues from birth. As an adult, he bravely dealt with intellectual disability and diabetes, and his mother, aptly named Grace, cared for him well into her 90s.

Alvin would regularly visit the church office, riding his bike several blocks from home. I quickly learned that if I needed to know what was going on around town, all I needed to do was ask Alvin for the latest news. Every day, Alvin had a ritual of visiting the local coffee shop, the grocery store, the pharmacy, the post office, and the mayor's office. Everyone in the community took time to speak with Alvin and keep him informed of neighborhood happenings. I remember getting stuck in traffic once, an unheard-of occurrence in our small town. As several cars and a semi-truck slowly crawled through town, the traffic broke when Alvin turned onto a side street with his bicycle.

Alvin was a trustworthy source for community history. He could tell you almost anything you wanted to know about the last 60 years in that town. The community loved Alvin and his family well, and people from both the Baptist and Methodist churches (the only ones in town) often delivered food to their home and filled their fuel tank in the cold winter months. Alvin was famously the official bell ringer at both congregations and would alternate between churches on Sundays to fulfill his duty of announcing the start of the Sunday worship hour.

Watching how the community loved Alvin and cared for his family was an inspiration. Alvin exuded individuality, and his differences could have been reason for people to reject or ignore him. Instead, he was celebrated as a part of the community, as was his dear family. Embracing Alvin's *individuality* was also a way for the town to embrace its own *individuality* as a community. No town has ever had anyone quite like Alvin, and Urbanna, Virginia, may never have anyone quite like him again. Alvin was a gift to all who knew him and to his community.

Individuality in Western Culture

Many who deride modern culture claim that the youngest generation is selfish. Some Baby Boomers say such things about Millennials and may forget that they were once called the "Me Generation" by their own elders. Individuality is perhaps not a generational trait as much as a Western one, and it is largely the basis of our culture in the United States. Our Constitution and Bill of Rights do not guarantee liberties for towns, counties, or companies. When the founders spoke and wrote of rights and liberties, they most often spoke of rights and liberties of the individual. In 1776, when the American colonies declared independence from Great Britain, they stated, *"We hold these truths to be self-evident: that all men are created equal; that they are endowed by their Creator with certain unalienable rights; that among these are life, liberty, and the pursuit of happiness."* The personal freedom and personal liberty they espoused were given by the Creator. Perhaps our ancestors knew something that we often miss. Our individuality and our freedom are gifts from God. Some of the best ideas and best progress the world has ever known have come from individual people, uniquely created, called, and gifted by God.

I am not arguing here that America is a so-called "Christian nation" or that the Declaration of Independence or the U.S. Constitution are somehow based on the Bible. What I do believe though is that the Enlightenment led people who had lived their entire lives under oppressive monarchies and empires to the (perhaps) inevitable conclusion that the worth and value of a person is not derived from a royal bloodline or decree. They, too, came to believe that the locust of God's design in human dignity and flourishing was not a nation state but individual people made by the Creator. This Western understanding of the self and the individual is arguably more of an outgrowth of Enlightenment philosophy (Kant, Locke, Hume) than from Scripture, as the Bible was written in a completely ancient, near-Eastern culture and context. Individuality then, while a distinctly Western value, is not an inherently biblical one. This is not to say, however, that individual giftedness and difference are not ordained and established by God. But let's be honest – for most of the men who signed the Declaration of Independence and ratified the United States Constitution and Bill of Rights, the individual rights they contended for only included white, male, land-owning gentry. The Bible tells a better story.

Individuality Versus Divine Uniqueness

In 1 Corinthians 12, Paul discusses human flourishing in terms of individual difference and giftedness within the Church. If everyone in the Church would do their part, then the whole body would function the way it's supposed to. Unity in the Church does not come from conformity, but from recognizing that in God's wisdom, each person is made with their own giftedness. Paul establishes that the Spirit of God has ordained particularity and diversity within the Church. He states,

Chapter Thirteen: THE TIDE OF INDIVIDUALISM: BRIDGING SPIRITUAL GIFTS WITH MINISTRY

"⁴ Now there are varieties of gifts, but the same Spirit; ⁵ and there are varieties of services, but the same Lord; ⁶ and there are varieties of activities, but it is the same God who activates all of them in everyone."

Individual gifts are divine gifts worth celebrating. In verse 4, the word translated "varieties of gifts" is χαρισμάτων. Karismatone *literally* means "gifts of grace" with the connotation that the one with the gift is either possessed by or possesses the gift.[275] The Scripture reads, "To each is given the manifestation of the Spirit for the common good." Whatever your spiritual gift, it is not just for your own benefit. It is for "the common good." If you are not using the spiritual gift God gave you, then you are either selfish or lazy as a Christian and your church is deprived of knowing the benefit of God's grace in your own life.

The unique gifts of believers at your rural church are meant to be used in conjunction with the gifts of other believers. The best way for God's grace and purposes to manifest in the church is when individuals use their own gifts for the benefit of the whole. When the body functions in this manner, God's grace is most fully realized through the church. Paul states in verse 12, "For just as the body is one and has many members, and all the members of the body, though many, are one body, so it is with Christ." Paul uses the analogy of the human body to describe the way spiritual gifts work in the church. In fact, this is one of the only places in Scripture where church "membership" is discussed.

Even in rural communities, many churches embrace a "country club" mentality. Membership in the church isn't about perks and privileges. Oftentimes, when people think of membership in a church, they only think of "what's in it for me." Membership in the body of Christ isn't about what we get out of church; it's about using our spiritual gifts for the common good. The fact is, you may be on the membership roll in your rural church, but biblically, if you aren't using your spiritual gifts for the benefit of the congregation, you're not functioning the way a member should function. Paul doesn't go here, but if you take the analogy to its logical end, sometimes there may be a negative growth in the body that sucks life from the rest of the body. What do we usually call that? Cancer. The moral here – be a blessing to your church and not a tumor.

Paul reminds the Church at Corinth that each person in the congregation has a divinely appointed role to play in the Body. He says, "[18] But as it is, God arranged the members in the body, each one of them, as he chose. [19] If all were a single member, where would the body be? [20] As it is, there are many members, yet one body." What role has God appointed for you at your church? Our churches suffer when any one of us does not use our spiritual gifts in service to God and others.

While our culture was largely founded on the Enlightenment understanding of individual rights (for white, male, landed gentry), *individualism* pervades our culture *to the point of sinfulness at times*. The great tide of individualism says that the only person that matters is you. The only opinions and truths that matter are your own. The relativistic notion, "Your truth is good for you, and my truth is good for me," stems from a high view of the individual. Small-church author and theologian David Ray points out that it has even been argued, "The presence of individualism [is] the central reality and problem of our culture, and the most serious threat to our future."[276] In some ways, the divine uniqueness that God gives each of us should lead to a greater sense of community and authenticity. Ray argues that instead of giving into the pressures of individualism in society, "Churches, particularly smaller ones, have capacity for caring that can serve as a needed alternative, one based on interdependence rather than individualism. Our world desperately needs that which we in the church are uniquely equipped to be and do."[277] The community that cared for and embraced Alvin and his family lived out this interconnectedness in a beautiful way.

Rural Diversity and Individualism

It is, of course, right to understand and acknowledge that different people live in different communities and experience different realities. A single black mother in my rural community has undoubtedly lived life a very different reality than that of my own as a white married male. So, how do we hold space for people with divergent life experiences and realities to come together in the Body of Christ, particularly in rural communities? Ray wisely and deftly points out, "Often the caring in small churches has to do with their lack of diversity. Many small churches are fairly homogenous. People in homogenous groups tend to care for each other more easily. Often people who are different have been weeded out and repelled."[278] Hence, the individualism that pervades our culture (even in rural communities) may be part of the reason people seek out churches filled with people like themselves. This is, ironically, like the high school kid who thinks he is fashionable and expressing his individuality by buying the same designer jeans all of his friends are wearing. One of the most readily named rural values is, after all, rugged individualism. Despite our own Western-based, Americanized sense of self-worth and rural self-sufficiency, the Scripture reminds us how God created us to live in community with one another as part of one Body.

One reality regarding the complexity of the emerging rural landscape is that diversity is on the rise in rural communities. It seems, "The diversity of town and country life has become more complex than most of the stereotypes of small-town USA lead us to believe."[279] Not long ago, it was discovered that in the United States, "fourteen of the thirty most diverse counties are rural."[280] This trend has only continued, and with many in urban centers relocating to rural communities as a result of the COVID-19 pandemic, this statistic is indicative of deep demographic currents. As this rural demographic complexity increases, the emerging diversity in rural culture presents unique challenges. Rural communities and churches may struggle with diversity because 1) unity in the community used to exist around likeness and similarity, 2) caring is easier in community when everyone else is like yourself, and 3) cultural individualism ironically leads us to gravitate toward people with our own likes and preferences. How can the rural church overcome these challenges and build congregations that more adequately reflect God's diverse Kingdom?

Perhaps it begins with seeing the rural "other" as made in God's image and with listening. Different people have different gifts to bring to the table in ministry and mission of the Church. Additionally, the divine uniqueness of spiritual giftedness should be celebrated and embraced to the extent that our individuality is a gift from God for service to the Body of Christ. Too many Christians in our churches buy into cultural individualism. Cultural individualism says, "I don't have to acknowledge your difference, I owe you nothing, and I will seek my own interest and my own pleasure to the detriment of yours." This view is self-centered (perhaps even hedonistic) and is not honoring God's design for the Body of Christ. Cultural individualism is often antithetical to the Great Commandment.

Chapter Thirteen: THE TIDE OF INDIVIDUALISM: BRIDGING SPIRITUAL GIFTS WITH MINISTRY

We should view our uniqueness as individuals as grace from God for the benefit of others. In this sense, diversity is a wonderful gift to the rural church, not only racially, culturally, and economically, but in terms of spiritual gifts. When Paul speaks of the beautifully diverse Body of Christ, he reminds the reader that each part of the body performs its part in contribution to the whole. One's usefulness (and uniqueness) in the Body of Christ comes not from one's *personal* individuality but from spiritual gifts bestowed by God's Spirit. You are not special in the body of Christ because of how pretty you are, how well you sing, what hobby or job you have, or because of your political persuasions. What makes people unique members of the body of Christ are the *spiritual* graces God freely bestows upon each believer. We should focus on allowing people who are uniquely gifted to serve in the ways God has spiritually gifted them.

Diversity in rural churches and communities should be embraced, not because of the trend toward inclusivity or the sweeping cultural tide of individualism, but because God has created the church to embody God's own divine originality in the beautiful patchwork we call humanity. Too often though, rural communities are still segregated with ethnic minorities "rarely living in integrated community; instead they live in separated social networks."[281] Many ethnic minorities who speak English as a second language may also feel like they live as "others" in their rural communities due to language barriers.

In the small town of Warsaw, Virginia, the Park family has a long standing ministry to Hispanic and Latino immigrants and farm workers. Many of the families they serve are largely living as outsiders in the community. The tide of cultural individualism can lead to many in the community existing with near invisible status. Remember the beautiful idea that rural churches should find rootedness in "interdependence rather than individualism?"[282] What would embracing rural diversity look like to that end? Many of those "othered" by rural churches, particularly by white/Anglo rural churches, are vital parts of the rural communities, working on farms and in restaurants and serving in construction and horticulture.

Who are the people and families in your own community with near invisibility to the prevailing culture? What would a refocus away from individualism toward interdependence mean for your church? By embracing the idea of interdependence, the rural community of Urbanna, Virginia, was able to provide love and support for Alvin and his family. A community that embraced cultural individualism may not have done the same. Contrary to rural mythology, rural communities are often places with beautiful diversity, and part of what it means for rural churches to deal with this emerging reality is to celebrate the divine uniqueness and giftedness of each person in the community. This moves beyond the tide of cultural individualism, which often places an unholy emphasis on the self to the detriment of others. Healthy church bodies arguably have room for people like Alvin to find a place of service and fulfill a function according to their own calls and abilities. God's people are called to live differently, and the body of Christ has many parts that are called to function in different ways. How can your rural church invite people to move beyond self-interest to the denial of self for the sake of Christ? How can your congregation celebrate the giftedness of all people in the community? Does your church even function as a healthy body or only as a group of self-interested individuals? Does the tendency of many rural individuals to embrace rugged individualism and self-sufficiency help or harm rural churches, and why?

Chapter Fourteen
THE TIDE OF SKEPTICISM: BRIDGING FAITH AND DOUBT

> *"When you draw a line in the sand,*
> *be careful it is not low tide."*
>
> — Dixie Waters

Key Text: 1 Corinthians 13

Skepticism as a cultural impulse is on the rise, playing out in any number of ways. A few years ago in 2016, the Oxford Dictionary famously selected the term "post-truth" as the word of the year. Oxford defines post-truth as "relating to or denoting circumstances in which objective facts are less influential in shaping public opinion than appeals to emotion and personal belief."[283] People are skeptical of truth claims made by those with differing opinions, skeptical of authority, skeptical of power and outside influence, and skeptical of those who are different from themselves. Skepticism also manifests itself in how people approach religious faith and truth claims. People who exhibit skepticism may question a wide variety of things, including climate science, vaccination, the benefits of capitalism, or a patriarchal culture. Skepticism is such a wide cultural impulse that it touches both conservatives and progressives – and all points in between.

The main impulse of skepticism is to approach all claims with intellectual suspicion and some measure of doubt. Consequently, people often hold doubts (perhaps both founded and unfounded) regarding medical claims, scientific claims, political claims, religious claims, and ethical claims – to name a few. Skepticism is classically understood as a form of epistemology (that segment of philosophy concerned with how to distinguish justified belief from opinion). Everett Fulmer of Loyola University writes of philosophical skepticism, "Skepticism involves doubt, or at least a reluctance to commit."[284] The doubt many rural residents express regarding science and COVID-19 or the hesitancy to get a COVID-19 vaccine is a well-documented example of skepticism in emerging rural culture.[285] Historically,

> In the ancient world, skepticism was recommended as a way of life. The general claim was that living with an attitude of skeptical doubt is superior (morally and/or practically) to living with an attitude of dogmatic certainty. In the modern world (i.e., the 1600s through the 1800s), skepticism was more often treated as something to be avoided, and considerable philosophical energy was put into strategies for doing so.[286]

Since we are emerging into a postmodern rural culture, a question arises regarding if we are moving beyond modernity, entering a kind of hyper-modernity, or reverting to forms of cultural pre-modernity. However the current shift may be characterized, evidence is increasingly mounting that in contemporary Western culture, living with skeptical doubt is indeed seen by many as superior to dogmatic certainty. Ironically, many may exhibit skepticism in one area of life while exhibiting dogmatic certainty in other areas. Take, for example, the number of rural Christians wrapped up in the recent conspiracy movement Q-Anon, skeptically questioning everything about reality and culture while also holding rigid and dogmatic beliefs concerning religion.[287] Alternately, some atheists who hold certainty regarding their non-theistic worldview are also part of the anti-vaccination movement.[288] Suffice it to say, people can hold great certainty in one area of their lives while exhibiting great skepticism in others.

Atheism in Rural Communities

In our youth ministry in one small church, a student began coming with his friends to our Wednesday night gatherings. The young man (and presumably his parents) were atheists. The teen came largely because his friends invited him, and he had a place of belonging. Our Bible study times were always interesting because he would bring deep and thoughtful questions regarding our lessons. This student loved to ask questions that would have made many Bible study leaders squirm – not to be the center of attention, but because of honest inquiry. I realized two things as our weekly discussions unfolded in front of his peers. The first is that he was incredibly well read. He would regularly refer to writers like Stephen Hawking or philosophers like Emmanuel Kant. Periodically, our discussions got so deep that I could tell the other students had trouble following along, and I would invite further conversation after our study that night concluded.

The second thing I learned as our conversations unfolded was that the other students were watching how I responded to someone in the middle of our church Bible study that questioned things like the existence of God, the virgin birth, and also the possibility of miracles. It seemed that for many of our students, this was the first time they had ever seen a grownup in their church not dismiss such questions outright or shy away from articulating a cogent and gracious answer. I don't communicate this story to make myself out as some kind of hero, but rather to remind us that 1) many people – both youth and grown-ups – who are atheists and agnostics may come to church because they value the fellowship and learning, 2) how we respond matters to the one asking the questions, 3) how we respond is instructive for others who may be watching. For theists, doubt is not the antithesis of faith as many surmise but an element of faith and part of the journey of faith. I do not know whatever became of that student in our youth group. His family moved out of our community the next school year. However, I am grateful my life's journey briefly overlapped with his own.

Famed scientist and agnostic Carl Sagan once quipped, "Who is more humble? The scientist who looks at the universe with an open mind and accepts whatever the universe has to teach us or somebody who says everything in this book must be considered the literal truth and never mind the fallibility of all the human beings involved?"[289] The Sagan's thinking here serves as an example of an impulse that has long been on the rise in our culture – skepticism toward claims made by many Christians concerning the nature of the Bible. Even for this Christian, Sagan's question is a fair one. Many are clearly turned away from Christianity when we make claims regarding the Bible that (in my view) the Bible never makes for itself. For readers subscribing to inerrantist views of Scripture, it may prove useful to consider how best to communicate your

Chapter Fourteen: THE TIDE OF SKEPTICISM: BRIDGING FAITH AND DOUBT

own deeply (and sincerely) held convictions regarding the Bible without alienating those who bristle at exclusivist truth claims. There are both conservative and progressive Christians that have not been humble in stating their own closely held convictions, and in an increasingly post-modern context with skepticism on the rise, believers of all stripes would do well to live out the humility of Christ in conversations where difference is apparent.

Worth mentioning here is that not all atheists are comfortable with the term skeptic as it may not accurately characterize their own self-understanding. John, a personal friend and atheist living in rural Virginia, graciously responded to a number of questions about his experience living in a rural community. In regard to the word skeptic as a personal descriptor, he states, "I can't speak to the skepticism community at large, but as an atheist with great admiration for the faith community, I want the same respect from those that believe for my non-belief. I'm not skeptical; that is the believer's perspective." In this regard, characterizing John as a skeptic would not be accurate since he holds certainty in his own non-theism. Interestingly, John often takes his own kids to a Christian skate night sponsored by a local church and speaks highly of how the pastor sincerely loves him and his family. Of living in rural community, he states, "In the end, I've learned to get offended less and expect less inclusion from the religious community." He concludes by stating that when engaged by sincere pastors with authentic friendship, "I feel all the richer and hope I can reciprocate." In terms of relating to people different from himself, John states:

> If we are truly wise, we can always change our minds. I could be a monk by the time I'm through, and you could be homeless, or vice versa. I imagine in any

of those extreme outcomes, we'd find ourselves with more time to cherish the great discussions and ponder the ones we accidentally omitted because of lines someone drew for us that we couldn't figure out how best to erase.

Perhaps rural churches might do well to consider what lines someone drew for them. Of course, it could be that many of those lines drawn in the sand were "drawn at low tide," as novelist Dixie Waters writes.

As the postmodern tide laps against the shoreline of rural life, rural communities may sense an increase in the number of those with non-theistic worldviews. This may not be because the number of non-theists is inherently on the rise, but rather that non-theists feel more comfortable openly discussing their own personal understandings and convictions. In rural communities, many atheists, skeptics, and agnostics may presently live with closeted beliefs due to the fact that they fear judgement or ostracization in their community. A large national study called the Secular Survey found that nearly 30 percent of all nonreligious respondents (including atheists, agnostics, humanists, freethinkers, and skeptics) live in rural communities and small towns.[290] Consider that finding in conjunction with U.S. Census data that 19.3 percent of the population lives in non-metro rural communities.[291] Taken in tandem, these statistics may be an indication that skepticism and non-theism are far more prevalent in rural communities than many living in religious bubbles may realize. The study also found that for participants living in highly religious rural communities, "The level of discrimination and stigmatization was dramatically higher."[292] One interviewee, a female from New York State, shared, "I had to hide my transformation for a very long time. Bangladesh is a very dangerous place for atheists still. I am living in the USA for last 28 years, still somewhat in the shadows. It is not safe for a nonwhite immigrant to be atheist in a rural community."[293] How then should rural churches respond when our neighbors feel unsafe for simply abiding by their own consciences? What would the Great Commandment to "Love your neighbor as yourself" look like for rural Christians in relation to secular neighbors?

Skepticism and Christlike Love?

Personally, I am thankful for those secularists, atheists, and agnostics in my own life – some of whom have often been more like Jesus than a number of Christians I know. I'm thankful too for those who know enough to know they do not know anything at all. At first, it may seem like a stretch to focus on skepticism when reading the great love passage in 1 Corinthians 13. However, Paul is quick to admit (when focusing on love) that he does not have all the answers. He admits that he only knows "in part." In the church, it often proves tempting to pretend like we have all of the answers to life's deepest questions or even that the Bible has all the answers. The Bible, however, says nothing about many of the most pressing cultural and ethical issues of our time. Admittedly, the last statement may be a stretch for many. What if ultimately having all the answers is not the point of faith? What if the point of Christian faith is learning to love like Christ?

Paul writes in verse 3, "If I give away all my possessions, and if I hand over my body so that I may boast, but do not have love, I gain nothing." Without love, we are nothing. Without love, we gain nothing. Christians who think they are something but don't embrace godly love do not know a thing about following Christ. Christians who think they gain something by hating others instead of loving don't know a thing about following Christ.

Having faith without love and having knowledge without love actually *drives people away* from God. Perhaps we should *love* the skeptics in our church and the secularists in our communities rather than try to convince them we have all the answers.

According to Paul, knowledge itself will come to an end, so knowledge cannot rightly become an end in following Christ. How can we minister in the midst of a rising tide of skepticism? Only through love. Paul tell us the kind of godly love we are to show to all people. We all know the words, "⁴ Love is patient; love is kind; love is not envious or boastful or arrogant ⁵ or rude. It does not insist on its own way; it is not irritable or resentful; 6 it does not rejoice in wrongdoing but rejoices in the truth. ⁷ It bears all things, believes all things, hopes all things, endures all things." I personally find it difficult to exhibit patience with the anti-vaxxer crowd or those who question climate change, but godly love demands something different than my gut response. The response of the church to skeptics (particularly agnostics and atheists), however, is often the opposite of love as Paul describes – impatient, mean-spirited, arrogant, rude, dismissive, combative, insisting on our own way, and even resenting that others might sincerely doubt beliefs we hold dear. Embedded in the love passage is a self-disclosure about Paul's own unknowing and willingness to admit to not having all the answers. In terms of your own faith or of the ministry of your rural church, can you, like Paul, admit you do not know it all?

Not everyone in rural America approaches religion with warm regard. Unfortunately, many have been wounded by the Church. Drew Dyke says in his book *Generation Ex-Christian: Why Young Adults Are Leaving the Church and How to Bring Them Back*, "In a postmodern world, no one story is large enough to contain the whole of reality, much less define it for all people."[294] The story of the Bible competes with the stories of other religions and the stories of culture, philosophy, and science in the contemporary

Chapter Fourteen: THE TIDE OF SKEPTICISM: BRIDGING FAITH AND DOUBT

context. Seventy years ago, Western people held few suspicions about the story of God as revealed in Scripture. One approach to people mistrusting the story of God in Christ as the only legitimate story might be to argue them into thinking the Christian story is the best story. It seems, however, that this approach often falls flat among those people we want to reach the most.

Paul reminds us that knowledge itself will one day end. Only one thing will last forever. He says, "⁸ Love never ends. But as for prophecies, they will come to an end; as for tongues, they will cease; as for knowledge, it will come to an end." Perhaps love alone is the key. I believe loving people into the Kingdom has always worked better than arguing them to death or prodding them with the tip of a sword. George Hunter, III, reminds us in the book *The Celtic Way of Evangelism* that belonging comes before believing in the emerging cultural context.[295] When we focus on love in our ministry, we do not have to worry about pretending we have all the answers. How can we help people belong even if they don't believe the same as us? Love them!

People categorized as "nones" and "dones" in your rural community don't yearn for theological answers and religious jargon spewed from the mouths of arrogant believers. They yearn for love. Worth mentioning here is that Paul reminds the Corinthians that not everyone will understand or embrace the cross (I Corinthians 1:18-25; 1:27-28; 14:20). He does state concerning believers, "⁹ For we know only in part, and we prophesy only in part." Why then do we act like we know everything? Some humility might serve the church well in an age of skepticism. Pretending to know it all is not the mark of a grownup faith. Paul writes, "¹¹ When I was a child, I spoke like a child, I thought like a child, I reasoned like a child; when I became an adult, I put an end to childish ways." Pretending that we know it all is the result of childish faith.

Sea Change | *Jonathan Howard Davis*

I once had a seminary professor named Dr. Mark Biddle. Biddle is arguably one of the preeminent Old Testament and Hebrew scholars in the world today. He once wrote a commentary on Deuteronomy that surpassed over 600 pages in length! Of all the professors I had in seminary, Dr. Biddle was one that, for many reasons, intimidated me and many of my peers. Although an incredibly humble and gracious man (and a gifted jazz musician), his intellect intimidated me. I will never forget one day at the beginning of class, Dr. Biddle walked into the room in a huff and set a large pile of books on the table. He sat in silence before the class for what seemed like an eternity with what seemed like a flustered and confused look on his face. Finally, when the room could handle the silence no longer, one seminarian colleague of mine asked, "Dr. Biddle, is everything okay?" Dr. Biddle shook his head as if in wonder and said, "I have given my entire life to studying and interpreting the Scriptures and biblical languages, and some days, I am keenly reminded of how little I actually know." I was floored. Dr. Biddle's statement sticks with me still and has reminded me often of Paul's words, "[12] For now we see in a mirror, dimly, but then we will see face to face. Now I know only in part; then I will know fully, even as I have been fully known." Paul reminds us that when we do not have all the answers, love is the key. When we do not understand life's difficulties and have a crisis of faith, facts are never good enough. Only love will do.

Even though we cannot know God fully in this life, God fully knows us. What greater love is there than to be fully seen and fully known and for the one who fully sees us to love us anyway? As Paul states, "[13] And now faith, hope, and love abide, these three; and the greatest of these is love." At the end of the day, love matters most because love is all that will exist.

Chapter Fifteen
THE TIDE OF GREEN: BRIDGING CREATION CARE WITH PRACTICAL MINISTRY

> *"For still there are so many things that I have never seen: in every wood in every spring there is a different green."*
>
> – J. R. R. Tolkien

Key Text: 1 Corinthians 15:35-49

The year was 1969, and Roger Waters was on the Mediterranean island of Ibiza, 49 miles off the coast of Spain.[296] The sky was blue, the water was crystal clear, and the sun's heat reflected off the sand. The lush green vegetation that covered the island added to the paradise scene, and Waters was inspired to write a song. His band Pink Floyd recorded the song in London later that year for the album *Soundtrack from the Film More*.[297] The lyrics are:

> *Heavy hung the canopy of blue*
> *Shade my eyes and I can see you*
> *White is the light that shines through the dress that you wore*
> *She lay in the shadow of the wave*
> *Hazy were the visions of her playing*
> *Sunlight on her eyes but moonshine beat her blind every time*
> *Green is the color of her kind*
> *Quickness of the eye deceives the mind*
> *Many is the bond between the hopeful and the damned*[298]

The last line, "Many is the bond between the hopeful and the damned," could very well be a prophetic proclamation concerning the tension between humans and the environment. An interesting question to consider in terms of ecology is who are the hopeful and who are the damned? The title of the song also speaks to our current context in many ways. Green is the color—the color of the emerging economy, the color of sustainability, the color of conscientious capitalism, and the color of political buzzwords. Society seems green with environmental concern, and the church needs a practical response.

Our world is a world that's going green. Environmental concern is a top value of the younger generation. Companies and philanthropists and even governments are taking the lead on cleaner energy, sustainable agriculture, renewable energy, and caring for creation. What is the church's role in all of this? If care for creation is a high value in our culture and care for creation is a biblical mandate, why is the church not leading this conversation? Paul writes:

> [35] But someone will ask, "How are the dead raised? With what kind of body do they come?" [36] Fool! What

you sow does not come to life unless it dies. ³⁷ And as for what you sow, you do not sow the body that is to be, but a bare seed, perhaps of wheat or of some other grain. ³⁸ But God gives it a body as he has chosen, and to each kind of seed its own body.

What happens when we die? Paul appeals to what God has revealed in the natural order to explain the resurrection. People in the ancient world placed an incredibly high value on things revealed in the natural order of the world.

Paul teaches about the resurrection by appealing to people's love of the natural world and by using examples from God's creation. Other early church fathers appealed to the natural world in their own understanding of God. Hear these words from some of the earliest Christian leaders. Irenaeus of the second century once wrote, "The initial step for a soul to come to knowledge of God is contemplation of nature."[299] Ambrose of Milan wrote in the fourth century, "Why does harm done to nature give you pleasure? The world was created for all, but you few rich try to keep it for yourselves. For not merely landed property but the heavens themselves, the air, the sea are claimed for the use of a few wealthy persons. This air, which you include in your widespread possessions — how many people can it provide for!"[300] During the eighth century, John of Damascus wrote:

> I do not worship matter, I worship the God of matter, who became matter for my sake, and deigned to inhabit matter, who worked out my salvation through matter. I will not cease from honouring that matter which works my salvation ... I honour all matter besides, and venerate it. Through it, filled, as it were, with a divine power and grace, my salvation has come to me.[301]

Do we care enough about creation that we could lead someone to Christ by using creation as an example of God's redemptive work? How can our level of care for creation serve as a witness to the world of God's goodness, grace, and glory?

Individual Christians as well as Christian institutions like our rural churches face several challenges concerning consumption. In the American economy, one's consumption may inherently come into conflict with one's loyalty to God. All social systems place moral and economic demands on their adherents and may come into conflict with faith daily. We must find ways to meet the challenges our social system presents to faithful discipleship, and "as we do these things, a narrative emerges in which words like restraint, sharing, limits, boundaries are central, and words like limitless, expansion, growth, development, which have ruled our personal, political, and market lives for centuries, move to the margins."[302] Part of a minister's task in a local church setting is then to invite people toward a new understanding of creation stewardship.

Many people appear to be in total denial of environmental change. Remember the tide of skepticism? Perhaps you are skeptical yourself of claims of climate change. In fairness, the issue is highly politicized, and to many, global warming and environmentalism seem like left-wing political agendas. Environmental policies are often written in urban office buildings by bureaucrats who know little about the local challenges of water, land management, or agriculture. This is part of the spatial relations between urban and rural places with people in cities sometimes thinking they know best how to embark upon environmental policy, often preventing local voices and regulators from having any input on public policy.

It seems part of the hesitancy of many in rural communities to embrace environmentally friendly practices stems from political leanings and a distrust of outsiders telling them what to do, but hesitancy also stems from a deep-seeded distrust of

Chapter Fifteen: THE TIDE OF GREEN: BRIDGING CREATION CARE WITH PRACTICAL MINISTRY

the academy. If the same scientists who believe in evolution also believe in global warming, then many in rural churches want nothing to do with it. As many studies have shown, "The religious right and transnational corporations, [...] each have vested interests in scientific outcomes," and both act as major players in the distrust some people have in science.[303] Any plan for bridging environmental ethics and creation stewardship in the local church needs to acknowledge these hurdles and find a way to depoliticize certain issues at play. In fact, rural pastors should be aware that "trust in science has not declined since the 1970s except among conservatives and those who frequently attend church."[304] This piece of knowledge deserves *careful* consideration because many rural churches are naturally full of conservatives, and all *healthy* churches are full of frequent attendees. Many people in our churches will have a difficult time considering theology in terms of environmental concern because of their politics or because of their own skepticism concerning science. That said, many rural communities are blessed with fine scientists who understand the challenges of rural communities in caring for 97 percent of the country's land mass.[305]

By appealing to nature itself, the early apostles and church fathers were able to explain concepts like salvation, resurrection, sin, and grace and even make arguments for or against things like the use of icons and symbols in worship. Continuing in his letter to the Church at Corinth, Paul writes:

> [39] Not all flesh is alike, but there is one flesh for human beings, another for animals, another for birds, and another for fish. [40] There are both heavenly bodies and earthly bodies, but the glory of the heavenly is one thing, and that of the earthly is another. [41] There is one glory of the sun, and another glory of the moon, and another glory of the stars; indeed, star differs from star in glory.

Here and in other places, Paul appeals to people's understanding of nature and love of the natural world in order to communicate the gospel. Paul's use of the word δόξα in verses 40-41 (translated "glory") indicates that each piece of nature listed has intrinsic worth. If God's creation has intrinsic worth and beauty, how much more do we have intrinsic worth and beauty as the only created beings made in God's image! Paul continues:

> [42] So it is with the resurrection of the dead. What is sown is perishable, what is raised is imperishable. [43] It is sown in dishonor, it is raised in glory. It is sown in weakness, it is raised in power. [44] It is sown a physical body, it is raised a spiritual body. If there is a physical body, there is also a spiritual body.

By appealing to the inherent and lasting beauty of sun, moon, and stars, Paul uses dualism in nature to explain the dualism of body and spirit as it pertains to the resurrection. Paul did not only appeal to nature in this instance to explain deep theological truth. By appealing to natural order and beauty embedded in creation, Paul makes appeals concerning everything from church health issues to daily life in Corinthian households. Paul also uses nature to appeal to people in other contexts, making appeals in Acts 14, Acts 17, Romans 1, and 1 Timothy 4:3-4.

In an increasingly secular and post-modern culture where people find spirituality in nature itself, appealing to people's sense of connection to and responsibility for nature may be one of the best evangelism tools the rural Church possesses in the 21st century. Paul appeals to people's understanding of and appreciation for nature in explaining something as basic as the resurrection. If one of the biggest values in our culture is care for the environment and the church is completely silent on the environment, we are missing a huge opportunity to witness to the world! Of all of the organizations that should have

Chapter Fifteen: THE TIDE OF GREEN: BRIDGING CREATION CARE WITH PRACTICAL MINISTRY

something to teach us about caring for creation and building a sustainable future, the church should be leading!

As a rural church, your congregation should highly consider how you may model creation care and stewardship as a Christian discipline and witness. *If the culture values something inherently that is already mandated in Scripture, then the church has a great opportunity for witness concerning a commonly held belief.* For clarity, this is not to drag the church into environmental politics. Far from it! Creation care is a priority throughout the Scripture. Numbers 35:33-34 states, "You shall not pollute the land in which you live; for blood pollutes the land, and no expiation can be made for the land, for the blood that is shed in it, except by the blood of the one who shed it. You shall not defile the land in which you live, in which I also dwell; for I the Lord dwell among the Israelites." In context, the passage is about polluting the land with bloodshed from violence among the tribes and because of revenge killings from family avengers, but what if the violence was *toward the land itself* which was a gift from YHWY?

An exciting study performed among Lutherans in Wisconsin recently identified a simple way to overcome the barriers of politicization, scientific distrust, and misunderstanding. They suggest that ministers move churches toward less consumption and environmentally friendly practices through cultivating a spiritual, communal, personal, and sacred "sense of place" using the church's property, based on creation-stewardship theology.[306] Through promoting a sense of place, Seifert and Shaw argue, "By scaling back the magnitude of God's creation to one's own patch, nurturing a congregation's sense of place at church could instill a sense of responsibility to care for the environment at the local level."[307] By focusing on the practices of a local congregation and appealing to the things that people passionately want to preserve in their local church/town, they show that Christians might willingly rally to conservationism and less consumption. The appeal to protect one's personal and communal place of worship is far less political than other types of environmental appeals, and "since studies have shown that religiosity may not preclude pro-environmental behavior as much as it precludes identification with liberal political ideologies, transcending this political association may be necessary to influence Christians who do not currently support political environmentalism."[308] The barriers to environmental ethics in the local church have potential to crumble with a little forethought. It seems clear from the Wisconsin study that "attitudes about environmental issues are situational, and situational attitudes are better predictors of behavior than broader, cross-situational attitudes."[309] In other words, "By situating care of creation in one's own place where its inherent closeness may motivate a heightened recognition of one's role and ability to protect it, active involvement in its protection may follow."[310] By appealing to a motivator other than political loyalty or scientific data, Christian leaders may be able to lead rural churches toward more robust creation-stewardship theologies and practices. This holy sense of place may indeed lead to a spirituality "not only about a one-on-one relationship with God, but about growing in relationship with others, including the natural world."[311] Rallying around the holy place that is the rural church calls people to view the church and its land as an outpost of God's Kingdom on earth and a safe environment for kenosis to gestate and grow. Because churches are part of larger communities, the influence of their actions in preserving sacred places will ripple outward.

Individuals can move toward practicing creation stewardship, not by convincing them that global warming is real or by convincing them to change their lifelong party loyalty but by appealing to their love for what makes their local community

Chapter Fifteen: THE TIDE OF GREEN: BRIDGING CREATION CARE WITH PRACTICAL MINISTRY

a unique representation of God's creation. If you pastor a small-town church, this is great news! When it comes to environmentalism and consumption, you do not have to play the political games of our culture which may definitely be a losing game for any pastor in a rural community. Small towns generally already have a strong sense of community, so under the model that Seifert and Shaw propose, a pastor can easily capitalize on existing norms in rural culture to lead a congregation toward positive environmental change.

In one rural congregation I pastored, as a result of cultivating a sense of sacred place, we stopped utilizing toxic fertilizers that would wind up in the creek due to runoff (the church was right next to a creek) and began a recycling program. At another church I pastored, after cultivating this sacred sense of place, a church member donated solar panels to place on the church pavilion which saved us thousands in energy costs each year and more importantly attracted a number of younger families to join our church. In fact, we were the first institution in our rural county to adopt solar energy!

Genesis teaches that God created all things *ex-nihilo* (out of nothing) and entrusted stewardship over all creation to humanity. Our first and only job was to care for creation. Leviticus 25 prescribes that the land should be given a sabbatical year of rest every seven years. Moreover, in the Jubilee year every fiftieth year, the Lord commanded, "The land shall not be sold in perpetuity, for the land is mine; with me you are but aliens and tenants. Throughout the land that you hold, you shall provide for the redemption of the land." (Leviticus 25:23-24, NRSV). If your church wants to return to the radical holiness prescribed by YHWY, then the church should consider what it means to redeem the land today. One former church is situated on nearly 30 acres of land, some of which is still farmed. The church is across the road from a major river which runs directly to the Chesapeake Bay, and the church is immediately south of a national wildlife refuge. If we wanted to reach younger people through taking creation care seriously, there was ample opportunity.

What if our care for creation became an evangelism tool, just like Paul's love and understanding of the natural order? Rural churches should care about creation as a church, not out of political concern but because all creation is the Lord's. We should care about creation, not out of motivation to save a few dollars on the church's utility bills but because it is an issue at the forefront of our young people's hearts – the same young people that leave churches in droves.

Paul concludes this particular discourse on nature and faith in verse 49, "Just as we have borne the image of the man of dust, we will also bear the image of the man of heaven." When the church cares for creation, we bear the image of God to the world. What does it mean to bear God's image to the world? Julian of Norwich once said, "Then I saw three properties. The first is that God made it, the second is that God loveth it, the third, that God keepeth it. But what is to me verily the Maker, the Keeper, and the Lover […]."[312] God made a beautiful world for us to care for. How can we as a church make it more beautiful? God keeps the world held together by His very being. As those made in God's image, how are we keeping and tending God's creation? Finally, if God is the lover of humanity and we have the promise of resurrection one day – resurrection of new life and an eternal home with Christ Jesus, how are we loving others, God, and God's creation presently? If we are made in God's image, how are we using our creative abilities to make, keep, and love God's creation for the next generation? Our love and care for God's creation may be a point of engagement and even a mark of authenticity to those who are skeptical of God

Chapter Fifteen: THE TIDE OF GREEN: BRIDGING CREATION CARE WITH PRACTICAL MINISTRY

and the church. How can your rural church appeal to people's love of nature for the sake of the gospel, imitating Paul? An important question for your church in light of emerging rural culture is, "Will we be the kind of church that loves our Lord and loves our neighbors by loving God's creation?"

Chapter Sixteen

THE TIDE OF SOLIDARITY: BRIDGING THE HEART OF GOD WITH CULTURE

"If solidarity is unity of purpose or togetherness, how to span this great divide of inequality, privilege, universal rights, political agency, and even our seeing things completely differently?"

– Ramor Ryan

Key Text: 2 Corinthians 8:1-15

In our rural community, the turnover in the school system was rampant. The school board blamed the county board of supervisors, and the board of supervisors blamed the school board. Some in the community blamed the teachers or poor families for the struggling school system. As the seasons changed, so too did the administrative staff at the school board office. When the new superintendent started his position, I stopped by the office one day to introduce myself and communicate our church's support for the school system. Before I left the superintendent's office, I offered to pray for him, which he accepted with gratitude. Right there in the school board office, we shared a holy moment.

A few months later, it was late in the evening when I received the call from the school superintendent's office. They were requesting my presence to help with a crisis counseling situation at school the next day. A teacher from Essex High School, Mr. Peters (a younger black man), had been killed in a police-involved shooting in Richmond, Virginia, while having a mental health crisis – and completely unarmed. Many of Mr. Peters' students had seen evening news footage of their teacher getting shot and laying naked and dead on a Richmond highway, not long after they got home from school. Needless to say, our entire rural community was in total shock and dismay.

The next morning, I showed up at the school, and six other crisis counselors and I (the only pastor in the bunch) were ushered into the school library and briefed on the situation. During each period of the day, students that had Mr. Peters would have the chance to come and talk through their own shock, grief, and trauma. The seven of us must have counseled nearly a hundred students that day, and the next day, the school asked us to return and counsel any more students that needed crisis counseling. I cannot express how raw the emotions of these students were. I was especially impacted by the perspectives of so many young black teenagers, who must have said in a thousand different ways, "It could have been me." For the first time in my life, I was confronted with the struggles that

Chapter Sixteen: THE TIDE OF SOLIDARITY: BRIDGING THE HEART OF GOD WITH CULTURE

often come with being a person of color in America. Many white students had a very different perspective. One told me, "Officers are trained to do that," and another even said, "He must have done something wrong if he got shot by the police." It seemed apparent to me that these students, particularly the white ones, were largely parroting whatever their own parents had said regarding the footage on the evening news.

The tragic death of Marcus-David Peters resulted in numerous investigations, sparked outcry and protests in Richmond, became a topic of conversation among politicians in a gubernatorial race, and inspired a law mandating changes to how Virginia police respond to incidents involving mental health. Over the next two years and especially after the killing of George Floyd, there were several local marches, demonstrations, and prayer vigils for racial justice. I was at one of the prayer vigils on the steps of an old church when someone driving by in a big truck with a giant "Keep America Great" flag honked and yelled, "All live matter, you f#*%ing n_____s!" I could tell by the looks of many of my black friends that it was not the first time they had heard such racist vitriol in their lifetimes. Sheepishly, I was more shocked than they were. At a racial justice march that took place on a warm summer day, white-nationalist militia stood guard over the town square with semi-automatic rifles in tow. I don't say any of this to "spill the beans" on that wonderful town, for every small town has what Richard Lischer terms "Open Secrets."[313] I say it to share that sometimes I struggled (as did the church) with how to show solidarity in such a highly politicized and charged environment. Paul invites the Church at Corinth to stand in solidarity with a congregation in Macedonia that was very likely being persecuted. In fact, he writes to the Corinthians that their solidarity with oppressed brothers and sisters is a mark of their own maturity as followers of Jesus.

The Oxford Dictionary defines solidarity as "unity or agreement of feeling or action, especially among individuals with a common interest; mutual support within a group."[314] In 2 Corinthians 8, Paul is encouraging the Corinthians to show solidarity with an impoverished sister church in Macedonia. In appealing to the Corinthians, Paul writes:

> We want you to know, brothers and sisters, about the grace of God that has been granted to the churches of Macedonia; [2] for during a severe ordeal of affliction, their abundant joy and their extreme poverty have overflowed in a wealth of generosity on their part. [3] For, as I can testify, they voluntarily gave according to their means, and even beyond their means, [4] begging us earnestly for the privilege of sharing in this ministry to the saints [...].

Sometimes, the most generous people are the ones possessing the least. Even in the midst of extreme poverty and potential persecution, the Macedonians generously shared so that the work of the gospel might continue. I have often witnessed the same in rural ministry, where some of the most kind and giving people I have ever encountered are not people of great means.

Audrey and I once traveled to a village in Ecuador on mission to a native people group. When we arrived in the mountain village, the people there gave us freshly roasted corn as a welcome gift. It was the sweetest corn I have ever tasted. I remember being struck by how people with so little could be so generous. Paul writes to the Corinthians, "[7] Now as you excel in everything—in faith, in speech, in knowledge, in utmost eagerness, and in our love for you—so we want you to excel also in this generous undertaking." He tells them to "excel in generosity." What would it look like your rural church to excel in generosity? Often, we consider generosity

Chapter Sixteen: THE TIDE OF SOLIDARITY: BRIDGING THE HEART OF GOD WITH CULTURE

only in terms of financial stewardship, but it can also be understood as an act of solidarity.

Paul encourages the Corinthian Church (which he has been in conversation with for several years at this point) that a mark of their maturity and commitment is their willingness to stand in solidarity with and support for hurting brothers and sisters in the faith. In comparison to the Macedonian Church, the Church at Corinth was quite wealthy. Remember the rich people who refused to share in communion with the poorer church members? Paul corrected that bad habit in a former letter, first addressing how the church internally handles great disparity and even oppression. Paul's appeal to the Corinthians to support an extremely poor (and perhaps persecuted) church may indicate the Corinthians had made progress in treating all people with love and dignity. *They had to get their own house in order before they could turn outward in healthy and missional ways.* Paul writes, "[8] I do not say this as a command, but I am testing the genuineness of your love against the earnestness of others. [9] For you know the generous act of our Lord Jesus Christ, that though he was rich, yet for your sakes he became poor, so that by his poverty you might become rich." Helping the poor is of utmost importance for Christians because we literally live the way Christ lived, where we are poured out and emptied for the sake of others.

Paul also appeals to the church to make good on plans it had for over a year to send support to the Macedonian church, writing, "[10] And in this matter I am giving my advice: it is appropriate for you who began last year not only to do something but even to desire to do something— [11] now finish doing it, so that your eagerness may be matched by completing it according to your means." Like many churches today, the Corinthian congregation began with the best of intentions but never followed through.

Sea Change | Jonathan Howard Davis

One of the marks of a mature congregation is identifying where the church should stand in solidarity and then *acting* on it. Perhaps a Corinthian voiced the desire to support the Macedonian Church, and the issue was passed off to the mission committee who tabled it until the church council meeting which tabled it because not enough people showed up at the church council meeting to make a significant decision, and so on. *Many churches get caught in cycles of never following through on excellent ministry plans, and as a result, the Kingdom suffers.*

The story of the Macedonians is reminiscent of the story of the Widow's Mite, where one without much of anything to give gave her all out of a generous heart toward God, trusting through faith for her own provision. How can we become poor so that others may be rich in Christ? Who is afflicted, in extreme poverty, or facing tribulation that we as a church can stand beside in prayer and material support?

In the last several years, incredible movements of solidarity have sprung up around the nation and the world. The Arab Spring, Occupy Wall Street, Black Lives Matter, Blue Lives Matter, the Women's March on Washington, the Right to Life March on Washington, Moral Mondays, and prayer vigils after attacks at places like San Bernardino, Sandy Hook, the Mother Emmanuel Massacre in Charleston, and Pulse Night Club Shooting (and many more) have all sprung up as solidarity movements. Some of these solidarity movements have even emerged as reactions to other solidarity movements. People of a particular political bent do not own solidarity as a deep cultural undercurrent. In these movements, people band together to express fellowship and unity around common causes and interests, often in the wake of tragedy. Many young people are slow to trust an institution of any type but quick to support a cause. As a value, solidarity has swept the nation like

Chapter Sixteen: THE TIDE OF SOLIDARITY: BRIDGING THE HEART OF GOD WITH CULTURE

a great tidal wave. One of the freedoms we enjoy in America is the freedom of expression and the freedom to peacefully assemble. Some solidarity movements have not always been peaceful, and the church should condemn violence as a form of political speech, following the non-violent way of Christ.

For the emerging culture, solidarity is a top value. Standing up for the oppressed, and coming alongside the downtrodden, the marginalized, and the persecuted is a badge of authenticity and legitimacy – especially for the church, which is supposed to care for the least of these. This may be a stretch for many, but I am convinced rural churches should think strongly about showing solidarity with certain causes, especially when they align with the teachings and ethics of Christ. Small-town churches may rightfully be judged as hypocritical when proclaiming to follow the teachings of Christ if also failing to exhibit care for the poor and marginalized. Not only is such care a mark of a mature church, such care is central to following Christ. Those who hear the words, "I never knew you; go away from me, you evildoers," (Matthew 7:23) are those who ignore the least of these.

How is God calling your own church to model the solidarity and generosity Paul called for in 2 Corinthians 8? What would Jesus say to us in terms of our own care for the least of these? Here you may want to take an opportunity to ask several questions regarding your church. How can our church come alongside the rural homeless? How can we come alongside a school system that needs community support? How can we come alongside suvivors of sexual abuse and assault? How can we fight against human trafficking and modern slavery? What are we doing in regard to racism in our community? What is our church's response to rural poverty? How can we use our abundant blessings to bless others? How can we excel in generosity and solidarity as a church?

Sometimes solidarity in rural communities is the opposite of what Paul writes about. Often, those who are crying out for justice do so from the margins of society and culture. Many smaller communities have a strong sense of who is in and who is out. Chances are, if you are hurting and crying out for justice, you are not part of the "in-group." Those who are not part of the "in-group" do not have the same social capitol and moral agency as those who are, and they may face backlash if they are perceived to be challenging the social norms and structure. It is important to realize:

> Such in-group solidarity generally results in the drawing of sharp boundaries between insiders and outsiders and may even result in the persecution of those who do not share (or who are perceived as not sharing) the values of the in-group. These distinctions between those who do and do not share the in-group's values are strongest when the out-group values are perceived as threats to the social order.[315]

In a sense then, this is the underlying reason why solidarity groups (particularly those calling for social change) often cause those in privilege to have a kind of solidarity with others in privilege.

For Paul, the issue of the Corinthians having solidarity with the Macedonians is not an issue of fairness but rather one of balance. We are often slow to help those in need because we say things like, "I worked hard for this money, and it's not fair that people who did not work for it might get it." Many have this attitude, not only in terms of taxation and social welfare programs but even of benevolence money. Paul calls the same attitude into question, arguing, "[13] I do not mean that there should be relief for others and pressure on you, but it is a question of a fair balance between [14] your present abundance and their need, so

Chapter Sixteen: THE TIDE OF SOLIDARITY: BRIDGING THE HEART OF GOD WITH CULTURE

that their abundance may be for your need, in order that there may be a fair balance. ¹⁵ As it is written, 'The one who had much did not have too much, and the one who had little did not have too little'." Here, in appealing to the people's notions of fairness, Paul quotes Exodus 16:17-18, which is a passage about the daily distribution of Mana. It reads, "¹⁷ The Israelites did as they were told; some gathered much, some little. ¹⁸ And when they measured it by the omer, the one who gathered much did not have too much, and the one who gathered little did not have too little. Everyone had gathered just as much as they needed." This poses a challenging passage for all of us in our consumeristic culture.

In rural communities where the values of hard work, rugged individualism, and self-sufficiency permeate culture, solidarity with the oppressed and the poor may prove especially difficult to build. This is deeply embedded in Western culture, perhaps more so in rural communities. It seems:

> As a nation, we seldom acknowledge the degree to which our culture is built upon an extremely moralistic set of doctrines, particularly the belief in the moral value of hard work and the doctrine of individual achievement. Such ideas as the individual's personal and moral responsibility for his or her own success or failure permeate our culture and our worldview. These moral ideas frequently become most important when other status markers are unattainable or unusable.[316]

The idea is sometimes popularly stated, "God helps those who help themselves." The cultural tide of solidarity, and in particular the solidarity Paul is calling the Corinthian church to, not only casts aside this old adage but demolishes it. Part of what it means to stand in solidarity with the poor and marginalized is to lay down the idol of cultural moralism (and the judgement and othering that often come with it) in order to follow Christ's command to love our neighbor as ourselves (Mark 12:31).

First-century Christian apologist and philosopher Justin Martyr recorded Christian love and solidarity extensively in his writings. He wrote:

> We who used to value the acquisition of wealth and possessions more than anything else now bring what we have into a common fund and share it with anyone who needs it. We used to hate and destroy one another and refused to associate with people of another race or country. Now, because of Christ, we live together with such people and pray for our enemies.

How is God calling your rural church to stand in solidarity with the marginalized in your community and in your own church? Standing with the oppressed and moving from mere presence to Christlike love in action is no small task. The greatest display of solidarity in history was Christ Jesus, coming to earth from heaven and showing sacrificial love for us, even while we were poor in our own sin. How will your rural congregation live like Christ lived and give like Christ gave? Loving like Jesus loved defies all of our political categories and also our cultural biases and assumptions.

Over the past several chapters, we have explored many tides of faith – great cultural shifts and movements we cannot control. The tides included the tides of Tolerance, Authenticity, Individualism, Skepticism, Green, and Solidarity. In studying Paul's letters to the Church at Corinth, we find encouragement to become a church that does not embrace tolerance but Christ's radical love and grace instead. We find encouragement to become a church that is genuine and authentic, not two-

Chapter Sixteen: THE TIDE OF SOLIDARITY: BRIDGING THE HEART OF GOD WITH CULTURE

faced and hypocritical, a church that celebrates God given individuality, encouraging all people to serve as God has gifted them, and a church that radically loves our secular neighbors while also embracing doubt and faith as two sides of the same coin. Rural churches, however, cannot thrive in the emerging culture if they shy away from tough questions. We have considered that God calls us to become a church that values care of God's creation because Scripture mandates it and because in the current cultural climate, creation care can serve as an avenue for evangelism. Finally, in his letter to the Church at Corinth, Paul invites us to become a church that stands in solidarity with the poor and marginalized.

Chapter Seventeen
REPORT FROM THE VOYAGE: ANALYSIS AND DISCUSSION OF FINDINGS

> "... a little of this, a little of that — a little of me, a little of you — put it together what do you have? Postmodern soup ..."
>
> — John Geddes

In our own rural congregation, Beale Memorial Baptist Church in Tappahannock, Virginia, we implemented a qualitative and quantitative questionnaire to measure the church's affinity for postmodern values verses modern and traditional ones. At the outset of this doctoral project (which was the inspiration for this book), I wanted to equip my own church to navigate the tides of cultural change. The following sections share the exciting results of the ministry project.

Quantitative Questionnaire

The quantitative test garnered responses from a diverse mixture of BMBC congregants and proved useful in assessing the congregation's comfort and readiness with emerging ministry. Over 40 individuals participated in two focus groups, making for enough participants to get an accurate picture of the church's pulse concerning the tides of change. The first focus group consisted of leaders in the church (deacons, church council members, and staff), and the second focus group consisted of a cross section of church members not in leadership. The questionnaire was delivered at the beginning of the project (a pre-test) and then again at the end of the project (post-test) so that results could be measured. There was notable differences between each focus group on both the pre-test and post-test, but each group moved into closer agreement as a result of the project. The quantitative questionnaire produced some interesting findings, including:

- The pace of change seemed greater among average attendees (Focus Group Two) than it did among our most committed leaders.
- There was definite movement among the congregation toward a realization that faith is dynamic rather than static in nature and a growing realization of their own deliberative faith history.
- In terms of congregational values, growth was more important than diversity, but diversity and growth were more important than tradition.
- It seemed the average congregant placed a higher value on diversity than her leaders. The survey also proved that the leaders of the church were more concerned with growth than

the average congregants.
- Love of community ranked higher than environmental concern.
- <u>Family was by far the highest value within the church.</u>
- Respect for the elderly tested as a very important value.
- Church leaders did not value authenticity as highly as the average churchgoer.
- The average churchgoer did not value friendliness to strangers as much as congregational leaders.
- The average congregant had slightly stronger affinity for traditional values than the leaders of the church.
- The church has grown less comfortable with pluralism over time.
- When asked to respond to the statement, "Our church is well prepared to meet the challenges of reaching the next generation," leaders and average congregants only slightly agreed overall, and many strongly disagreed.
- Those born from 1961-1980 felt more strongly than any other group that their values were under attack in today's culture.
- Congregants born from 1915-1945 agreed the most that "our church is well prepared to meet the challenges of the next generation." Each younger generation progressively agreed less, with the youngest generation of respondents disagreeing the most.

Regarding the project pre-test and post-test with each focus group, while the focus groups clearly showed several differences on both tests, overall the groups moved in to greater agreement from the first test to the second. Not only did the deacons and church council move into closer proximity with other laity, varying generations moved toward cohesion. This shows that *the project led to an overall increase in cohesion and unity as a church.* By addressing cultural shifts head-on, we were able to build the church's capacity for facing cultural change and thriving in the future, and rural culture continued postmodern emergence. In my estimate, that is an exciting outcome!

The focus groups, however, did not show cohesion or unity in every way. Based on the findings of the questionnaire, some helpful questions for the church's leaders to ask (and probably your church's leaders) include the following:

- What does it mean that the leadership of the church is less concerned about diversity and more concerned about growth than the rest of the church family?
- How do we help families, and in what ways do we as a church compete with families instead of complementing them?
- Why do our leaders not value authenticity as much as, if not more than, the average churchgoer, and why does the average churchgoer not value friendliness to strangers as much as the average leader?
- How do we build respect for the elderly into our ministries and teach our kids this value?

By asking these and other tough questions of themselves, rural church leaders and laity can continue to navigate the shifting cultural tides.

As mentioned above, one of the most interesting findings is that younger generations seemed more comfortable with rising pluralism (no surprise perhaps) but feel less confident than older generations that our church was prepared to meet the challenges of ministry in the 21st century. One concern moving forward is that the church equip younger members to feel more confident

Chapter Seventeen: REPORT FROM THE VOYAGE: ANALYSIS AND DISCUSSION OF FINDINGS

about the church's future. Perhaps the generational gap in confidence concerning the church's future comes down to the question, "Who owns the vision?"[317] It is possible leaders who have been in the church for many years feel more ownership over the church and her vision than younger generations. Much of what has occurred in the church over the last two decades has indeed been the vision of the older generations of leaders. One example of this was the vision to move the church two miles north of town to an updated facility which was a move largely orchestrated by people now in their early 80s. Many younger adults in the church were only children when this vision was birthed and when it came into fruition. Many were not yet members of the church or even the local community. Some older members already mourn the fact that their vision may no longer carry the church forward, but it is still the primary and most influential vision of the church. Many younger members may not have any sense of ownership in the church's vision, thereby decreasing their confidence in the future of the congregation. Moving forward, the congregation should seek to create a shared vision among generations.

Also interesting to note is that the pace of change seemed greater among average attendees (Focus Group Two) than it did among our most committed leaders (Focus Group One). This finding likely has several factors. First, people most heavily involved in leadership of any organization may not sense that change is happening rapidly because they are doing the tough work of leading the organization and realize how slowly change may occur. Deacons and church council members talk about the change in monthly meetings and often deliberate any major congregational changes over many months. By the time a change occurs or is proposed more broadly to the entire church, leaders seem well aware of the coming shift. This means, for average congregants, change may not only prove more surprising but also more sudden, thereby increasing the overall perception concerning the pace of change as fast. One lesson here is that more people in the congregation could participate in high-level leadership discussions before major decisions are made.

An example of when this did not happen comes in the formation of our church's contemporary worship service. The service was launched largely because of a push by an interim pastor and was initially sold as a temporary summer service. After the summer, the interim pastor simply led the contemporary service to continue, and there was never a church-wide vote on if it *should* continue. Among many congregants who are not currently deacons or church council, this created a heightened sense that change was not only rapid but also beyond their input or influence. In a congregational system, this surely caused anxiety among many, and unfortunately, I was left with a pastoral leadership issue of healing wounds that seemed unnecessary. Overall, however, the project seemed to have measurably lowered the anxiety concerning change within the life of the church.

Another encouraging result was that from the pre-test to the post-test, people moved from perceiving faith as static to perceiving faith as dynamic. By discussing cultural change openly (as in discussing nearly anything openly), it seems that something like a pressure valve was released within the church, thereby reducing anxiety. *One may then conclude that talking about change and giving people a chance to tell their stories and dream about the future may at once bring healing from the past and hope toward the future.*

The project also helped people realize that their own faith had shifted through the years. If change is perceived as external and acute, change may seem more distressing. If one realizes that change has been internal and gradual, not only in the church but in the individual heart and mind, then change is perhaps viewed

Chapter Seventeen: REPORT FROM THE VOYAGE: ANALYSIS AND DISCUSSION OF FINDINGS

as a natural process and not as the enemy. *One pastoral lesson here is that to minimize the anxiety of change, people need space to process change.* The more people process cultural tides, the more measured and less emotionally driven their feelings concerning those tides. Part of this measured approach may even mean that some become more realistic and less idealistic. The data from the quantitative questionnaires indicated that before the project, Focus Group One was slightly more optimistic concerning change, perhaps even idealistic, and Focus Group Two proved more pessimistic concerning change. As a result of the project, each group moved closer to the other, meaning that the idealists and the pessimists may now be more closely grounded in a commonly shared reality.

Another significant finding is that over the course of the project, both focus groups moved significantly from believing that Christians should seek to accommodate culture to overwhelmingly thinking that Christians should seek to transform culture. This proves positive in many regards. The culture of accommodation may prove useful in many instances, particularly in a pluralistic world, but it may also lead to syncretism, causing the church to lose unique voice in the world. If rural church members "are able to deal with the pluralism of their world without eroding their Christian identity, they will help forge a vision of Christin belief and behavior that will make a powerful and constructive contribution to the global church in the twenty-first century."[318] In some ways, transformational ministry may prove inherently more missional. In the transformational approach to culture, as per Niebuhr, one thing that distinguishes conversionists "is their more positive and hopeful attitude toward culture."[319] It seemed that the church shifted in some ways as a result of the project, from viewing culture negatively to viewing culture as something worth redeeming for the glory of God.

In the second section of the questionnaire, respondents ranked traditional values overall more importantly than modern or postmodern values. The second test showed a decrease in the affinity for traditional values but showed a marked increase in affinity for postmodern values. Throughout this book, it has been proposed that traditional and rural values may prove compatible in many ways and modern values may not find strong embrace in an emerging rural culture. The results of the project seem to clearly indicate that members of the church consistently prefer traditional rural and emerging postmodern values to modern values. What seems remarkable is that over the course of the project, participant's affinity for postmodern values increased by 24.5 percentage points! This seems to indicate a clearly measurable and significant increase in the comfort of the church with postmodern values. While BMBC remains a congregation strongly rooted in traditional rural cultural values, there is evidence to support the idea that the church seems well positioned for the continued transition to a postmodern rural culture.

Tides of Faith Message Series

The *Tides of Faith* sermon series (the catalyst for chapters ten through fifteen) was well received overall. Attendance during this series was slightly up from 150 people, with roughly 175 people attending on Sundays over the course of the series. In certain ways, the series moved the mark of people's perceptions regarding cultural change and the church's response. The sermon on tolerance presents a good example here. At face value, tolerance is a value that appeals to many in our culture. The sermon focused on tolerance attempted to show that tolerance is quite different from the radical love of Christ. That is, we can tolerate things and people we hate, even if briefly. Disciples of Christ, however, love their enemies and pray for them. While tolerance might seem like a good value from a secular perspective, it is not so from a discipleship perspective. In the pre-test quantitative questionnaire, respondents ranked "tolerance" on question twelve slightly higher than the modern value of achievement. On the post-test, tolerance ranked lower, weighing equally with achievement. Both values lost out over the traditional value of respect for the elderly. This seems to indicate that the message on tolerance may have measurably lowered the weight of tolerance as an embraced value among respondents. Each sermon was posted online in the sermon archive and shared across social media platforms each week.[320]

Church Vision Day and Qualitative Questionnaire

Twenty laypeople plus three staff members attended the churchwide Vision Day. People from the focus groups who had taken the pre-project questionnaire were overwhelmingly those in attendance. The day was filled with wonderful conversation and storytelling. In sharing these research results, the "community can also be thought of as a way of weaving theological reflection and interpersonal connections in the life of the group. The threads of the weaving are the stories – the yarns – that the community offers."[321] Much storytelling and theological reflection happened as a result of participation in Vision Day, which is itself a positive end.

As an added way to garner feedback concerning Vision Day, I crafted a brief questionnaire titled *Vision Day Feedback Form* that was distributed at the end of the event. The form appears in full in Appendix 4 (see page 270). According to the feedback form, Vision Day arguably caused a 29.2 percent increase in optimism concerning our church's future among Vision Day participants, compared with where they tested before Vision Day on the quantitative pre-test. *This is a significant observation because it shows how the power of story and positive questioning may influence hope in the lives of congregants experiencing rapid cultural change.*

After the implementation of the project, church deacons participated in a retreat in the spring of 2018 to better train for the task of pastoral care and visitation. This not only helped them fulfil their duties as deacons but also freed me as the pastor (in some ways) to do the work of cultural shifting and visioning needed in the emerging rural cultural context.

Vision Day

Greek philosopher Heraclitus famously quipped, "No man ever steps in the same river twice, for it's not the same river and he's not the same man."[322] With cultural tides constantly shifting and evolving, a church that engages culture today will not look the same as a church that engages culture 100 years from now. By taking time to vision and dream as a church family, we were able to imagine a shared reality where the church fully engages the emerging culture around us.

Our Church Vision Day workshop was a very positive experience overall, and all who came seemed to enjoy themselves and take away good ideas. Cooperation was built around how the church may respond to and even thrive in cultural change. The provocative proposals were personally quite encouraging. Each small group at Vision Day named a future

Chapter Seventeen: REPORT FROM THE VOYAGE: ANALYSIS AND DISCUSSION OF FINDINGS

where the congregation is more innovative, highly relational, intentional, and diverse in every way. The provocative proposals and dialogical sessions proved useful in getting participants to dream of God's potential futures for BMBC.

In the weeks following the project, each provocative proposal was printed off on large poster-size paper and hung in the church library for eight weeks. The library is the space were nearly every committee in the church meets to do its business. Each provocative proposal was prominently displayed for two months so our leaders could reflect on them in their meetings. Additionally, the proposals were read in worship over the course of several weeks, and people in the church were invited to dream and pray about how God might be calling us to walk into these visions. A full schedule for our Vision Day Retreat is in Appendix 3 on page 267.

Chapter Eighteen
CHARTING A NEW COURSE THROUGH THE TIDES: SUMMARY AND CONCLUSIONS

> *Someday, after mastering the winds, the waves, the tides, and gravity, we shall harness for God the energies of love, and then, for a second time in the history of the world, man will have discovered fire.*
>
> – Pierre Teilhard de Chardin

Harnessing the Tide Instead of Fighting It

Postmodernity is a tide that will not turn back for the foreseeable future – like climate change. While humans can arguably take steps to reduce and even reverse climate change,

I am convinced that nothing will reverse the postmodern wave. The tide is a force that can destroy. Tidal waves regularly kill people and destroy property in their furious might. Tides can also prove useful as often as they are studied, understood, interpreted, and even embraced. The book at hand has been a labor of love, and the ministry project at Beale Memorial Baptist Church was a joy to implement. BMBC's people were gracious and loving in their response to the endeavor, and the results seem to have better equipped the congregation for the tides of cultural change. While there is much to take away from the data reported and the analysis in the previous chapter, overall, the project proved significant in several ways.

First, in my knowledge, this is the first ministry project (or certainly among few) that has attempted to wrestle with what postmodernity means for a rural congregation like BMBC. At the outset of this book, I observed the number of rural congregations in the United States has been estimated at nearly 200,000 churches.[323] This means BMBC is only one of nearly a quarter-million churches in the United States alone that presently wrestle with emerging rural values and culture.

In terms of emerging cultural values in the rural tidal basin of eastern Virginia, BMBC seems primed to hold a positive outlook on cultural change and take a redemptive view of culture rather than regarding culture as the enemy. The church has a strong presence and reputation in the community, and as it continually adapts to cultural emergence, it may thrive in the future world. For Christians, however, talk of the future may prove problematic in that the future arguably never really exists. It seems, "In a very real sense for the Christian's work, there is no time to call the future. Even as we speak of it, by the time we say it, it is the present. Thus so far as the Lord's work is concerned, the future is now!"[324] Postmodernity is not some far

Chapter Eighteen: CHARTING A NEW COURSE THROUGH THE TIDES: SUMMARY AND CONCLUSIONS

away social trend that might begin impacting us two decades from now. The tide is rising rapidly. So rapidly in fact, there was nearly a 25 percent increase in BMBC's affinity for postmodern values over the course of a six-week doctoral ministry project. By continuing to talk about the tides of cultural change, in openly discussing ways the Church has historically responded to culture, through exploring how the early church responded to life in a pagan Roman colony, and through positively visioning the Church's response to cultural tides, BMBC may enjoy solid footing for days ahead.

Where many churches may get into trouble here is in delaying discussion of change and resisting any form of acknowledgment that cultural change is all around. It remains prophetically true, "In any way that we view the future, it is fraught with problems. We live in a problem-perplexed present. And the future promises no relief from these problems. Instead they're likely to become more expansive and intensive. And they will become increasingly a challenge for God's people."[325] These words, penned 40 years ago by master communicator and preacher Herschel Hobbs, still ring with profound insight and clarity. As God's people, there is no time like the present to bridge vast cultural difference with godly grace, show authentic witness to neighbors near and far, embrace individual Spiritual giftedness as believer-priests, bridge faith and doubt in a tide of skepticism, bear witness to the world through biblical creation care, and show solidarity with the victimized and downtrodden – no matter their nationality, sex, political party, or creed. Only by living faithfully in the present can any church live into her future calling.

For a fairly moderate church like BMBC in a highly conservative county, "It's one thing to affirm and clarify our theology, and it's quite another to live by our theology so that it shapes and guides our ministry. To understand the theology of the rural church begins by putting it in the context of rural people."[326] At this juncture, it seems safe to say that the rural people of BMBC may embrace postmodern values at an increasingly rapid pace, along with other people in the region. Among the un-churched and de-churched, this proliferation of emerging values may prove even more precipitous. For centuries, many people have wrongly understood rural people as a residual population colonized by urban power centers and as backwards and slow to embrace change. Nothing could be further from the truth.

In early Baptist life, there is a fine example of rural Christians leading on the cutting edge of social, theological, and philosophical change. The Enlightenment and the Protestant Reformation brought much excitement and upheaval in the 16th and 17th centuries. One change brought about by this upheaval was the radical understanding of the priesthood of *all* believers. That is to say, "Women probably first began to preach in Holland in the 1630's in the Baptist churches, whose congregations had always included a large number of their sex."[327] While the main Baptist presence existed in Amsterdam with John Smyth's congregation, other congregations peppered the countryside in small rural hamlets. Some of the earliest women preachers were rural Baptist women who had become political refugees fleeing persecution and violence in their country of origin. Ironically, at the precipice of massive cultural change, rural Baptist women led in ways that still seem cutting edge in many Baptist circles. Their conviction, bravery, theological clarity, and even willingness to face harassment and imprisonment helped spur the Reformation forward and still inspire hope that a church like BMBC may, through embracing her own identify as rural and as Baptist, may ride the cultural wave of postmodernity in creative and inspired ways.

Chapter Eighteen: CHARTING A NEW COURSE THROUGH THE TIDES: SUMMARY AND CONCLUSIONS

Tides can be ridden and managed, or tides can cause great waves that crush and bring destruction. Scientifically speaking, even the changing climate has impact on tidal movements. As the climate of culture continually changes and outside forces pull and push on congregations nationwide, leaning into our identity and heritage may inspire us to navigate the waters of postmodernity. The story of 16th century Baptist "shepreachers" and "preacheresses" (as they were called)[328] is the story of every Baptist and therefore the story of BMBC. To live as a pioneering people in the present, we owe a great debt to the pioneering ones on whose shoulders we stand.

Since the Project

In continuing to follow through on provocative proposals arising from Vision Day and with the information gleaned from the congregational questionnaires, we worked diligently to build on the successes and learning of the ministry project. Several ministry opportunities and conversations have materialized since the project which can trace their origins back to the content and sequence of the project. Some of these conversations touch on themes directly addressed in the *Tides of Faith* sermon series, and some deal with practical and theological shifts in ministry strategy.

Essex County Homeless Organization

The Essex County Homeless Organization (ECHO) attempts to serve homeless individuals living in the county. Primarily, they function as a temporary hypothermic shelter in winter months.

Some fire code laws changed at a statewide level that made it difficult for a shelter to meet in a small congregation due to a square-footage requirement dictating that a temporary shelter cannot occupy more than 10 percent of the square footage in a building zoned as a house of worship. In urban areas with multiple large churches, this is not a problem. In a small county, the current state fire code makes it impossible for most churches to meet the requirements. For instance, if the shelter housed eight people with different sleeping areas for men and women and had a common area for people to eat, such an operation might occupy 20-30 percent of a small church building, thereby making the church and ECHO not in compliance with fire code. BMBC is one of the only churches in the county large enough to house up to ten people a night and have the shelter's use fall under the 10 percent requirement. Less than three weeks after the project, the deacons of BMBC voted unanimously to recommend that the church house ECHO for the winter while they looked for a more permanent location. In conversation, multiple deacons mentioned the sermons on solidarity and authenticity as motivating factors in their decision.

National Baptist – Muslim Dialogue

In the spring of 2018, Dr. Robert Sellars, one of my doctoral professors and chair of the Parliament of the World's Religions, invited me to participate in a delegation of Baptists at the Third National Baptist–Muslim Dialogue. The invitation was in part to represent rural Baptists from across North America at this historic meeting. Upon taking the idea to the deacons of the church and explaining the event and its purpose, the deacons voted unanimously to approve my participation in the dialogue. A few mentioned the need for BMBC to acknowledge

Chapter Eighteen: CHARTING A NEW COURSE THROUGH THE TIDES: SUMMARY AND CONCLUSIONS

the diversity existing in our own community and the trend of increasing tolerance in our country. One deacon who drives a local school bus route mentioned that he picks up several Muslim students each day and drops them off at the local high school. Upon my return from the dialogue, a report was given during the sermon time on Sunday, emphasizing the need for religious liberty for all people and God's command to love our neighbor, no matter their faith. Church members seemed receptive to the message, and the congregation entered discussions with regional Muslim leaders about doing cultural exchange between an urban mosque and our rural church. This is truly a unique opportunity that would have likely never materialized if the project had not led people to consider cultural change as a gift from God rather than a curse from the enemy.

A Rural Church Going Green

Until the Sunday focused on the *Tide of Green*, I had no idea a deacon in our church owned and operated a solar installation company. I incorrectly thought the deacon worked on the family farm! Immediately following the sermon, the individual approached me and offered to meet to discuss the church incorporating solar energy into our campus power grid. Since the initial conversation, the individual wrote out a plan for how the church could obtain solar panels and installations through grant proposals and green energy incentives. As of February 14, 2019, BMBC adopted solar power with the installation of 64 solar panels to offset our energy footprint. This conversation also spurred the properties committee to install new LED bulbs and fixtures in our high-use areas, like the office wing. The church is now discussing recycling and moving away from all Styrofoam products for food service. Finally, several individuals in the church started a community garden as a way to support the local food pantry and families in need. All of these conversations came out of the initial conversation during the *Tides of Faith* series and the ensuing conversations around creation care.

Teacher Appreciation Banquet

After the ministry project at the end of the school year, BMBC's church council led the church to host a Teacher Appreciation Banquet for all county teachers. Over 30 volunteers cooked, set up, secured donations and door prizes from local businesses, served food, or helped cleanup. Around 30 teachers and their families came to enjoy an evening of delicious food and live music. Nursery care was also provided for young children so teachers could truly enjoy the meal and evening entertainment. As far as anyone can tell, this was the first event of its kind in the county. It is worth noting here that all three Essex County Public Schools were (at that time) unaccredited by the State Department of Education due to low test scores attributable to high childhood poverty rates in the district. Many teachers left the banquet with joyful tears, saying this is the first time anyone in the community had ever thanked them for teaching. In the following week, the church received several hand-written thank-you notes from teachers, expressing their thanks for a lovely evening. This outreach helped BMBC people use their spiritual gifts in different ways, helped build trust with under-appreciated educators, and helped BMBC people begin to imagine how they might help transform and redeem the local culture to reflect the Kingdom of God. All three schools in Essex County are now accredited, and they arguably could not have done so without feeling community support.

EPILOGUE

Overall, exploring the postmodern tide at our rural church and dealing with it head on proved quite fruitful, and new and creative ministry continues to happen as a result. BMBC has a rich history of mission, witness, and strong leadership overall. If they continue to creatively address the needs of the emerging rural culture surrounding the church, then BMBC has a bright future, and as Herschel Hobbs suggested, the future is today. The best way to address anxiety concerning change in a church is calm pastoral presence and addressing the anxiety directly. To make it through tall waves in the ocean, one needs to steer the craft directly into the wave's path. The same is often true in congregational life. Cultural waves and movements will continue to happen until Christ returns, but thankfully, Christ promises His presence, "Always, to the end of the age."[329] Christ, of course, did not specify the end of which age, but He has indeed been present in the Imperial Age, the Medieval Age, the Renaissance and Enlightenment Age, the Revolutionary and Colonial Age, the Gilded Age, the Industrial Revolution Age, the Modern and Nation Building Age, and the Globalization and Post-Colonialization Age. Surely He is with us to the end of the Post-Modern Age. If we truly believe that Christ is with us and we are Christ's hands and feet for the world, then rural churches everywhere can ride the tides of cultural change in this age or any other. Today is the future, and now is the time to once again set sail.

Appendix 1. Quantitative Questionnaire

Beale Memorial Baptist Congregational Questionnaire

Instructions: Please fill out this questionnaire to the best of your ability.

SECTION 1) Questions 1-2: Please tell us a little about yourself. Circle one.

1. I was born between:

a. 2001-2016   b. 1981-2000   c. 1961-1980   d. 1946-1960   e. 1915-1945

2. I have lived in this town/county for...

a. 51+ years   b. 35-50 years   c. 20-34 years   d. 6-19 years   e. 0-5 years

SECTION 2) Questions 3-6: Circle <u>one</u> response for each of the following questions:

3. The statement I agree with the most is...
    a. In our church, things never change.
    b. Change occurs in our church, but it happens very slowly.
    c. Things are constantly changing in our church.

4. In terms of my own faith...
    a. My approach to faith has never changed.
    b. My approach to faith has slightly changed over time.
    c. My approach to faith has changed significantly over time.

5. When it comes to change in the church...

   a. Our church hates change.

   b. Our church grudgingly tolerates change.

   c. Our church embraces change.

6. When it comes to change in culture...

   a. Christians should resist culture.

   b. Christians should accommodate culture.

   c. Christians should seek to transform culture.

SCORING: *For each "a" answer, add one point. For each "b" answer, add five points, and for each "c" answer, add 10 points.*

Total _____

SECTION 2) Questions 7-14: Please rank each set of values 1-3 in order of importance to you with 1 being the most important.

7.	___ Cultural Heritage	___ Self-Sufficiency	___ Efficiency
8.	___ Solidarity	___ Love of Nature	___ Reason
9.	___ Diversity	___ Tradition	___ Growth
10.	___ Environmental Concern	___ Love of Community	___ Order
11.	___ Individual Identity	___ Family	___ Innovation
12.	___ Tolerance	___ Respect for the Elderly	___ Achievement
13.	___ Authenticity	___ Friendliness to Strangers	___ Progress
14.	___ Beauty	___ Legacy	___ Structure

C.1 Total _____   C.2 Total _____   C.3 Total _____

SCORING: *Add the totals for each column. Column one is postmodern values, column two is traditional values, and column three is modern values. The highest scoring column represents the value system with which you most readily sympathize.*

If your highest score was in column 1, write the number 30 on the "Total" line below. If your highest score was in column 2, write the number 20.

If your highest score was in column 3, write the number 10.

Total _____

SECTION 3) Questions 15-20: Please circle one response based on your level of agreement or disagreement with the following statements with 10 meaning "Strongly Agree" and one meaning "Strongly Disagree."

15. I feel like my generation has many of the same values as other generations.

    1   2   3   4   5   6   7   8   9   10

16. Various generations are represented in the leadership of our church.

    1   2   3   4   5   6   7   8   9   10

17. I am comfortable with the rising pluralism in our world.

    1   2   3   4   5   6   7   8   9   10

18. I do not feel like my values are under attack in today's culture.

    1   2   3   4   5   6   7   8   9   10

19. Our church is well prepared to meet the challenge of reaching the next generation.

    1   2   3   4   5   6   7   8   9   10

SCORING: *Add up the numbers you circled for 15-19.*

Total _____

SECTION 4) Follow-Up (Your personal information is kept confidential.)

PLEASE PRINT

Name_____ Phone _____

Email _____

Thank you for taking the time to complete this questionnaire. Upon completion, please return it to the church office or to Pastor Jonathan at your earliest convenience.

Appendix 2. Qualitative Questionnaire

Vision Day Group Discussion Questions

SECTION 1) Interviewee Information – Fill out this information before arriving for the interview.

Facilitator Name: _____

People around the Table:

_____

_____

SECTION 2) Ask these questions and see where the conversation leads. Do not feel the need to ask every question as it may detract from the stories the interviewees need to tell.

1. What are some of the biggest changes in culture you've witnessed in your lifetime? Can you think of positive ways Beale has responded to cultural change over the years?

_____

_____

2. Reflecting on your entire experience at Beale Memorial Baptist, recall a time when you felt engaged, alive, and passionate about our church's ministry. What happened? Who was involved? How were you impacted?

_____

_____

3. Describe a time you were proud of our church for handling change in a positive way. What was the change? Who set the pace for this change? How did it impact your view of the church?

_____
_____
_____

4. What aspect of our church's ministry has contributed the most to your spiritual life? For example, would you name relationships or a program, ministry, trip, or conference? How/why did this aspect of the ministry impact you so much?

_____
_____
_____

5. How are the values of your generation different from the values of other generations? Real world example? Is this difference positive or negative?

_____
_____
_____

6. Considering the shifting culture we live in, what are your feelings about the future of the church?

_____
_____
_____

7. If you could wish two or three things for our church's future, what would they be, and why? If we tried something and there was no possibility of failure, what would you dream for the church?

_____

_____

_____

8. What are a few important characteristics about our church's culture that make us unique? How can we build on those qualities in the future?

_____

_____

_____

9. Is there anything else you would like to say concerning how you feel about... (only ask about one or two):

_____ Change in the world?

_____ The values you hold versus the values the world holds?

_____ How our church can adapt to change?

_____ Your own history with the congregation?

Post Survey Notes:

_____ Responses have been typed   _____ "Thank you" notes sent

Appendix 3. Vision Workshop

Workshop Name: *Riding the Tide – Our Ability to Thrive in the Midst of Cultural Change*

Pre-Workshop:
1. Contact leaders and recruit at least 10 people to help for the day.
2. Facilitate training for deacons willing to assist in administering the ethnographic questionnaires. Discussion facilitators will be briefed on ethnographic methods, appreciative inquiry, and provocative proposals during a 30-minute training session (offered twice before the Vision Workshop).
3. Run announcements in bulletins, advertising workshop for three weeks prior to the event.
4. Secure supplies needed for the day – pencils, notepads, giveaways, and door prizes to entice attendance and participation, etc.
5. Print off handouts and schedules for the event.
6. Design power-point slides to complement the event.

8:00 a.m.	Arrival and setup
8:30 a.m.	Staff registration table with a volunteer.
9:00 a.m.	Kickoff Vision Day with a brief welcome, two worship songs, and a short explanation of the schedule for the day.
9:15 a.m.	Have people move toward sitting at round tables, encouraging them to make

	sure there is a diverse mix of people at the table. Make sure there is a trained facilitator at each table.
9:30 a.m.	Explain the metaphor of the tide and expound on the purpose of appreciative inquiry as a method of growing as a congregation. Lead the tables to do an adult-friendly ice-breaker game so people begin to feel comfortable with one another.
10:00 a.m.	Get people to sit back at their tables and invite lay leaders to begin the process of administering the qualitative questionnaire with people at their table – Questions 1-4.
10:40 a.m.	Break and Refreshments
10:50 a.m.	Qualitative Questionnaire: Part 2, Questions 5-9
11:20 a.m.	Help the group process their stories. Ask someone from each table to report on themes that emerged in conversation.
11:30 a.m.	After identifying micro-stories and themes emerging from the group, identify what ideas around which the church is feeling positive synergy.
12:00 p.m.	Break for Lunch. While people are eating, explain the idea of provocative proposals, perhaps using the example from the book:

Epilogue

"Beale Memorial Baptist Church is the most racially diverse congregation within a 40-minute drive from Tappahannock. Their commitment to welcoming people of all backgrounds became apparent several years ago when they leaned into their call to become a church of regional influence and embrace the shifting demographics of their community. When Beale hired a young African-American as a minister to seniors, people really began to notice a change in the passion the church had for reflecting the true diversity of the Body of Christ."

12:30 p.m.	Invite each table to create its own provocative proposal based on all we've learned during the day. Encourage everyone to consider naming a positive future for Beale as a church.
1:00 p.m.	Invite a representative from each table to read the provocative proposal that came out of their conversation.
1:15 p.m.	Give final encouragement to the people. Explain that our church can build on our shared dreams, weathering the tides of cultural change through bold and positive thinking and a creative commitment to furthering God's Kingdom.
1:20 p.m.	Closing Prayer

Appendix 4. Vision Day Feedback Form

Please rank the following questions on a scale of 1-10 (1 meaning *Strongly Disagree* and 10 meaning *Strongly Agree*).

1. Vision Day was helpful in facilitating discussion about our church's future.

    1   2   3   4   5   6   7   8   9   10

2. If Beale had another Vision Day in the next few years, I would make plans to attend.

    1   2   3   4   5   6   7   8   9   10

3. I am hopeful that positive vision for the church will result from today's conversation.

    1   2   3   4   5   6   7   8   9   10

4. I feel that Beale will effectively adapt to the culture as it shifts and changes.

    1   2   3   4   5   6   7   8   9   10

5. Do you have any comments or feedback concerning today's event?

    _____

    _____

    _____

    _____

    _____

REFERENCES

Works Consulted

1. Adams, Rachel Swann. *The Small Church and Christian Education*. Philadelphia: The Westminster Press, 1961.

2. Anderson, Rebecca M. Ottmar. "New Life off The Beaten Track: A Study of Congregational Redevelopment in Small, Rural PCUSA Churches." D.Min. diss., Union Theological Seminary, 2008.

3. Ashley, Jennifer, Ed. *The Relevant Church: A New Vision for Communities of Faith*. Lake Marley, FL: Relevant Books, 2004

4. Austin, Richard Cartwright. *Baptized into Wilderness: A Christian Perspective on John Muir*. Atlanta: John Knox Press, 1987.

5. Bass, Diana Butler. *Christianity for the Rest of Us: How the Neighborhood Church Is Transforming Faith*. San Francisco: HarperSanFrancisco, 2006.

6. Bernanos, Georges. *The Diary of a Country Priest*. New York: The Macmillan Company, 1937.

7. Berry, Wendell. *Jaber Crow*. Berkeley: Counterpoint, 2000.

8. Bosch, David. *Transforming Mission: Paradigm Shifts in Theology of Mission*. New York: Orbis Books, 2005.

9. Bugg, Charles B. and Alan Redditt. *Preaching That Connects*. Macon, GA: Smyth & Helwys, 2016.

10. Buttrick, David. "Preaching to the Elderly." In *Transitions: Leading Churches through Change*. Davis Mosser ed. Louisville: Westminster John Knox Press, 2011.

11. Byassee, Jason. *The Gifts of the Small Church*. Nashville: Abingdon Press, 2010.

12. Callahan, Kennon L. *Visiting in an Age of Mission: A Handbook for Person-to-Person Ministry*. San Francisco: HarperSanFrancisco, 1994.

13. Campbell, Barry. *Healthy and Growing Smaller Churches: Extraordinary Ministry*. Nashville: LifeWay Press, 1998.

14. Canada, David. *Spiritual Leadership in the Small Membership Church*. Nashville: Abingdon Press, 2005.

15. Cannato, Judy. *Field of Compassion: How the New Cosmology Is Transforming Spiritual Life*. Notre Dame, IN: Sorin Books, 2010.

16. Chilcote, Paul W. and Laceye C. Warner, Eds. *The Study of Evangelism: Exploring a Missional Practice of the Church*. Grand Rapids: William B. Eerdmans Publishing Company, 2008.

17. Claypool, John R. *The Hopeful Heart*. New York: Morehouse Publishing, 2003.

18. Coles, Robert. *Harvard Diary: Reflection on the Sacred and the Secular*. New York: Crossroad, 1992.

19. Convergence U.S. "Charter," Accessed April 13, 2015. www.convergenceus.org/charter.

20. Corcoran, Kevin, Ed. *Church in The Present Tense: A Candid Look at What's Emerging*. Grand Rapids: Brazos Press, 2011.

21. Crabtree, Charles T. *The Contemporary Pastor*. Springfield, MO: Gospel Publishing House, 1992.

22. Dale, Tony, Felicity Dale, and George Barna. *Small Is Big! Unleashing the Big Impact of Intentionally Small Churches*. Brentwood, TN: Barna Publishing, 2009.

References

23. Earp, Edwin L. *The Rural Church Movement*. New York: The Methodist Book Concern, 1914.

24. Essex Woman's Club Executive Committee, *Essex County Virginia: Its Historic Homes, Landmarks, and Traditions*. Richmond: The Williams Printing Company, 1940.

25. Estock, Beth Ann and Paul Nixon. *Weird Church: Welcome to the Twenty-First Century*.

26. Cleveland, OH: The Pilgrim Press, 2016.

27. Felton, Ralph A., and Arthur Raper. *Rural Churches and Pastors*. New York: Committee for the Training of Negro Pastors of the Phelps-Stokes Fund and the Home Missions Council of North America, 1946.

28. Francis, Leslie J. and Mandy Robbins, eds. *Rural Life and Rural Church: Theological and Empirical Perspectives*. Bristol, CT: Equinox, 2012.

29. Gibbs, Eddie. *Church Next: Quantum Changes in How We Do Ministry*. Downers Grove, IL: InterVarsity Press, 2000.

30. Gill, C.O., and Gifford Pinchot. *The Country Church*. New York: The Macmillan Company, 1913.

31. Gooder, Paula. *Searching for Meaning-An Introduction to Interpreting the New Testament*. Louisville: Westminster John Knox, 2009.

32. Groothuis, Douglas. *The Soul in Cyber-Space*. Grand Rapids: Baker Books, 1997.

33. Gudorf, Christine, E. *Comparative Religious Ethics: Everyday Decisions for Our Everyday Lives*. Minneapolis: Fortress Press, 2013.

34. Hall, Warner L. *Symbols of the Faith*. Richmond: The CLC Press, 1965.

35. Handy, Charles. *The Age of Paradox*. Boston: Harvard Business School Press, 1994.

36. Hart, David Bentley. *Against Postmodernity.* W.B. Eerdmans, 2003.

37. Hart, D.G. *That Old-time Religion in Modern America: Evangelical Protestantism in the Twentieth Century.* Chicago: Ivan R. Dee, 2002.

38. Hassinger, Edward W., John S Holik, and J. Kenneth Benson. *The Rural Church: Learning from Three Decades of Change.* Nashville: Abingdon Press, 1988.

39. Heine, Susan. *Women and Early Christianity: A Reappraisal.* Translated by John Bowden. Minneapolis: Augsburg Publishing House, 1988.

40. Hesselgrave, David J. *Scripture and Strategy: The Use of the Bible in Postmodern Church and Mission.* Pasadena, CA: William Carey Library, 1994.

41. Hicks, Rick, and Kathy Hicks. *Boomers, Xers, and Other Strangers: Understanding Generational Difference That Divide Us.* Wheaton: Tyndale House Publishers, 1999.

42. Hill, Samuel S. Jr. *Southern Churches in Crisis.* Boston: Beacon Press, 1967.

43. Hitchens, Peter. *The Rage against God.* New York: Continuum, 2010.

44. Hoeft, Jeanne, L. Shannon Jung and Joretta Marshall. *Practicing Care in Rural Congregations and Communities.* Minneapolis: Fortress Press, 2013.

45. Hunter, George G., III. *How to Reach Secular People.* Nashville: Abingdon Press, 1992.

46. Hunter, Kent R. *Move Your Church to Action.* Nashville: Abingdon Press, 2000.

47. Isaac, Rhys. *The Transformation of Virginia: 1740-1790.* Chapel Hill: University of North Carolina Press, 1989

48. Jensen, David H. *Living Hope: The Future of Christian Faith.* Louisville, KY: Westminster John Knox Press, 2010.

49. Jewett, Robert. *Christian Tolerance: Paul's Message to the Modern Church.* Philadelphia: The Westminster Press, 1982.

50. Johnson, Charles. *To Stem This Tide: A Survey of Racial Tension Areas in the United States.* Boston: Pilgrim Press, 1943.

51. Jung, Shannon, ed. *Rural Ministry: The Shape of Renewal to Come.* Nashville: Abingdon, 1998.

52. Kimball, Dan. *Emerging Worship: Creating Worship Gatherings for New Generations.* Grand Rapids, MI: Zondervan, 2004.

53. Landis, Benson Y. *Rural Church Life in the Middle West.* New York: George H. Doran Company, 1922.

54. LaRocque, Kathleen. "Understanding Growth as the Body of Christ: A Study of Small Congregations and the Elements That Determine 'Success' or 'Failure.'" D.Min. diss., Union Theological Seminary, 2008.

55. Lawson, John. *Green and Pleasant Land.* London: SCM Press LTD, 1955.

56. Lee, Bernard J., and Michael A. Cowan. *Gathered and Sent: The Mission of Small Church Communities Today.* New York: Paulist Press, 2003.

57. Lindstrom, David Edgar. *The Church in Rural Life.* Champaign, IL: The Gerrard Press, 1939.

58. Loughlin, Gerald. *Queer Theology: Rethinking the Western Body.* Malden: Blackwell Publishing, 2007.

59. Massey, Don W., and Sue Massey. *Colonial Churches of Virginia.* Charlottesville: Howell Press, 2003.

60. McLaughlin, Henry W. *Christ and the Country People.* Richmond: Presbyterian Committee of Publication, 1928.

61. McLaughlin, Henry W., Ed. *The Country Church and Public Affairs*. New York: The Macmillan Company, 1930.

62. McLeod, Cliff Hill, Jr. "Congregational Narrative: Its Implication for Forming And Transforming Congregational Identity." D.Min. diss., Union Theological Seminary, 1996.

63. McNeal, Reggie. *The Present Future: Six Tough Questions for the Church*. San Francisco: Josey Bass, 2003.

64. Miller, Mark. *Experiential Storytelling: (Re)Discovering Narrative to Communicate God's Message*. El Cajon: Emergent Ys, 2003.

65. Mills, Harlow S. *The Making of a Country Parish: A Story*. New York: Missionary Education Movement of the United States and Canada, 1914.

66. Mohler, R. Albert, Jr. Ed. *The Southern Baptist Journal of Theology: Responses to Universalism and Inclusivism* Vol. 2, no. 2 (Summer 1998).

67. Nash, Robert N., Jr. *An 8-Track Church in a CD World: The Modern Church in the Postmodern World*. Macon, GA: Smyth and Helwys Publishing, 1997.

68. Norris, Kathleen. *Dakota: A Spiritual Geography*. Boston: Houghton Mifflin Company, 1993.

69. Osmer, Richard R. *Practical Theology: An Introduction*. Grand Rapids: William B. Eerdmans Publishing Company, 2008.

70. Pappas, Anthony G. *Entering the World of the Small Church*. Bethesda, MD: Alban Institute, 2000.

71. Parry, Alan, and Robert E. Doan. *Story Re-Visions: Narrative Therapy in the Postmodern World*. New York: The Guilford Press, 1994.

72. Phillips, Kim M. and Barry Reay, eds. *Sexualities in History: A Reader*. New York: Routledge, 2002.

73. Powe, F. Douglas, Jr., and Jasmine Rose Smothers. *Not Safe for Church: Ten Commandments for Reaching New Generations.* Nashville: Abingdon Press, 2015.

74. Quinn, Bernard. *The Small Rural Parish.* New York: The Parish Project of The National Council of Catholic Bishops, 1980.

75. Raschke, Carl. *GloboChrist: The Great Commission Takes a Postmodern Turn.* Grand Rapids: Baker Academic, 2008.

76. Ray, David R. *The Big Small Church Book.* Cleveland, OH: Pilgrim Press, 1992.

77. Ray, David R. *The Indispensable Guide for Smaller Churches.* Cleveland, OH: Pilgrim Press, 2003.

78. Ried, Robert Stephen. "Responding to Resistance during a Change Process." In *Transitions: Leading Churches Through Change.* Davis Mosser ed. Louisville: Westminster John Knox Press, 2011.

79. Roads, Charles Roads. *Rural Christendom.* Philadelphia: American Sunday School Union, 1909.

80. Rossouw, G. J. 1993. "Theology in a postmodern culture: ten challenges." *HTS Teologiese Studies/Theological Studies* 49, no 4 (Winter): 894-907, Accessed October 19, 2018. https://hts.org.za/index.php/hts/article/view/2528/4341.

81. Rouse, Rick, and Craig Van Gelder. *A Field Guide for the Missional Congregation: Embarking on a Journey of Transformation.* Minneapolis, Augsburg Fortress, 2008.

82. Rutledge, Christopher J. "Burnout and the Practice of Ministry among Rural Clergy." In *Rural Life and Rural Church: Theological and Empirical Perspectives*, eds. Leslie J. Francis and Mandy Robbins. Bristol, CT, Equinox Publishing, 2012.

83. Sartorius, Peter. *Churches in Rural Development: Guidelines for Actions.* Geneva: World Council of Churches, 1975.

84. Sevier, Melissa Bane. *Journeying toward Renewal: A Spiritual Companion for Pastoral Sabbaticals*. Bethesda, MD: Alban, 2002.

85. Shah, Timothy Samuel, Thomas F. Farr, and Jack Friedman, eds. *Religious Freedom and Gay Rights: Emerging Conflicts in the United States and Europe*. New York: Oxford University Press, 2016.

86. Shook, John R. *The God Debates: A 21st Century Guide for Atheists and Believers (and Everyone in Between)*. Malden, MA: Wiley-Blackwell, 2010.

87. Smith, Huston. *Beyond the Post-Modern Mind*. Wheaton: The Theosophical Publishing House, 1982.

88. Snyder, Howard A., and Daniel V. Runyon. *Decoding the Church: Mapping the DNA of Christ's Body*. Grand Rapids: Baker Books, 2002.

89. Sorenson, Stephen W. *Like Your Neighbor? Doing Everyday Evangelism on Common Ground*. Downers Grove: Intervarsity Press, 2005.

90. Spindle, Grace Dryden. *Beale Memorial Baptist Church: The First Hundred Years, 1875-1975*.

91. Sweet, Leonard. *Soul Tsunami: Sink or Swim in the New Millennium Culture*. Grand Rapids: Zondervan Publishing House, 1999.

92. Temple, Gray. *Gay Unions: In the Light of Scripture, Tradition, and Reason*. New York: Church Publishing, 2004.

93. Thompson, Wayne E., and David L. Cummins, *This Day in Baptist History: 366 Daily Devotions Drawn from the Baptist Heritage*. Greenville: Bob Jones University Press, 1993.

94. Tickle, Phyllis. "Progressive vs Emergence Christianity: From Where I Sit." Accessed April 23, 2015. http://www.patheos.com/Resources/Additional-Resources/Progressive-vs-

Emergence-Christianity-From-Where-I-Sit-Phyllis-Tickle-06-13-2011?offset=1&max=1.

95. Vance, J.D. *Hillbilly Elegy: A Memoir of a Family and Culture in Crisis.* New York: Harper Publishing, 2016.

96. Vidich, Arthur J. and Joseph Bensman. *Small Town in Mass Society: Class, Power and Religion in a Rural Community,* Revised Ed. Princeton: Princeton University Press, 1968.

97. Vines, Matthew. *God and the Gay Christian: The Biblical Case in Support of Same-Sex Relationships.* New York: Crown Publishing Group, 2014.

98. Virginia Baptist Historic Society. "Gold Tried in the Fire: The Baptists of Virginia's Northern Neck." *The Virginia Baptist Register*, no. 56 (2017).

99. Weatherhead, Leslie D. *The Christian Agnostic.* New York: Abingdon, 1965.

100. Westermann, Claus. *Basic Forms of Prophetic Speech.* Translated by Hugh Clayton White. Louisville: Westminster John Knox Press, 1991.

101. Wilson, Jim L. *Future Church: Ministry in a Post-Seeker Age.* Nashville: Broadman and Holeman Publishers, 2004.

102. Woodward, J.R. *Creating a Missional Culture: Equipping the Church for the Sake of the World.* Downers Grove: IVP Books, 2012.

103. Woodward, J.R., and Dan White Jr. *The Church as Movement: Starting and Sustaining Missional-Incarnational Communities.*

104. Zvi, Ehud Ben and Christoph Levin, eds. *Centers and Peripheries in the Early Second Temple Period.* Tubingen: Mohr Siebeck, 2016.

Endnotes

Works Cited

1. Robert A. Petrin, Kai A. Schafft, Judith L. Meece, "Educational Sorting and Residential Aspirations Among Rural High School Students: What Are the Contributions of Schools and Educators to Rural Brain Drain?", *American Educational Research Journal*, Vol 51, Issue 2, (April, 1, 2014): page(s): 294-326.

2. David L. Brown and Kai A. Schafft, *Rural People and Communities in the 21st Century: Resilience and Transformation* (Cambridge, UK: Polity Press, 2011), 10.

3. Catholic Rural Life Conference, *Manifesto On Rural Life*, 3rd ed. (Milwaukee: Bruce Publishing Company, 1939), 112.

4. Lee Shapiro, "The Unprecedented Pace of Change," *Forbes*, February 25, 2021.

5. Paul Cloke, "Conceptualizing Rurality," in *The Handbook of Rural Studies*, eds. Paul Cloke, Terry Marsden, and Patrick Mooney (Thousand Oaks, CA: Sage Publications, 2006), 18.

6. Willem Roper, "COVID-19 is Pushing Americans Out of Cities and Into the Country," *World Economic Forum*, January, 19, 2021. (Accessed March 15, 2021, https://www.weforum.org/agenda/2021/01/rural-life-cities-countryside-covid-coronavirus-united-states-us-usa-america/).

7. Ibid., 19.

8   Ibid., 19.

9   Genesis 1:26, NRSV

10 Proverbs 28:16, NRSV.

11 Proverbs 28:16, NIV.

12 Luke 16:10, NRSV.

13 Ibid., Brown and Schafft, *Rural People and Communities in the 21st Century*,11.

14 Ibid., 10.

15 Ibid., 35.

16 Ibid., 35.

17 Ibid., 96.

18 Amos 5:11-12, NRSV.

19 Amos 5:24, NRSV.

20 Leonard Edloe, "There Are a Lot of Theo-Ethical Issues," The rural Black Church blog, entry posted December 10, 2019, http://www.theruralblackchurch.com/2019/12/there-are-lot-of-theo-ethical-issues.html.

21 Ibid., Brown and Schafft, *Rural People and Communities in the 21st Century*,109.

22 Ruth Panelli, "Rural Society," in *The Handbook of Rural Studies*, eds. Paul Cloke, Terry Marsden, and Patrick Mooney (Thousand Oaks, CA: Sage Publications, 2006), 67.

23 Ibid., 114-117.

24 Ibid., Brown and Schafft, *Rural People and Communities in the 21st Century*,157.

25 Ibid., 158.

26 Jennifer Sherman, *Those Who Work, Those Who Don't: Poverty, Morality, and Family in Rural America* (Minneapolis: University of Minnesota Press, 2009), Loc. 1157, Kindle.

27 Ibid., Loc. 1244, Kindle.

28 Ibid., Loc. 1280, Kindle.

29 Ibid., Loc. 266, Kindle.

30 Ibid., Loc. 291, Kindle.

31 Ibid., Loc. 291, Kindle.

32 Ibid., Brown and Schafft, *Rural People and Communities in the 21st Century*, 194.

33 Lawrence W. Farris, *Dynamics of Small Town Ministry* (Herndon, VA: The Alban Institute, 2000), 3.

34 Nancey C. Murphy, *Beyond Liberalism and Fundamentalism: How Modern and Postmodern Philosophy Set the Theological Agenda*, The Rockwell Lecture Series (Valley Forge, PA.: Trinity Press International, 1996), 13.

35 "Postmodernism," *Stanford Encyclopedia of Philosophy*, accessed October 19, 2018, https://plato.stanford.edu/entries/postmodernism/.

36 Hans Küng, *Christianity: Essence, History, Future* (New York: Continuum, 1996), 771.

37 Drew Dyck, *Generation Ex-Christian: Why Young Adults Are Leaving the Faith…And How to Bring Them Back,* (Chicago: Moody, 2010), 15-31.

38 Google Search, https://www.google.com/#q=postmodern+church, accessed February 8, 2015.

39 Murphy, *Beyond Liberalism and Fundamentalism*, 109.

40 James N. Barnes and Kalyn Coatney, "Progress on Broadband Adoption in Rural America," *Choices-The Magazine of Food Farm, and Resource Issues*, 1st Quarter 2015, accessed February 8, 2015, http://www.choicesmagazine.org/magazine/pdf/cmsarticle_405.pdf.

41 Küng, *Christianity*, 775.

42 *It's a Wonderful Life*, directed by Frank Capra, (Liberty Films, 1946), DVD (Paramount, 2006).

43 Town Planning Commission, *Town of Tappahannock Comprehensive Plan 2014* (Tappahannock, 2014), 11, accessed March 11, 2019, http://www.tappahannock-va.gov/pdflib/comp-plan-revised-v4.pdf.

44 Troy Bronsink, "The Art of Emergence: Being God's Handiwork," in *An Emergent Manifesto of Hope: Key leaders Offer an Inside Look*, Doug Pagitt and Tony Jones, eds. (Grand Rapids: BakerBooks, 2007), Chapter 5.

45 Jonathan Murdoch, "Networking Rurality: Emergent Complexity in the Countryside," in *The Handbook of Rural Studies*, eds. Paul Cloke, Terry Marsden and Patrick Mooney (Thousand Oaks, CA: Sage Publications, 2006), 172.

46 Rodolpho Carrasco, "A Pound of Social Justice: Beyond Fighting for a Just Cause," in *An Emergent Manifesto of Hope—Key leaders Offer an Inside Look*, eds. Doug Paggit and Tony Jones (Grand Rapids: Baker Books, 2007), 254.

47 Dan Kimball, *They Like Jesus But Not the Church* (Grand Rapids: Zondervan, 2007), Kindle, Location 405.

48 Larry S. Chowning, *Images of America: Urbanna* (Charleston: Arcadia, 2012), 9.

49 Special relations serves as an approach in sociology that explores the intersectionality of geographic spaces, like rural bedroom communities and metropolitan areas. See Thomas et. al., *Critical Rural Theory: Structure, Space, Culture* (New York: Lexington Books, 2011).

50 Sherman, *Those Who Work, Those Who Don't*, Location 223-225, Kindle.

51 Previously cited, *The Handbook of Rural Studies* (Sage Publications, 2006), is an excellent example. Over thirty premier rural studies scholars contribute thoughtful essays, totaling over five-hundred pages, and only a handful of contributors explore postmodernity in rural communities.

52 Chris Peterson, comment in Emerging Village Community's online discussion group in response to an article shared from www.smalltownchurches.org, February 9, 2015 (1:44 p.m. ET), accessed February 9, 2015, https://www.facebook.com/groups/176519765766429/.

53 Ibid.

54 Murphy, 94.

55 Thomas, Lowe, Fulkerson and Smith (2011), Flora and Flora (2013), Jung and Agria (1997), Hoeft, Jung and Marshall (2013). See Works Cited and Works Consulted.

56 Glenn Daman, *The Forgotten Church: Why Rural Ministry Matters for Every Church in America* (Chicago, IL: Moody Publishers, 2018), 29.

57 Ibid., 30.

58 Paul Cloke, "Rurality and Racialized Others: Out of Place in the Countryside?," in *The Handbook of Rural Studies*, eds. Paul Cloke, Terry Marsden, and Patrick Mooney (Thousand Oaks, CA: Sage Publications, 2006), 381.

59 Paul Cloke, "Rurality and Otherness," in *The Handbook of Rural Studies*, eds. Paul Cloke, Terry Marsden, and Patrick Mooney (Thousand Oaks, CA: Sage Publications, 2006), 450-54.

60 Fritz Kling, *The Meeting of the Waters: 7 Global Currents That Are Shaping the World* (Colorado Springs: David C. Cooke, 2010), Kindle, 108.

61 Thomas, et.al., 62.

62 Nancy Murphy, *Beyond Liberalism and Fundamentalism: How Modern and Postmodern Philosophy Set the Theological Agenda* (Harrisburg, PA: Trinity Press International, 2007) 88-94.

63 Alexander R. Thomas, Brian M. Lowe, Gregory Fulkerson, and Polly J. Smith, *Critical Rural Theory: Structure, Space, Culture* (New York: Lexington Books, 2011), 62.

64 Éva G. Fekete, and Katalin Liptak, "Postmodern Values in Rural Peripheries," *Journal of Settlements and Spatial Planning* vol. 2, no. 1 (2011) 1-7.

65 Éva G. Fekete, and Katalin Liptak, "Postmodern Values in Rural Peripheries," 2-3.

66 Thomas, Lowe, Fulkerson, and Smith, *Critical Rural Theory*, 9.

67 Ibid..

68 Ibid..

69 Ibid., 31.

70 Éva G. Fekete, and Katalin Liptak, "Postmodern Values in Rural Peripheries," 6-7.

71 Thomas, Lowe, Fulkerson, and Smith, *Critical Rural Theory*, 64.

72 Ibid., 126.

73 Cornelia Butler Flora and Jan Flora, *Rural Communities: Legacy and Change*, 4th Ed. (Boulder, CO: Westview Press, 2013), 13.

74 Flora and Flora, 3.

75 Ibid..

76 Ibid..

77 Bob Dale and Bill Wilson, *Weaving Strong Leaders: How Leaders Grow Down, Grow Up, and Grow Together* (Macon, GA: Nurturing Faith Publishing, 2016), 9-48.

78 Ibid., 9.

79 Howard W. Stone and James O. Duke, *How to Think Theologically*, Second Edition (Minneapolis, MN: Fortress Press, 2006), Kindle, Loc. 269.

80 Dale and Wilson, *Weaving Strong Leaders*, 9.

81 Tod Bolsinger, *Canoeing the Mountain: Christian Leadership in Uncharted Territory* (Downers Grove, IL: IVP Books, 2015), Book sub-title.

82 Ibid., 31.

83 Ibid., 101.

84 Ibid., 19.

85 Edward H. Hammett, *Spiritual Leadership in a Secular Age: Building Bridges Instead of Barriers* (St. Louis, MO: Chalice Press, 2005), 77.

86 Hammett, 77.

87 Ibid., 75.

88 Shannon L. Jung and Mary A. Agria. *Rural Congregational Studies: A Guide for Good Shepherds*, (Nashville: Abingdon Press, 1997), 102.

89 Ibid., 90-91.

90 Alan Hirsch, *5Q: Reactivating the Original Intelligence and Capacity of the Body of Christ* (Columbia: 100Movements, 2017), 182.

91 Ibid., 189.

92 William H. Willimon, *Worship as Pastoral Care* (Nashville: Abingdon Press, 1979), 95-96.

93 George Barna, *Effectively Building Lay Leadership Teams* (Ventura, CA: Issachar Resources, 2001), 152.

94 Edward Farley, *Deep Symbols: Their Postmodern Effacement and Reclamation* (Valley Forge, PA: Trinity Press International, 1996), 11.

95 Cloke, "Rurality and Racialized Others," 380.
96 Farley, 11.
97 Ibid..
98 Ibid., 14.
99 Ibid..
100 Ibid., 14-15.
101 "Jefferson's Bible: The Life and Morals of Jesus of Nazareth," The Smithsonian's National Museum of American History, accessed January 14, 2018, http://americanhistory.si.edu/exhibitions/jefferson-bible.
102 Farley, 16.
103 James W. Watts, *Ritual and Rhetoric in Leviticus: From Sacrifice to Scripture* (New York. NY: Cambridge University Press, 2007), 214.
104 Watts, 214.
105 Ibid., 215.
106 "U.S. Public Becoming Less Religious," Pew Research Center, accessed January 14, 2018, http://www.pewforum.org/2015/11/03/u-s-public-becoming-less-religious/.
107 Watts, 217.
108 Farley, 19.
109 J. B. MacKennon, "America's Last Ban on Sunday Shopping," *The New Yorker*, February 7, 2015, accessed October 19, 2018, https://www.newyorker.com/business/currency/americas-last-ban-sunday-shopping.
110 Farley, 27.
111 Bolsinger, 101.
112 Prov 29:18 (KJV).

113 Michael Frost and Christina Rice, *To Alter Your World: Partnering with God to Rebirth Our Communities* (Downers Grove, IL: IVP Books, 2017), 45.

114 Frost and Rice, 45.

115 Farley, 68-70.

116 Ibid., 68.

117 Ibid., 68-70.

118 Ibid., 70.

119 James Davison Hunter, *To Change the World: The Irony, Tragedy, and Possibility of Christianity in the Late Modern World* (New York, NY: Oxford University Press, 2010), 215.

120 Ibid., 215-16.

121 Ibid., 217.

122 Ibid., 217.

123 Frost and Rice, 56.

124 "Do Church 'Publicity Stunts' Send the Wrong Message?: Rifle raffles. Pastor boxing matches. How far is too far when it comes to church marketing?", *Relevant*, accessed on January 14, 2018, https://relevantmagazine.com/god/church/do-church-publicity-stunts-send-wrong-message.

125 Frost and Rice, 52.

126 Mary Clark Moschella, *Ethnography as Pastoral Practice: An Introduction* (Cleveland, OH: The Pilgrim Press, 2008), 237.

127 Ibid., 255.

128 *Keep Us All Close*, Eastlake Community Church Bandcamp webpage, https://eastlakecommunitychurch.bandcamp.com/track/keep-us-all-close, accessed September 7, 2018.

129 See *Against Postmodernity* by David Bentley Hart (W.B. Eerdmans, 2003), and G. J. Rossouw, "Theology in a

postmodern culture: ten challenges," *HTS Teologiese Studies/ Theological Studies* 49, no 4 (January 1993): 894-907, accessed October 19, 2018, https://hts.org.za/index.php/hts/article/view/2528/4341.

130 See Henry W. McLaughlin, *Christ and the Country People* (Richmond: Presbyterian Committee of Publication, 1928) or John Lawson, *Green and Pleasant Land* (London: SCM Press LTD, 1955) or Charles Roads, *Rural Christendom* (Philadelphia: American Sunday School Union, 1909).

131 Used in this sense, the word "Queer" is not derogatory in that the term is preferred by LGBTQIA theologians and is thus a standard term for gay theology. See Paula Gooder, *Searching for Meaning-An Introduction to Interpreting the New Testament* (Louisville, Westminster John Knox, 2009).

132 Exodus 7:8; 8:16; 9:8; 12:1; 12:43; 16:9 (NRSV).

133 James Strong, *The New Strong's Expanded Exhaustive Concordance of the Bible, Red Letter ed.* (Nashville: Thomas Nelson Publishers, 2001), 22.

134 James D. Findlay, *From Prophet to Priest: The Characterization of Aaron in the Pentateuch* (Bristol, CT: Peeters, 2017), 125.

135 Findlay, 132.

136 Exodus 32:22 (NRSV).

137 Findlay, 177.

138 Deborah W. Rooke, *Zadock's Heirs: The Role and Development of the High Priesthood in Ancient Israel* (Oxford: Oxford University Press, 2000), 16.

139 Lev 9 (NRSV).

140 Matt 3:13-17; Mark 1:9-11; Luke 3:21-23; John 1:29-33 (NRSV).

141 Heb 5:1-6 (NRSV).

142 Num 20:22-29 (NRSV).

143 Num 20:12 (NRSV).

144 Findlay, 301.

145 Matt 28:16-20 (NRSV).

146 Mark 1:14-15 (NRSV).

147 Strong, 481.

148 George Eldon Ladd, *A Theology of the New Testament* (Grand Rapids, MI: Wm. B. Eerdmans Publishing Company, 1974), 63-64.

149 Strong, 162.

150 Mark 1:15 (NRSV).

151 Matt 13:31-32 (NRSV).

152 Strong, 165.

153 Warren C. Trenchard, *Complete Vocabulary Guide to The Greek New Testament* (Grand Rapids: Zondervan, 1998), 3.

154 Matt 13:32 (NRSV).

155 Henk P. Medema, and Lytton John Musselman, "Mustard," Old Dominion University Plant Site, April 11, 2017, accessed May 19, 2018, http://ww2.odu.edu/~lmusselm/plant/bible/mustard.php.

156 Carol Howard Merrit, *Reframing Hope: Vital Ministry in a New Generation* (Herndon, VA: Alban, 2010), 112.

157 Ladd, 113.

158 Doug Pagitt, "The Emerging Church and Embodied Theology" in *Listening to the Beliefs of Emerging Churches*, ed. Robert Webber (Grand Rapids, MI: Zondervan, 2007), 124-25.

159 Dick Keyes, *Chameleon Christianity: Moving beyond Safety and Conformity* (Grand Rapids, MI: Baker Books, 1999), 61.

160 Ibid., 60.

161 See John R. Shook, *The God Debates: a 21st Century Guide for Atheists and Believers (and Everyone in Between)* (Malden, MA: Wiley-Blackwell, 2010) and Peter Hitchens, *The Rage Against God* (New York: Continuum, 2010).

162 Consider Leslie D. Weatherhead, *The Christian Agnostic* (New York: Abingdon, 1965).

163 Walter L. Liefeld, "Introduction to Ephesians," in *Today's New International Version Study Bible*, eds. Kenneth L Barker, John H. Stek, and Ronald Youngblood (Grand Rapids, MI: Zondervan, 2006), 1982.

164 Eph 2:1-10 (NRSV).

165 See *Centers and Peripheries in the Early Second Temple Period*, eds. Ehud Ben Zvi and Christoph Levin (Tubingen, Mohr Siebeck, 2016). This collection of essays provides a wonderful example of the dynamics between center and periphery in various Bible texts.

166 Matt 27:37 (SLBGNT).

167 Matt 27:37 (NRSV).

168 Matt 27:46 (NRSV).

169 Craig Nash, "Whatever happened to the Emerging Church?" (2018, The Baptist Standard), https://www.baptiststandard.com/opinion/voices/voices-whatever-happened-emerging-church/

170 Owen Strachen, "The Emergent Church Called, and it Wants its Wobbly Tables Back," (Reformanda, 2020), https://www.reformandamin.org/articles1/2020/3/11/the-emergent-church-called-and-it-wants-its-wobbly-tables-back

171 RELEVANT Magazine, "How to Deconstruct Your Faith Without Losing It," August 6, 2020 (Accessed March 14,

2021, https://www.relevantmagazine.com/magazine/how-to-deconstruct-your-faith-without-losing-it/)

172 Gerardo Marti and Gladys Ganiel, *The Deconstructed Church: Understanding Emerging Christianity* (Oxford: Oxford University Press, 2014), 70, Kindle.

173 Ibid, 70, Kindle.

174 Marti and Ganiel, *The Deconstructed Church: Understanding Emerging Christianity*, 6, Kindle.

175 Ibid., 26, Kindle.

176 Ibid., Marti and Ganiel, 34, Kindle.

177 Ibid., 60, Kindle.

178 Ibid., 79, Kindle.

179 Ibid., 111, Kindle.

180 Phyllis Tickle, personal correspondence, May 10, 2014.

181 Brian McLaren, personal correspondence, June 10, 2014.

182 Tim Conder, *The Church In Transition—The Journey of Existing Churches into the Emerging Culture* (Grand Rapids: Zondervan, 2006), 41.

183 Conder, *The Church In Transition—The Journey of Existing Churches into the Emerging Culture*, 40.

184 "World Vision: Why We're Hiring Gay Christians in Same-Sex Marriages," Christianity Today, Accessed May 10, 2014, http://www.christianitytoday.com/ct/2014/march-web-only/world-vision-why-hiring-gay-christians-same-sex-marriage.html.

185 Albert Mohler, "Pointing to Disaster—The Flawed Moral Vision of World Vision.", *AlbertMohler.com blog*, accessed May 10, 2014, http://www.albertmohler.com/2014/03/25/pointing-to-disaster-the-flawed-moral-vision-of-world-vision/.

186 John Piper, "World Vision: Adultery No, Homosexual Practice Yes," *Desiring God Blog*, accessed May 10, 2014, http://www.desiringgod.org/blog/posts/world-vision-adultery-no-homosexual-practice-yes.

187 Dan Kimball, *They Like Jesus but Not the Church* (Grand Rapids: Zondervan, 2007), Kindle Edition, Location 405.

188 Éva G. Fekete and Katalin Liptak, "Postmodern Values in Rural Peripheries," pgs. 2-3.

189 Jonathan Murdoch, "Networking Rurality: Emergent Complexity In the Countryside," in *The Handbook of Rural Studies*, eds. Paul Cloke, Terry Marsden, and Patrick Mooney (Thousand Oaks, CA, Sage Publications, 2006), 172.

190 Rodolpho Carrasco, "A Pound of Social Justice: Beyond Fighting for a Just Cause," in *An Emergent Manifesto of Hope—Key leaders Offer an Inside Look*, eds. Doug Paggit and Tony Jones (Grand Rapids, Baker Books, 2007), 254.

191 Samuel S. Hill, Jr., *Southern Churches in Crisis – A probing study of the white Protestant "Southern accent in religion,"* (Boston: Beacon Press, 1966), 76-77.

192 Philip Clayton, *Transforming Christian Theology—For Church and Society* (Minneapolis: Fortress Press, 2010), Kindle Edition, 150.

193 Ibid., Kindle Edition, 150.

194 Dan Kimball, *They Like Jesus but Not the Church* (Grand Rapids: Zondervan, 2007), Kindle Edition, Location 405.

195 Jennifer Sherman, *Those Who Work, Those Who Don't: Poverty, Morality, and Family in Rural America* (Minneapolis: University of Minnesota Press, 2009), Location 223-225, Kindle Edition.

196 David L. Brown and Kai A. Schafft, *Rural People and Communities in the 21st Century: Resilience and Transformation* (Cambridge, UK: Polity, 2011), 41.

197 Esther 3:8, NRSV.

198 Alexander Green, " Power, Deception, and Comedy: The Politics of Exile In the Book of Esther," *Jewish Political Studies Review*, 2011., 61, JSTOR Journals, EBSCO*host* (accessed February 10, 2015).

199 Brown and Schafft, *Rural People and Communities in the 21st Century*, 18.

200 Mary Chilton Calloway, "1 Maccabees Introduction" in *The New Oxford Annotated Bible with the Apocryphal/ Deuterocanonical Books*," 3rd ed., ed. Michal D. Coogan (New York: Oxford University Press, 2001), 201 Apocrypha.

201 1 Maccabees 1:44-49, NRSV.

202 Guy G. Stroumsa, "The End of Sacrifice-Religious Mutations of Late Antiquity," in *Empsychoi Logoi — Religious Innovations in Antiquity*, ed. Alberdina Houtman, Albert De Jong, and Magda Misset-Van De Weg (Boston: Brill, 2008), 29.

203 Ibid., 29-30.

204 Travis Collins, "Fresh Expressions Training Presentation" (training seminar, Rosalynn Retreat Center, Richmond, March 28, 2015). Collins quoted Lisa Smith, a Fresh Expressions Pioneer in Alexandria, VA. Fresh Expressions is an international movement of Christians concerned about reaching people who would never come through the doors of a traditional church. In the Anglican Church particularly, Fresh Expressions functions as the emerging edge of Christianity.

205 Hebrews 6:19, NRSV.

206 Jonathan Merritt, "Does Russell Moore Really Represent Southern Baptists (Commentary)," *Washington Post*, accessed August 23, 2016, https://www.washingtonpost.com/national/ religion/does-russell-moore-really-represent-southern-

baptists-commentary/2016/02/03/8b5b2576-cac1-11e5-b9ab-26591104bb19_story.html.

207 John N. Wall Jr., Ed., *George Herbert: The Country Parson, The Temple* (New York: Paulist Press, 1981), pg. 109.

208 "I Just Don't Trust the New Pastor Yet," *Onion*, June 23, 1999, accessed January 20, 2017, http://www.theonion.com/blogpost/i-just-dont-trust-the-new-pastor-yet-10925.

209 Gilbert R. Rendle, *Leading Change in the Congregation: Spiritual and Organizational Tools for Leaders* (Arlington: Alban Institute, 1998), 43.

210 Ibid., Rendle, 43.

211 Ibid., 44.

212 Ibid., Gilbert, *Leading Change in the Congregation*, 44.

213 Israel Galindo, The Hidden Lives of Congregations: Discerning Church Dynamics (Herndon, VA: The Alban Institute, 2004), 81.

214 Shannon L. Jung and Mary A. Agria, *Rural Congregational Studies: A Guide for Good Shepherds* (Nashville: Abingdon Press, 1997), 89.

215 Ibid., Jung and Agria, 89.

216 Christopher J. Rutledge, "Burnout and the Practice of Ministry Among Rural Clergy," in *Rural Life and Rural Church: Theological and Empirical Perspectives*, eds. Leslie J. Francis and Mandy Robbins (Bristol, CT, Equinox Publishing, 2012), 321.

217 Jung and Agria, *Rural Congregational Studies*, 92.

218 Ibid., Rutledge, 323.

219 Rutledge, "Burnout and the Practice of Ministry Among Rural Clergy," 323-324.

220 Bruce Sangiun, *The Emerging Church: A Model for Change and a Map for Renewal* (Kelowa, BC, CopperHouse Publishing, 2008), 23.

221 Sanguine, *The Emerging Church*, 144.

222 Ephesians 4:12 (NRSV).

223 Robert Stephen Ried, "Responding to Resistance During a Change Process," in *Transitions: Leading Churches Through Change*, ed. Davis Mosser (Louisville, Westminster John Knox Press, 2011), 180.

224 Jim Herrington, Mike Bonem and James H. Furr, *Leading Congregational Change: A Practical Guide for the Transformational Journey* (San Francisco, Jossey-Bass, 2000), 13.

225 Ibid., 13.

226 Ibid..

227 Jung and Agria, *Rural Congregational Studies*, 93.

228 Jung and Agria, *Rural Congregational Studies*, 115.

229 Ibid..

230 Ibid., 115.

231 Ibid..

232 Mark Lau Branson, *Memories, Hopes, and Conversations: Appreciative Inquiry and Congregational Change* (Herndon, VA, Alban, 2004) 19.

233 Ibid., 39.

234 Sanguin, *The Emerging Church*, 23.

235 Herrington, Bonem and Furr, *Leading Congregational Change*, 7.

236 Jung and Agria, *Rural Congregational Studies*, 118.

237 Reid, "Responding to Resistance During a Change Process," 178.

238 Ibid., 188.

239 David Buttrick, "Preaching to the Elderly" in *Transitions: Leading Churches Through Change,* ed. Davis Mosser (Louisville, Westminster John Knox Press, 2011), 88.

240 Buttrick, "Preaching to the Elderly," 88.

241 Fekete and Liptak, "Postmodern Values in Rural Peripheries," 4.

242 Ibid., 2-3.

243 Lee Tylor, *Urban-Rural Problems* (Belmont, CA: Dickenson Publishing Company, 1968), 6.

244 Ibid., 53.

245 Gerardo and Ganiel, *The Deconstructed Church,* 5, Kindle.

246 Alexander R. Thomas, Brian M. Lowe, Gregory Fulkerson, and Polly J. Smith., *Critical Rural Theory: Structure, Space, Culture* (New York: Lexington Books, 2011), 61.

247 Murphy, *Beyond Liberalism and Fundamentalism,* 88-94.

248 Thomas, Lowe, Fulkerson, and Smith, *Critical Rural Theory,* 62.

249 Margaret D. LeCompte and Judith Preissle, *Ethnography and Qualitative Design in Educational Research,* Second Ed. (New York: Academic Press, 1993), 32.

250 Judith Bell, *Doing Your Research Project: A Guide for First-Time Researchers in Education, Health and Social Science,* 4th ed. (Maidenhead, England: Open University Press, 2005), 138-142.

251 Moschella, *Ethnography as Pastoral Practice,* 78.

252 Marti and Ganiel, *The Deconstructed Church,* 96, Kindle.

253 George G. Hunter III, *The Celtic Way of Evangelism: How Christianity Can Reach the West-- Again,* 10th ed. (Nashville: Abingdon Press, 2010), Loc. 1967, Kindle.

254 Marti and Ganiel, *The Deconstructed Church,* 96, Kindle.

255 Branson, *Memories, Hopes, and Conversations*, 77.

256 Ibid., 86.

257 Ibid., 87.

258 Moschella, *Ethnography as Pastoral Practice*, 15-36.

259 "About Us," Survey Monkey Webpage, accessed May 24, 2018, https://www.surveymonkey.com/mp/aboutus/.

260 Dale and Wilson, *Weaving Strong Leaders*, 2.

261 Oxford Dictionary of the English Language Online, "Tolerance," accessed January 1, 2018, https://en.oxforddictionaries.com/definition/tolerance.

262 1 Cor 10:14-17 (NRSV).

263 G.R. Beaseley-Murray, "Evangelising the Post-Christian Man" (Diamond Jubilee Lecture, The London Baptist Preachers' Association meeting, March 21, 1969).

264 Pew Research, "In U.S., Decline of Christianity Continues at Rapid Pace: An update on America's changing religious landscape," https://www.pewforum.org/2019/10/17/in-u-s-decline-of-christianity-continues-at-rapid-pace/ (Accessed, March 15, 2021).

265 Outreach Magazine, "7 Startling Facts: An Up Close Look at Church Attendance in America," Church Leaders, April 10, 2018, https://churchleaders.com/pastors/pastor-articles/139575-7-startling-facts-an-up-close-look-at-church-attendance-in-america.html, (Accessed March 15, 2021).

266 John Leland, "A Chronicle of His Time in Virginia," *The Writings of the Later Elder John Leland*, published in 1845, http://www.brucegourley.com/baptists/quotesscs.htm (Accessed, March 15, 2021).

267 Sherman, *Those Who Work, Those Who Don't*, Kindle Location 191.

268 Ibid.

269 "What Doesn't Kill Us," Phycology Today, accessed 10/15/17, https://www.psychologytoday.com/blog/what-doesnt-kill-us/201608/7-qualities-truly-authentic-people.

270 Oxford Dictionary of the English Language, "Authentic," accessed January 2, 2018, https://en.oxforddictionaries.com/definition/us/authentic.

271 David Kinnaman and Gabe Lyons, Unchristian: What a New Generation Thinks About Christianity… and Why it Matters (Grand Rapids, MI, Baker Books, 2007), 27.

272 Kate Blackman, "Addressing Pregnancy Among Rural Teens," *National conference of State Legislators* Vol. 23. No. 27, July 2015. https://www.ncsl.org/research/health/addressing-pregnancy-among-rural-teens.aspx (Accessed March 16, 2021).

273 Julia L. DeClerque and Trude Bennett, "An Overview of Adolescent Pregnancy in rural Areas," the *Journal of Rural Health* Vol. 14, Winter, 1998, Abstract, https://www.researchgate.net/publication/227872645_An_Overview_of_Adolescent_Pregnancy_in_Rural_Areas (Accessed March 16, 2021).

274 Levi Morgan, Facebook Post, October 14, 2017, accessed January 2, 2017, https://www.facebook.com/levi.morgan.142?ref=br_rs.

275 James Strong, *The New Strong's Expanded Exhaustive Concordance of the Bible*, Red Letter Ed. (Nashville, Thomas Nelson Publishers, 2001), 270.

276 David R. Ray, *The Big Small Church Book* (Cleveland: The Pilgrim Press, 1992), pg. 104.

277 Ibid., pg. 104-105.

278 Ibid., pg. 110.

279 Jeanne Hoeft, L. Shannon Jung, and Joretta Marshall, *Practicing Care in Rural Congregations and Communities* (Minneapolis: Fortress Press, 2013), pg. 87.

280 Cornelia Butler Flora and Jan L. Flora, *Rural Communities: Legacy and Change*, 4th ed. (Boulder: West View Press, 2013), pg. 8.

281 Hoeft, Jung, and Marshall, *Practicing Care*, pg. 89.

282 Ray, *The Big Small Church Book*, pg. 104.

283 Oxford Languages, "Word of The Year 2016," https://languages.oup.com/word-of-the-year/2016/ (Accessed March 18, 2021).

284 Everette Fulmer, "Skepticism," PhilPapers, https://philpapers.org/browse/skepticism (Accessed, March 18, 2021).

285 Sarah Jane Tribble, "Rural Americans, Who Doubted the Pandemic, Now Hesitant to Get Vaccinated," Weekend Edition Sunday, *NPR*, March 14, 2021.

286 Fulmer, "Skepticism."

287 Jawkeed Kaleem, "QAnon and other conspiracy theories are taking hold in churches. Pastors are fighting back," Los Angeles Times, March 4, 2021.

288 "Atheist vs Agnostic s Skeptic vs Humanist," *Skeptical Science*, https://www.skeptical-science.com/atheism/atheist-agnostic-skeptic-humanist/ (Accessed March 18, 2021).

289 Skepticism, Good Reads, https://www.goodreads.com/quotes/tag/skepticism (Accessed March 17, 2021).

290 United States Secular Survey, *Reality Check: Being Nonreligious in America* (Cranford, NJ, American Atheists, 2019), pg. 15.

291 United States Census Bureau, "One in Five Americans Live in Rural Areas," August 9, 2017, https://www.census.gov/library/stories/2017/08/rural-america.html (Accessed March 18, 2021).

292 United States Secular Survey, *Reality Check*, pg. 9.

293 Ibid., pg. 41.

294 Dyke Drew, *Generation Ex-Christian: Why Young Adults Are Leaving the Church and How to Bring Them Back* (Chicago: Moody Publishers, 2010), 27.

295 George Hunter III, *The Celtic Way of Evangelism: How Christianity Can Reach the West...Again*, Rev. ed. (Nashville, TN, Abingdon, 2010), Loc. 824-837, Kindle.

296 Green Is the Colour, Wikipedia article, accessed on March 31, 2014, http://en.wikipedia.org/wiki/Green_Is_the_Colour.

297 Ibid..

298 Ibid..

299 Irenaeus of Lyons, quoted in *The Sermon of All Creation: Christians on Nature*, eds. Judith Fitzgerald and Michael Oren Fitzgerald (Bloomington, IN: World Wisdom, 2005), 69.

300 Martin R.P. McGuire, trans., *S. Ambrossii de Nabuthae*, in *Ambrose: Early Church Fathers*, by Boniface Ramsey O.P., (New York, NY: Routlege, 1997), 120. Per Ramsey, McGuire's translation is the only known English translation of St. Ambrose's sermon on the story of Naboth and Ahab in 1 Kings. The translation appears in "S. Ambrosii De Nabuthae, A Commentary, With an Introduction and Translation," which is Martin R.P. McGuire's 1927 PhD dissertation, housed in the Mullin Library at Catholic University of the America's in Washington D.C.. The dissertation has not yet been digitized, making it problematic in citing it as a primary source.

301 St. John of Damascus, *Apologia Against Those Who Decry Holy Images*, trans. Mary H. Allies (London: Thomas Baker, 1898), accessed January 1, 2018, https://sourcebooks.fordham.edu/basis/johndamascus-images.asp.

302 Sally McFague, *Blessed Are the Consumers: Climate Change and the Practice of Restraint* (Minneapolis, Fortress Press, 2013), Location 30, Kindle Edition.

303 Gauchat, Gordon, "Politicization of Science in the Public Sphere: A Study of Public Trust in the United States, 1974 to 2010," *American Sociological Review* 77, no. 2 (April 2012): 171. SocINDEX with Full Text, EBSCOhost (accessed April 5, 2014).

304 Gordon, "Politicization of Science in the Public Sphere," 182.

305 Ibid., United States Census Bureau, "One in Five Americans Live in Rural Areas."

306 Jenny M. Seifert and Bret R. Shaw, "Tending Our Patch of Creation: Engaging Christians in Environmental Stewardship through Sense of Place." *Journal For The Study Of Religion, Nature & Culture* 7, no. 3 (September 2013): 265-288. Academic Search Complete, EBSCOhost (accessed April 5, 2014).

307 Ibid., 268.

308 Ibid., 269.

309 Ibid..

310 Ibid., 268.

311 McFague, *Blessed Are The Consumers*, 18, Kindle.

312 Julian of Norwich, *Revelations of Divine Love*, trans. Grace Warrack (London: Methune & Company, 1901), Loc. 1108-1109, Kindle.

313 Richard Lischer, Open Secrets: A Memoir of Faith and Discover (Easton, PA: Harmony Press, 2002), title.

314 Oxford Dictionary of the English Language Online, "Solidarity," accessed January 1, 2018, https://en.oxforddictionaries.com/definition/solidarity.

315 Flora and Flora, *Rural Communities*, pg. 120.

316 Sherman, *Those Who Work, Those Who Don't*, Kindle Loc. 193.

317 Chuck Harrison, *What Happened to Our Church? And Where Do We Go from Here?* (Newport News, VA: Clear Vision Publishing, 2015), 107.

318 Milton J. Coalter, John M. Mulder, and Louis B. Weeks, *Vital Signs: The Promise of Mainstream Protestantism* (Grand Haven, MI: FaithWalks Publishing), 58.

319 H. Richard Niebuhr, Christ and Culture, (New York, Harper One, 1951), 191.

320 "Tides of Faith Series," accessed June 18, 2018, https://www.bealembc.org/series/tides-of-faith/.

321 Moschella, 215.

322 Stanford Encyclopedia of Philosophy, "Heraclitus," https://plato.stanford.edu/entries/heraclitus/ (Accessed March 18, 2021).

323 Lawrence W. Farris, *Dynamics of Small Town Ministry* (Bethesda, MD: Alban Institute, 2000), 3.

324 Herschel Hobbs and E.Y. Mullins, *The Axioms of Religion*, Revised Ed. (Nashville: Broadman, 1978), 163.

325 Ibid., 164.

326 Daman, 159.

327 Antonia Fraser, *The Weaker Vessel* (New York: Alfred A. Knopf, 1984), 245.

328 Ibid., 246-49.

329 Matthew 28:20 (NSRV).

www.ingramcontent.com/pod-product-compliance
Lightning Source LLC
Chambersburg PA
CBHW020830160426
43192CB00007B/595